NAVY SEALS

ALSO BY DICK COUCH

NONFICTION

The Warrior Elite: The Forging of SEAL Class 228

The U.S. Armed Forces Nuclear-Chemical-Biological Survival Manual

The Finishing School: Earning the Navy SEAL Trident

Down Range: Navy SEALs in the War on Terror

Chosen Soldier: The Making of a Special Forces Warrior

The Sheriff of Ramadi: Navy SEALs and the Winning of al-Anbar

A Tactical Ethic: Moral Conduct in the Insurgent Battlespace

Sua Sponte: The Forging of a Modern American Ranger

Always Faithful, Always Forward: The Forging of a Special Operations Marine

FICTION

SEAL Team One

Pressure Point

Silent Descent

Rising Wind

The Mercenary Option

Covert Action

Act of Valor (Novelization)

OpCenter: Out of the Ashes

Act of Revenge

ALSO BY WILLIAM DOYLE

Inside the Oval Office: The White House Tapes from FDR to Clinton

An American Insurrection: James Meredith and the Battle of Oxford, Mississippi, 1962

A Soldier's Dream: Captain Travis Patriquin and the Awakening of Iraq

A Mission From God (with James Meredith)

American Gun: A History of the U.S. in Ten Firearms (with Chris Kyle)

NAVY SEALS

THEIR UNTOLD STORY

DICK COUCH AND
WILLIAM DOYLE

Including Interviews by Carol L. Fleisher

Afterword by Rear Admiral Garry J. Bonelli (USN Ret.),
Ninth Force Commander, Naval Special Warfare Command

WM
WILLIAM MORROW
An Imprint of HarperCollins*Publishers*

Portions of chapters six and seven previously appeared in Dick Couch's books *Down Range* and *The Sheriff of Ramadi*.

FIRST EDITION

Designed by Jamie Lynn Kerner

Library of Congress Cataloging-in-Publication Data has been applied for.

ISBN 978-0-06-233660-6

14 15 16 17 18   OV/RRD   10 9 8 7 6 5 4 3 2 1

I will never quit. I persevere and thrive on adversity.
My Nation expects me to be physically
harder and mentally stronger than my enemies.
If knocked down, I will get back up, every time.
I will draw on every remaining ounce of
strength to protect my teammates
and to accomplish the mission.
I am never out of the fight.

FROM THE SEAL ETHOS

You are not alive unless you are living on the edge.
And living on the edge like these swimmers and the
rest of those men, you are alive. I mean, you are alive.
I think that was the most fun I had in my life.

WALTER MESS, WORLD WAR II

OSS MARITIME UNIT OPERATIVE

It's just the way we were, the teams and the men, the camaraderie, it lives with you forever. I mean, you never forget your buddy. You never forget your shipmate. You never forget the team. You never forget the operations.

That's what comes back, memories of all of the good times and the bad times, but always the good times.

I'm very proud and happy to have been part of the military, part of the SEALs, part of special warfare and if I was a younger man I would still love to be back in there with them.

RETIRED LIEUTENANT JOSEPH DIMARTINO (USN RET.)

D-DAY VETERAN AND ORIGINAL MEMBER OF SEAL TEAM TWO

They just vanished. They came out of darkness and disappeared back into it. I mean, it's incredible.

JESSICA BUCHANAN, AID WORKER
RESCUED BY SEALS IN SOMALIA

We must remember that one man is much the same as another, and that he is best who has training in the severest school.

Then I heard the voice of the Lord saying, "Whom shall I send? And who will go for us?" And I said, "Here am I. Send me!"

CONTENTS

NAVAL SPECIAL WARFARE COMMAND ORGANIZATIONS

UNITE

NAVAL SPECIAL

NAVAL SPECIAL WARFARE CENTER
Coronado, CA

Basic Training
Command
Coronado, CA

Advanced Training
Command
Imperial Beach, CA

NSW GROUP 1
Coronado, CA

SEAL Teams
1/3/5/7
Coronado, CA

Logistics Support
Unit 1
Coronado, CA

NSW Unit 1
Guam

NSW Unit 3
ASU, Bahrain

NSW GROUP 2
Little Creek, VA

SEAL Teams
2/4/8/10
Little Creek, VA

Logistics Support
Unit 2
Little Creek, VA

NSW Unit 2
Stuttgart, Germany

NSW Unit 4
Little Creek, VA

NSW Unit 10
Stuttgart, Germany

NSW GROUP 3
Ford Island, HI

SDV Team 1
Pearl City, HI

Logistics Support
Unit 3
Pearl City, HI

SDV Det. 1
Little Creek, VA

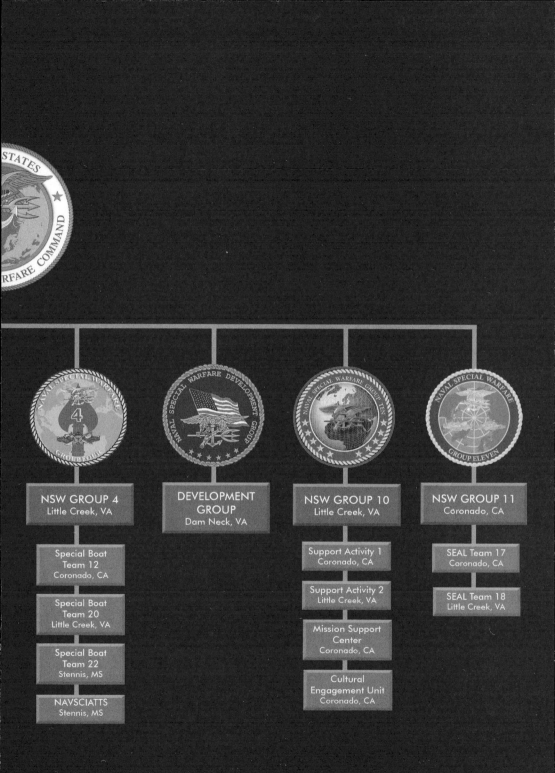

NSW GROUP 4
Little Creek, VA

Special Boat
Team 12
Coronado, CA

Special Boat
Team 20
Little Creek, VA

Special Boat
Team 22
Stennis, MS

NAVSCIATTS
Stennis, MS

DEVELOPMENT
GROUP
Dam Neck, VA

NSW GROUP 10
Little Creek, VA

Support Activity 1
Coronado, CA

Support Activity 2
Little Creek, VA

Mission Support
Center
Coronado, CA

Cultural
Engagement Unit
Coronado, CA

NSW GROUP 11
Coronado, CA

SEAL Team 17
Coronado, CA

SEAL Team 18
Little Creek, VA

PREFACE

by William Doyle

This book is a battle history of the U.S. Navy SEALs from their origins through today. Based in large part on interviews with more than one hundred former Naval Special Warfare members, it is our effort to tell the story of a remarkable elite fighting force and its ancestors, a group of warriors who have contributed directly to critical moments in American military history from the landings at D-Day and battles in the Pacific, through the Korean and Vietnam Wars, Iraq, Afghanistan, and the battles against international terrorism.

I learned military history from my father, in a lifetime of conversations about his experiences in the South Pacific during World War II as a U.S. Army intelligence and military police sergeant.

He survived Japanese air raids, helped protect General Douglas MacArthur in the jungle of New Guinea, rode on PT boats, and suffered from tropical diseases that brought him to the edge of death on several occasions. He met hundreds of people whom he found utterly fascinating, including GIs and sailors from every corner of the United States, highly proper British officers and beautiful Australian nurses, native islanders who seemed to have stepped out of the Stone Age, and a friendly Japanese POW who spoke fluent English and had served as a conductor on a Tokyo trolley car before the war.

I once asked him, "Why was it such an amazing time for you?"

"Because every morning when you woke up," he said, smiling, "you had no idea what was going to happen that day. Absolutely anything could happen!"

Today, there can be few American service personnel who experience that feeling more intensely than the U.S. Navy SEALs. When they awake every day, they know there's a chance they'll be called upon to conduct some of America's most complex, dangerous, and far-flung military missions, and to do so in a veil of anonymity and secrecy.

I first became fascinated with the U.S. Navy SEALs during the course of writing *A Soldier's Dream: Captain Travis Patriquin and the Awakening of Iraq,* published in 2011. It told the story of one American army soldier's work with Iraqis and the U.S. military during the Battle of Ramadi, a turning point in the Iraq War.

During my research interviews for the book, I heard an increasingly common refrain from American and Iraqi veterans of that event: the Navy SEALs, they said, were silent heroes of that battle. The American commander of that battlespace in 2006, then-Colonel Sean MacFarland, told me the SEALs were among the most effective fighters and most professional teammates he had ever worked with. The central figure of my book, Captain Travis Patriquin, admired the SEALs so much that he spent as much of his time as he could at their "Shark Base" special operations compound at Camp Ramadi, trading intelligence, tactical tips, and breaking bread with the men he called his "super-friends."

Then, in 2008, when I read a remarkable book by former Navy SEAL Dick Couch about the SEALs in Ramadi, called *The Sheriff of Ramadi,* it became even more clear to me that the SEALs helped provide the critical muscle, targeted application of force, and Iraqi police training needed by Patriquin, MacFarland, and their American military colleagues to help the Iraqi tribes largely expel al-Qaeda from the strategic province of al-Anbar, and to give their people a chance, however fleeting and fragile, at a better life.

In 2012, I was introduced to another hero of the Battle of Ramadi, SEAL Team Three Chief Chris Kyle, the top sniper in U.S. military history and author of *American Sniper.* Chris served from 1999 to 2009 and saw action in almost every major battle of the Iraq War. He and I wound up writing a bestselling book together, *American Gun: A History of the U.S. in Ten Firearms.* Tragically, while we were writing the book, Chris and his good friend Chad Littlefield were killed in the course of trying to help a fellow Iraq War veteran. I will always treasure Chris Kyle's patriotic self-sacrifice, enthusiasm, humility, and humor, and his great passion for American history, an interest he shared with many of the SEAL veterans I've met.

In 2013, the TV director Carol Fleisher, my writing and production partner on an award-winning A&E documentary on the history of White House tape recordings, suggested we team up to explore the possibility of a PBS network documentary and companion book on the history of the U.S. Navy SEALs. We realized it could be an important, essential program and book. Many of the SEALs' greatest battle stories have rarely or never been told, and the SEALs were among the most intriguing modern warriors well before the operation that killed Osama bin Laden in Pakistan in 2011 and made them legendary in the popular consciousness.

Great idea, I thought, but nearly impossible to pull off, given the SEALs' historical aversion to publicity. But then we checked with sources in what's called "the Naval Special Warfare Community" (read: SEALs) and we realized that it might be possible to do it, and do it right, but only if we had a strong partner. Ideally that person would be a former SEAL, someone who could give us a true insider's perspective, who could introduce us to some of the critical players in SEAL history, and who could open doors for us to tell the story the way it deserved to be told.

It didn't take us long to figure out that one man fit that bill perfectly. His name was Dick Couch. He'd written eighteen books, many of them on the SEALs and on special operations. He was a combat leader in Vietnam and a longtime SEAL officer on active duty and the reserves. And he was highly respected by the many veterans and serving SEALs he stayed in close touch with over the years. Pretty soon, Dick teamed up with Carol as a consultant on the PBS special, for which we obtained a Production Assistance Agreement with the U.S. Department of Defense as well as the cooperation of the Public Affairs Office of the Naval Special Warfare Command, and with me as coauthor for this companion book. That's how this book wound up in your hands.

Any book about the SEALs is by definition only part of the story, since many moments and operations in SEAL history remain in the shadows of classification and secrecy, and SEALs are by nature very averse to revealing details of their operations to outsiders. In this book, we've done our best to tell as much of the full declassified story as best we can, through the eyes of the SEALs in the midst of combat, and through the window of some of the most illustrative and historic engagements and operations of the SEALs and their predecessors. This is by no means a complete history of the SEALs' operations, nor is it a tactical or top-down administrative history.

We have done our best to verify and cross-check the information in this book with firsthand witnesses, third-party accounts by historians and journalists, and declassified government documents, as indicated in the source notes. But it is important to understand that much of the history of the SEALs is classified and therefore out of reach for responsible authors, including ourselves. Also, different people can remember events quite differently; that's just a fact of journalism and history.

The early history of the SEALs is obscured by the fact that much of it simply was not written down in the form of after-action reports or other documents for the "institutional memory," and SEALs often did not even share much information with each other about their operations at the time, as they were too busy and too discreet. As former SEAL Bob Gormly noted, "SEALs and UDTs [Underwater Demolition Teams] have been excellent at never writing anything down on paper. I tell people we're like an Indian tribe: information gets passed down to the younger troops from legends being told around the fires. That's okay, but when all your old chiefs go out, their experience goes with them." In light of this, we are donating interview transcripts from our project to U.S. Navy historians, to add to the historical record.

This book was a collaborative effort and we did our best to help the reader see the history of the U.S. Navy SEALs through the words of those who experienced it. We hope you enjoy reading this book as much as we have been honored to write it.

Visit William Doyle at www.facebook.com/williamdoylenyc

PREFACE
by Dick Couch

My sole connection to William Doyle before he called and asked me to help with this project was through his work. The research for my book, *The Sheriff of Ramadi; Navy SEALs and the Winning of al-Anbar*, brought me into contact with Captain Travis Patriquin and the role he played in the Battle of Ramadi. I had read Bill's book *A Soldier's Dream: Captain Travis Patriquin and the Awakening of Iraq*, which I found to be a marvelous documentary on the life and death of this worthy warrior. Now he was calling *me* about a book on the history of the Navy SEALs.

I'm not a historian; my nonfiction works (I'm also a novelist) chronicle current special operations training and operations. Historians are old guys with longish hair, half-moon reading glasses, and faded corduroy jackets—the ones with the frayed elbow patches. But I listened to what Bill had to say and considered the prospect of us working together on a history of the SEALs. He told me of the PBS special on SEAL history, and the opportunity we would have to help with that production. The more we talked, the more I warmed to the project, both the prospect of working with Bill and working with those individual Navy "frogmen" and SEALs whose stories would form the basis of this history. And I'm a sucker for a good war story. My work as a novelist and with nonfiction books on special operations has taught me that, regarding SEALs and frogmen, the real thing is far more compelling than any of my fiction.

A few years ago, I attended the fiftieth anniversary of the SEAL teams. If we go back to our roots of our community, the frogmen of World War II, we are but seventy years old. It was the over 3,000 Marine casualties at the Battle of Tarawa in November 1943 that documented the need for pre-invasion intelligence and helped spawn the Navy frogmen of the Naval Combat Demolition Units and Underwater Demolition Teams—the forebears of today's SEALs. I was born one month before the Battle of Tarawa. So what you are about to read in *Navy SEALs* all took part during my lifetime. And I was privileged to be a part of it.

I'm often asked why a kid from southern Indiana wanted to be a Navy frogman. I think I was captured when I read *The Silent World* by Jacques Cousteau and watched the Lloyd Bridges TV series *Sea Hunt*. In high school I built an aqualung and began diving in the cold clear waters of the limestone quarries near my home. I dove alone for two years before I found a dive buddy. When I was appointed to the U.S. Naval Academy I thought I might be a little closer to my goal of becoming a frogman. That was in the summer of 1963 and few people, including myself, had heard of these new teams with warriors called SEALs. But when I graduated from Annapolis in 1967, Naval Academy graduates were not allowed to be frogmen, let alone SEALs.

While I attended Annapolis, the superintendent was a distinguished admiral by the name of Draper Kauffman. He was a legendary figure who had much to do with the development and training of the Naval Combat Demolition Units during World

War II. When he was at the helm of the Naval Academy, we midshipmen were in awe of him.

In the spring of 1967, I was a first-class midshipman just a few months from graduation. That April my company mates and I were required to attend a reception at the home of our revered Academy superintendent. When it was my turn to meet Admiral Kauffman, he asked me, "Mr. Couch, what will be your choice on Service Selection Night?"

"A destroyer out of Japan to begin with, sir," I replied. "But as soon as I can, I'm going to request orders to the Underwater Demolition Teams."

The great man put his arm around me like he was my dad and said, "Son, you're regular Navy. You have a wonderful career ahead of you in the fleet. You can be a destroyer man, an aviator, or a submariner, but there's no future for you in underwater demolition. That's not why you're here at Annapolis." Back then, a career in UDT or SEALs was not considered a viable path for a career naval officer.

"I appreciate the advice, sir," I told him, "but I'm going to do it anyway." He smiled, I smiled, and he moved on to speak with the next midshipman in line. I think that to this day, I'm the only Navy SEAL who had one of the original UDT leaders personally try to discourage him from becoming a Navy SEAL.

Following graduation from the Naval Academy in 1967, I served aboard a Navy destroyer with duty in Vietnam. And after reporting aboard, I immediately put in for orders for Basic Underwater Demolition/SEAL Training, or BUD/S. My skipper passed my request along as *"forwarded, not recommended."* Yet in the fall of 1968 and following my tour aboard ship, I found myself in Little Creek, Virginia, and in the east coast version of BUD/S Training, suffering alongside other officers and enlisted sailors who wanted to be frogmen as badly as I did. There were seventy-nine of us who began that BUD/S class; thirteen of us graduated.

In early 1969 I checked into my first team, UDT-22. Within hours of my arrival, I met Joe DiMartino. Here I was, a green junior-grade lieutenant being welcomed aboard by a man who had been on Omaha Beach ahead of the first waves of infantrymen. And he treated me like a brother. Wow! I might have been alive (just) when it all began, but I was serving with men who were there when it all started.

I'm honored to have served in the UDTs as well as the SEAL teams. Indeed, all of us who were in the teams are proud of our heritage. We are also immensely proud of the current generation of Navy SEALs. We stand in the shadow of their accomplishments and professionalism. And we are very proud to have played a part in the development of what is now modern Naval Special Warfare.

In this book, Bill has asked me to share some of my experiences in Vietnam. I agreed to this to document just how capable and courageous my brother SEALs were, to illustrate how critical the proper training and experience were to our work, and to be completely candid about some of the difficulties I faced as a platoon commander who tried his best and sometimes came up short. I was a "one tour wonder" in Vietnam, a SEAL who had but a single six-month hitch in the combat zone and then came home. There are other SEALs and Americans who had three, four, and five tours in the combat zones of Vietnam, and there are 58,000 Americans who never came back. The magnitude of their service and sacrifice, and that of all the Naval Special Warfare heroes who have given that last full measure, is beyond the power of words to express.

Shortly after Bill and I began this project, a number of folks, including my agent and current publisher, asked why I was undertaking this work. There was and is, I'm happy to report, a good deal of interest in my other works—the novels and the nonfiction that address special operations and special operations training. So I had to ask myself, why *am* I doing this? It's certainly not that I don't have plenty of work, along with time that needs to be allocated to fishing, skiing, and hiking here in Idaho.

Those of us who are, or have been, Navy SEALs see our community through two foci. One focus is our personal experience on active duty—what we did, our teammates at the time, and the times in which we served. The other is the current operational posture of the Navy SEALs. Certainly today, there is no mystery about SEALs nor, within the constraints of classified tactics, techniques, and procedures, what they do. And there are more than a few current-day SEALs who are out there writing books about *their* personal experiences. So for me, it's only been recently that I've thought about those other times, and the men who served before my time and those who came to the teams after I left active service. During my work on this book, I've become increasingly aware that ours is a rich history with colorful and courageous men who served their teams, their teammates, and their nation well. Like many of our sister special operations components, the SEALs were born out of necessity, and over their brief life span have continued to evolve to meet the new direct and asymmetrical threats in combating insurgency and terrorism. It's a worthy history—one deserving of a PBS documentary and our best efforts with this book.

So I'm now an apprentice historian. I'm definitely what the young SEALs consider an old guy. I need my reading glasses, and I do in fact have an old corduroy sports coat with elbow patches. And I hope you find these pages as compelling in the reading as we did in the writing. Thank you, Bill, for allowing me to be a part of telling this story.

Visit Dick Couch at www.dickcouch.com

AUTHORS' NOTE

This book has been cleared for publication by the Department of Defense and the Central Intelligence Agency. The book underwent an additional security review by Naval Special Warfare Command. In the course of these reviews, we were asked to not reveal classified details of certain components of the Special Operations Command, including special mission units. We have complied with that request.

The information for this book has been taken from personal interviews, declassified and historical documents, memoirs, journalistic accounts, and other available public sources, and contains the personal perspective and opinions of the authors. Where errors may exist, we apologize for the oversight; where opinions may differ, we welcome your comment.

This work is, by necessity, highly selective and cannot possibly cover every action, individual, development, or relevant discussion concerning the history of the UDTs and SEALs. It is our hope and intention that the following will help to document and celebrate all those who served in Naval Special Warfare, and provide the reader with an overview of the rich history of this very special breed of warriors.

NAVY SEALS

CHAPTER 1

THE FANTASTIC HOUR

OMAHA BEACH,
JUNE 6, 1944, 6:33 A.M.

THE FORCE:
175 Naval Combat Demolition Unit (NCDU) demolitioneers, 500 Army Combat Engineers and 150,000 Allied soldiers and sailors

THE MISSION:
Spearhead the Allied assault to liberate Europe

His job was to blow things up, and fast.

Seaman Second Class Ken Reynolds and his teammates in the joint U.S. Army-Navy Gap Assault Teams had less than thirty minutes to blast open the gates of Western Europe. If they failed, thousands of American soldiers would be trapped and slaughtered in the water, the assault on Omaha Beach would stop at the shoreline of Normandy, and the D-Day invasion would lurch sideways into a disaster of unknown dimensions. The weather was overcast, the seas choppy and the winds were whipping up four-foot waves along the coast of Normandy, which to Reynolds looked like "the longest and flattest beach I'd ever seen."

Their mission was to open sixteen fifty-foot-wide corridors through a wall of steel, and they had to do it inside a hurricane of machine gun and artillery fire. They were supposed to follow an initial wave of tanks and infantry onto the shore, but in the chaos of the operation, some of the demolition men were the very first to hit Omaha Beach.

Before they could even get out of the landing craft, the Americans were engulfed in a storm of shells and machine-gun fire from German positions dug into the heights overlooking the beach.

A few simple thoughts bounced around in the brain of Ken Reynolds as he jumped out of the landing craft: "Blow the obstacles. Do the job. Don't get killed. Get to the beach."

"The team right next to us was all killed except one," Reynolds told us of his teammates in Boat Team 11, "when a shell landed right in their rubber boat and set off their explosives." Nearby, a shell hit the landing craft deck and ignited the explosives of Boat Team 14 before the commandos could even offload their rubber boat, killing many of them. Another shell scored a direct hit on Team 15's boat and detonated their explosives, killing three men and wounding four.

"It was crazy," Reynolds said. "We were dodging bullets and shells, and if you didn't improvise you didn't survive."

"I saw people dying, I saw dead people in the water, I heard the noise," he remembered. "I saw the whole gamut, but it didn't bother me. I knew what we had to do."

The scene marked a milestone in the prehistory of the U.S. Navy SEALs in combat, as their direct ancestors, the little-remembered Naval Combat Demolition Units, or NCDUs, launched the assault on the beaches of Normandy, the spearhead of an operation that combat historian S. L. A. Marshall described as "an epic human tragedy which in the early hours bordered on total disaster."

Unlike today's SEALs, who enter battle prepared by an entire year or more of broad-based commando and maritime training and a wide spectrum of high-tech weapons, vehicles, and communications equipment, Reynolds and many of his colleagues had only basic training at Fort Pierce, Florida, a demolition course, and a bare minimum of tools needed to try to blow gaps in the obstacles that Hitler built on the shores of Western Europe. And in sharp contrast to the modern SEALs, the NCDUs were not trained combat swimmers—they were dropped off in shallow water and were expected to do their work mostly as they walked and crawled through the cold surf.

The young warrior's brain switched off the violence and chaos, and focused only on the pair of pliers and the knife in his pocket, and the two canvas satchels of explosives slung over his shoulders. Each satchel was stuffed with sixteen 2.5-pound sausage-shaped packs of C-2 plastic or tetrytol explosive, for a total of thirty-two charges. The ingenious new explosive delivery system was called the "Hagensen Pack" after its inventor, Naval Reserve Seabee Lieutenant Carl P. Hagensen, who was NCDU-trained at Fort Pierce and officer-in-charge of NCDU-30. The packs could be quickly attached to any type of obstacle by a hook-and-line design. Other men in Reynolds's team carried blasting caps and detonation cord to wire the charges together.

Incoming U.S. Army infantry troops could feel bullets beating on the drop ramps of their landing craft as the ramps were being lowered, ribbons of bullets raked the surf as the troops tumbled into the water, and many drowned from being overloaded with supplies. Some men scampered over the sides or dove underwater to escape the hail of bullets.

"They just slaughtered us, it was unbelievable," recalled Ken Reynolds. "There were bodies, body parts, and blood everywhere," remembered Seaman First Class Robert Watson. "There were more killed and wounded on the beach than those of us left alive." Joe Amorelli, an Army engineer who landed nearby, said "a guy beside me had his arm blown off, and while he was looking at it, he was shot again. He went right down. They were dying all around me."

When he jumped into the cold, waist-high water of the English Channel just after 6:33 A.M. on June 6, 1944, U.S. Navy Seaman Second Class Ken Reynolds was the length of two football fields away from the coast of France.

For an instant, he sensed the staggering scale of the spectacle he was at the front of: "It was a fantastic, unbelievable sight," he remembered. "I couldn't imagine that there were that many naval vessels in the world." It was one of the biggest armadas in history, with nearly 5,000 vessels, 11,000 planes, and 150,000 Allied sailors and soldiers striking the coast of Normandy.

Reynolds was eighteen years old, barely out of high school in Providence, Rhode Island, and hadn't had time to find a sweetheart or have much of a life yet. He was assigned to Naval Combat Demolition Unit 42, Boat Team 5, part of a force of twenty-one "Gap Assault Teams" that included detachments of U.S. Army combat engineers, who were ordered to spearhead the five-mile-long Omaha Beach assault. The job was split at the waterline: sailors would cut fifty-yard-wide gaps in the seaward obstacles, the army engineers would handle the landward barriers. The overall mission was to clear sixteen fifty-foot-wide pathways at each of the U.S. landing zones, Omaha Beach, and Utah Beach, where there were eleven more NCDU teams.

In his brief life as a civilian Reynolds had worked as a commercial fisherman and a welder, and today he was one the volunteer naval demolitioneers who were riding the tip of the spear of the Allied attempt to invade Western Europe and overthrow Adolf Hitler. Ken Reynolds came to England as a regular seaman on Easter 1944 and was one of a group of sailors who were selected to beef up the NCDU forces that came over from the NCDU's training base at Fort Pierce, Florida. At first, Reynolds remembered, "I thought it [the acronym NCDU] meant 'Non-Combat Demolition,' and my mother was elated because it was non-combat! But, I soon found out that's not what it meant."

Reynolds went into training immediately at different sites around the English coast. "The training was focused on how to handle a rubber boat and explosives," he recalled, "what to do, how to tie it on, how to charge it. There wasn't too much to it. If you could swim, fine, it was a plus, but it wasn't mandatory, as long as you weren't afraid of water."

In the minutes before approaching Omaha Beach, Reynolds and many other Allied military personnel figured this would be a pretty smooth operation. "Our officers told us the Air Force was going to bomb and clear the beachhead," he recalled. His superiors said, "They're going to obliterate everything on the beach. When you land there should be nobody there to bother you. There should be sporadic fire, that's about all."

But here they were, being greeted instead by a torrent of German fire from hidden machine-gun nests that "just riddled the devil out of us," he recalled. Meanwhile they were simultaneously coming under "heavy, heavy, constant fire" from mortars and 88 mm high-velocity antiaircraft artillery, which the Germans were highly effective at using on surface targets.

A Navy after-action report described what Reynolds and his colleagues faced: "The artillery and machine guns were generally sited for enfilading fire along the beaches. In some cases they were completely concealed from a direct view from seaward by concrete walls covered with earth, which extended well beyond the muzzle of the gun. This acted as a blast screen and prevented them from being located by the dust raised near their muzzles, so that when used with flashless, smokeless, powder, and without tracer bullets, as they were in defense of OMAHA Beaches, they were exceedingly difficult to detect."

As Reynolds quipped, "The Germans had it made."

"The shells and rockets from our warships were screaming over our heads," recalled then-nineteen-year-old Tom Koester, another sailor on an incoming landing craft. "You could feel the heat on the back of your neck," said Koester, "and we had to watch out for rockets that could fall short and explode right on us."

Expecting to face a lower-grade German coastal defense regiment and assorted East European conscripts in German uniforms, Allied intelligence planners missed the fact that elements of the German 352nd Infantry Division were stationed near the landing areas in greater strength than expected.

Ken Reynolds had no rifle, no sidearm, and no grenades. He wore a green Navy uniform and a steel-pot helmet with "USN" marked on top. "We looked just like the Army," he recalled to us. "Army boots, no weapons, no toothbrush, and no food, that's what we hit the beach with." He added, "We had a wraparound life preserver that was charged with two canisters of CO_2 to inflate them. You had to make sure they were under your arms or they would strangle you to death. And we wore a web belt that carried a water can and this knife and a pair of pliers. Other than that, that's all we had, nothing."

Some of the NCDU men carried .45 pistols or carbines for self-defense, but Reynolds had neither. His job was strictly to blow things up, hence the stripped-down gear.

At six feet, six inches tall, Reynolds stood out like a tree in the ocean to German machine gunners dug into the cliffs. He crouched down as low as he could in the shallow water as he and five fellow demolitioneers dragged a rubber boat packed with explosives and supplies toward their destination, a vast labyrinth of partially submerged obstacles tipped with thickets of pressure mines, box mines, anti-boat mines and other explosives. Machine-gun bullets were slicing into the little boat, so they grabbed as many explosive satchels as they could wrap around their shoulders, let the boat go, and scampered forward in the surf. Reynolds and many of his colleagues were feeling sick from the cold, choppy ride across the English Channel that morning, and their bodies were stiff and sore from sleeping in the open air on the steel boat decks for the past five days.

The twenty-five-foot tide was rushing in at a rate of a foot every eight to ten minutes, and if the sailors couldn't open a path through the obstacles and mines before the water covered them up, incoming Allied landing craft and infantrymen would be impaled and the boats sunk before they could touch French soil. Nearly 175 Navy demolition personnel were hitting the water to clear the waterside of Omaha Beach, followed by hundreds of Army engineers who would blow through the obstacles on land, then mark the open lanes with flags.

Even by the usually chaotic standards of combat, everything was falling apart and the intricate invasion plan was in danger of totally collapsing. The pre-assault Allied naval and air bombardments seemed to make little impact. Airborne paratrooper drops hours earlier were badly scattered over the French countryside. Scores of landing craft were being pushed eastward in the unexpectedly strong lateral current, so thousands of incoming infantry were bunching up toward the wrong landing points.

In a nearby scout boat, a horrified Navy lieutenant, junior grade named Phil Bucklew was frantically calling his superiors on a radio, beseeching them not to launch amphibious tanks into the maelstrom. Phil Bucklew was one of the few over-the-beach veterans headed for Omaha Beach that day. A seasoned combat leader in the joint Army-Navy Amphibious Scouts and Raiders beach reconnaissance force, former pro football player Bucklew later went on to command the Navy's Naval Operations Support Group, Pacific, forerunner of today's Naval Special Warfare Group One. The Scouts and Raiders were formed in August 1942 at the Amphibious Training Base at Little Creek, near Norfolk, Virginia, and trained in amphibious reconnaissance and commando operations. In that sense, the Scouts and Raiders are symbolic ancestors of the modern U.S. Navy SEALs.

Phil Bucklew himself earned a Navy Cross for helping guide, under intense enemy fire, the Allied landings on Sicily on July 10, 1943, and he would receive another Navy Cross for his actions in support of the D-Day operations. In the months preceding D-Day, Phil Bucklew personally led hazardous reconnaissance missions along the beaches of Normandy, paddling up to the waterline in small boats in the dark of night, taking depth soundings, scooping up sand samples from enemy territory and sneaking back into the darkness. Now, in the opening moments of D-Day, as Bucklew witnessed the heavy seas and murderous fire in the waters off the Omaha Beach landing zone, he quickly realized that the experimental duplex-drive amphibious Sherman tanks that were supposed to accompany the advance wave of American infantry were doomed.

He pleaded with his commanders by radio to call off the tanks, but it was too late. Thirty-two American Sherman tanks spilled into the surf from landing craft into the choppy sea, and their flimsy water-wing flotation collars were quickly shredded by wind, surf, and German fire. They were supposed to lead the Gap Assault Teams onto the beach but twenty-seven tanks floundered or sank in the shallow ocean, taking many of their crewmen with them. Bucklew reached into the water from his craft to save several of the drowning tank men, and stayed in the line of fire all day, helping to guide landing craft.*

The landing zones were a logistical nightmare, according to a later Navy analysis: "Slit trenches were dug for defending riflemen, and tank traps and antitank ditches intervened between beaches and road exits. In addition, there had been installed in the tidal area, between high and low water, several rows of underwater obstacles consisting of hedgehogs, tetrahedrons, Element C [nicknamed Belgian Gates], and pole ramps all interconnected by barbed wire and thickly sown with mines. The obstacles actually encountered were much more numerous than Intelligence Reports had indicated." As Ken Reynolds later described, "Everything they could think of to make it miserable for us, they stuck on the beach."

The toughest barriers were the Belgian Gates, which were massive three-ton, ten-foot-tall interlocking solid steel platforms that were designed to be pushed into the surf on wooden ramps to block the beach. The gates were spotted weeks earlier in reconnaissance missions, and for weeks Reynolds and his teams had been practicing on replicas of the barriers at English training bases.

They discovered that if they detonated charges on the Belgian Gates at the wrong points, they'd just create a jumble of twisted steel and flying shrapnel that would make things worse

---

* A notable earlier naval combat operation occurred in September 1942, when a small team of handpicked Navy salvage divers led by Lieutenant Mark Starkweather was put through a cram course in demolition and commando-raiding techniques and then sent across the Atlantic to spearhead Operation TORCH, the Allied invasion of North Africa. The team disabled a massive cable-and-net barrier blocking the Wadi Sebou River in Morocco, enabling shipborne U.S. Army troops to capture the strategic Port Lyautey airdrome, and earning a Navy Cross for each of the demolition team members.

for the thousands of infantrymen who had to pass over the debris. After many experiments, Allied planners found the trick was to blow sixteen charges at sixteen key points of the structure at the exact same time, which would collapse it flat-down instead of in pieces, so the incoming infantry and vehicles could just pass over them in an open lane onto the beach.

Once through the Gates, there were other dangers, like the Teller mine, a plate-shaped, pressure-triggered German anti-tank mine. Reynolds got to a steel post and hooked up a charge right next to a Teller mine that was fixed on top. The trick was to blow up the post and the mine at the same time, so American infantrymen wouldn't walk on the unexploded mines. "To accomplish this," recalled one Navy officer, "men shinnied up the stakes and stood on each other's shoulders, all in the face of heavy enemy gunfire."

Reynolds pulled a tassel cord to ready the explosive for firing, and repeated the move on more charges on two more posts close by. A teammate hooked up all the charges on the multiple posts together with a long string of primacord, set the fuse, called out the warning "Fire in the hole!" and hauled off.

Next, Reynolds wired up a series of steel hedgehogs. The hedgehogs looked like giant children's jacks stuck in the surf. They blocked any large craft or vehicles trying to pass through, and they were interlaced with explosives. From Reynolds's vantage point, "there was a world of those damn hedgehogs."

Reynolds kept concentrating on the universe under his nose, and the theoretical fifty-yard-wide lane he was trying to open up on the beach. Despite the withering fire, it looked like they might eventually do it. Small sections of their gap seemed open all the way to the beach, and they were making some progress wiring up the myriad of remaining obstacles.

But it was a bloody, often fatal business, virtually a suicide mission for the Navy and Army demolition men on Omaha Beach.

The NCDU officer in charge of Omaha Beach, Lieutenant Commander Joseph H. Gibbons, recalled that an officer from one boat team on the beach "was standing by to pull the fuses after the charges had been placed when rifle fire cut his fingers off and the fuse assemblies." Nearby, "enemy rifle fire set off the charges which had been placed on the obstacles which cleared the gap but unfortunately also caused casualties. One unit was decimated, with the exception of three men, by enemy sniper fire. Throughout the entire operation the loyalty and bravery and devotion to duty of the men were most outstanding. All of those who were killed died with their faces toward the enemy and as they moved forward to accomplish their objectives."

Seaman First Class Robert Watson was on the first landing craft to head to Fox Green Beach, and the vessel came under fire two hundred yards from the shore. "Our craft hit a mine that blew the front of the boat clear out of the water at the same time we were hit with 88 mm shells from the beach," he recalled. "It was then that I found myself in the water over my head with a full pack on my back. Somehow I made it to the beach behind a hedgehog, which gave me some cover. There were bodies, body parts, and blood everywhere."

One demolition team man sprinted through the labyrinth without a scratch, successfully wiring and blowing up obstacles as a voice yelled at him to keep down.

An exuberant *"F—k!"* was all he had to say, and he ran off to continue his work.

In horror, a wounded naval demolition man lying on the beach witnessed panicked GIs spilling out of a landing craft, falling on top of each other and disappearing in the water. "Twenty to forty guys drowned there," recalled the injured seaman, Alfred Palacios. "Nobody was even hit." He recalled standing up and screaming helplessly to no avail, then crying, and finally passing out.

A landing craft was impaled on a steel tetrahedron barrier just five hundred yards from the beach, offering a stationary target for German gunners. "I ordered all hands to inflate their life belts," recalled Ensign Herbert Duquette, officer-in-charge of NCDU 128, "then carrying forty pounds of TNT apiece we swam for the beach. Only seven of my men made it in."

As he continued attaching explosives to the German obstacles in the water, Ken Reynolds saw incoming American boats and vehicles slicing through some of the priming wires, rendering the charges useless. Scattered infantry troops were tripping through and disabling the wires as well, and enemy fire was shredding other sections of wire.

Then, out of the corner of his eye, Ken Reynolds glimpsed a horrifying sight.

American infantrymen were taking cover behind the obstacles his team had just wired up with explosives. Their landing craft were coming in and unloading too fast, before the gaps could be blown open.

When fired, the charges would explode in 120 seconds, creating flying shrapnel of steel fragments that would be deadly for over one hundred yards. And the Army troops were only inches away from the charges.

"Get out of there! Get out!" screamed Reynolds. "We're going to blow it!"

But more Army troops crowded behind the obstacles, too terrified to move forward into the blizzard of German bullets and mortar fire.

Instead of killing Germans, the U.S. sailors were about to kill their fellow Americans.

It was nearly 7 A.M. on Omaha Beach. No matter how hard Ken Reynolds screamed, some U.S. Army troops would not budge from the explosives-charged obstacles. Reynolds grabbed one GI and shoved him away with a foot on his backside. "The Army guys were hanging on the obstacles," Reynolds said. "We'd boot them in the butt to give them two minutes to get away from there, but you really couldn't talk to them, some of them were so scared," Reynolds recalled, "so you'd grab and push them away from the obstacle, but after a while you got tired of doing that and tried to save yourself." Reynolds and his teammates were forced to abandon the attempt to blow the remaining obstacles and head for the beach. By 7:30 A.M., Reynolds staggered to the beach, ran this way and that, and finally collapsed in the shelter of a small ridge. Reynolds was finally able to turn around and absorb what he'd accomplished, plus everything else that was going on. "It was a fantastic hour," he recalled. "There were ships and bodies all over the place." Thousands of American, British, Canadian, and German troops lay dead and wounded around the landing beaches and in the waters off the Allied landing zones of Omaha, Utah, Sword, and Juno Beaches.

Of the 175 NCDU men who went ashore on Omaha Beach, 31 were killed and 60 were wounded. Some of the boat teams were obliterated before they could even start their work that morning. Casualties suffered by the demolition teams at Utah Beach were much lighter, with 6 killed and 11 wounded. D-Day remains the bloodiest day in the history of U.S. naval special warfare. Looking out to the water, Ken Reynolds could see that he and his colleagues in Boat Team 5 had opened up a narrow lane, an opening that they would steadily expand as the day wore on. But for now, he recalled, "We were quite fortunate, we were able to blow most of the obstacles. Some of them we missed. Our gap was wide enough for about two landing craft to come in and land side by side." Of the sixteen corridors the NCDUs and Army combat engineers were supposed to blast open, only five full lanes and three partial gaps were opened by the time the first high tide rushed in, and most of them were inadequately marked. But that was enough to allow the landings at Omaha Beach to proceed. It was sufficient to pry open the gates of Europe. That afternoon, when the tide went down, the surviving demolitioneers went back to the beach and got to work steadily widening the gaps over the next few days to allow the full-scale invasion and liberation of Europe to proceed.

ON A SUMMER DAY in 2012, former U.S. Navy Seaman Second Class and Naval Combat Demolition Unit sailor Ken Reynolds sat in his home in Fort Pierce, Florida, a mile or so from a museum that honors the exploits of the U.S. Navy SEALs and their predecessors.

On his wall was a framed Presidential Unit Citation. It was awarded to the Naval Combat Demolition Units by the secretary of the Navy on behalf of the president of the United States, to honor the work Reynolds and his colleagues did on D-Day in the bloody sands of Omaha Beach.

Reynolds thought back to that morning in June 1944, and he told us there was one thing he couldn't figure out. It had puzzled him for the last sixty-eight years.

"I think I did my job very well and I survived. Some guys did their jobs well and didn't survive. I managed to survive. Why? I don't know." Reynolds showed us the Ka-Bar knife he carried onto Omaha Beach on D-Day.

"This was the only thing we carried on the day of the invasion," he explained. "The knife was important to us to cut cords, wires, and so forth. It was never used as a weapon, it was just strictly Navy issue. It was a good knife, it served us well.

It's a memento of what little we had on the invasion that day. That's all that we had to work with when we were charging all the obstacles to blow them out of the way." It is one of countless thousands of similar knives issued to U.S. military personnel from World War II to today, and is a particular favorite of today's Navy SEALs.

When he returned from Europe, Reynolds reported back to the Navy base at Fort Pierce, Florida, in September 1944, where he met his future wife. "We met in the USO. She was with her mother. She noticed me first, she said she liked my view from the rear. So anyway, that sparked a conversation. The conversation led to me taking them both to a movie in Fort Pierce, mother, daughter and me, and it went on from there. We stayed married for sixty-one years, and had three children."

After World War II, Ken Reynolds became a diesel mechanic, worked for Caterpillar to help construct the Interstate Highway System, and managed eleven steel mills. For many decades, he never talked about the war, including to his family. Then in his final years, Reynolds volunteered at the Navy UDT-SEAL museum at Fort Pierce, where he began telling the story of his work on Omaha Beach to any visitors who were interested in learning about it.

Over the years, it bothered him a bit that in all the stories he read and movies he saw about D-Day, he never came across the story of the NCDUs, who were among the earliest combat ancestors of the U.S. Navy SEALs. "But we were there," he told us, "very much so, we were there."

A few days after the seventieth Anniversary of D-Day, Ken Reynolds died at the age of eighty-eight. He had recently been inducted into the French National Order of the Legion of Honour.

CHAPTER 2

DAWN OF THE NAKED WARRIORS

SAIPAN, JUNE 14, 1944, 9:00 A.M.

THE FORCE:

300 U.S. Navy Underwater Demolition Team (UDT) personnel

THE ENEMY:

Japanese Imperial Navy and Army troops

THE MISSION:

Reconnaissance and demolition of landing beaches to spearhead the assault to liberate Asia and the Pacific

Lieutenant Commander Draper Kauffman braced himself and slipped into the water. He and three hundred demolitioneers of the U.S. Navy's Underwater Demolition Teams (UDT) 5, 6, and 7 were about to try something no one had ever done before: a large-scale combat swimmer reconnaissance and beach survey while under enemy fire.

They were going to swim toward the shore of a heavily fortified strategic outpost of the Japanese Empire, practically into the muzzles of enemy guns, conduct a complex beach reconnaissance and survey mission while under intense enemy fire, and try to make it back to their ships in one piece.

It was a clear summer morning in the waters west of the tropical island of Saipan, and through his thick eyeglasses Kauffman could glimpse the coral lagoon and lush sandy beach that formed his target. Onshore, scores of Japanese gunners easily spotted the approaching Americans and prepared to open fire.

The next day, only eight days after the D-Day landings in Europe, the UDTs would try to blow open a path for the Second and Fourth Marine Divisions to land on the southwest beaches of Saipan and sweep northward to advance the final liberation of Asia and the Pacific. Even though they were backed up by an armada of over 500 American vessels bearing over 100,000 men, including sixteen destroyers, four battleships, and six cruisers patrolling behind them, monitoring their communications, and providing massed fire support, Kauffman feared that the first wave of demolitioneers would be incredibly conspicuous and exposed to Japanese fire. When he first heard of the plan, Kauffman, who was in charge of UDT-5, figured he'd be lucky if his men sustained only 50 percent casualties.

The island of Saipan is 1,300 miles south of mainland Japan and was technically a Japanese mandate of the impotent League of Nations. But it had become an integral outpost of the Japanese war machine, home to a garrison of thirty thousand Japanese Imperial Navy and Army troops. It was considered a linchpin in the empire's main defense perimeter guarding the Japanese Home Islands. Crucially, if the Americans captured the island, Japanese cities would fall within range of the United States' B-29 Superfortress bombers.

As the landing craft dropped Draper Kauffman and the UDT

teams off at hundred-yard intervals along the beach, American warships plastered the shoreline and beyond with covering fire. The barrage seemed unusually intense, and some of the demolitioneers had a theory as to why.

Commander Kauffman, a tall, bespectacled, sunburned twenty-eight-year-old officer, had a friend in a very high place in the Navy. One of the UDT men, Ed Higgins, later explained: "Draper's father was Admiral Kauffman and he was not only an admiral, he was COMCRUDESPAC (Commander, Cruisers, Destroyers, Pacific). It could have been normal, paternal concern on the part of Draper's father that resulted in our getting very extensive fire support covering us. Especially since most of the fire seemed to come from cruisers and destroyers."

As a symphony of bullets and shells raged above them, the UDT men got to work surveying the underwater landing zones with anchors, buoys, and weighted measuring string made of fishing line, writing their findings down with grease pencils on Plexiglas slates.

The demolitioneers hitting the water off Saipan resembled strange warriors from another world. "They looked fantastic," recalled Commander Francis Douglas Fane, later commander of UDT-13, "clad in blue sneakers, kneepads for crawling on coral, swim trunks, canvas work gloves to protect their hands from poisonous coral scratches, glass-fronted face masks, and helmets." He added, "Adding a final surrealistic touch, each man was camouflaged blue and was painted from toe to chin, and down each arm, with horizontal stripes of ordinary black paint a foot apart, with shorter lines between. This war paint was not an imitation of the Indian naked warriors; it was Kauffman's idea for quick measurement of lagoon and reef depths." Another UDT man wrote that "men from Mars had nothing on us for grotesque appearance." SEAL historian Tom Hawkins explained, "The 'naked warrior' was the UDT operator in the

Pacific who went to the beach just in swim trunks, a Ka-Bar knife, a slate around his neck and a stubby pencil to take a string line reconnaissance of the beach, taking depth soundings and then recording it on their slates. They had no weapons with them at all. They had no way to protect themselves as they would go up to the beach."

To make the scene even stranger, Commander Kauffman and five other swim-trunked platoon and assistant platoon leaders were gliding around the water on two-man surfboard-type rubber mats, powered by their swim fins, with the officers giving orders on waterproof radios. A Japanese soldier watching the spectacle from shore would have good reason to be befuddled.

IN NOVEMBER 1943, THE need for an outfit like the Underwater Demolition Teams became tragically obvious when a disaster unfolded on a shallow coral reef off a Pacific atoll named Tarawa. Six months after the attack on Pearl Harbor, Japanese naval power was crippled at the Battle of Midway, and Japan's advance in the Pacific was finally checked in land and sea actions around Guadalcanal. This is when U.S. forces began the long drive across the Pacific to the Japanese Home Islands, which was to be an island-hopping-and-landing campaign. The first of the island landings was to be on Tarawa Atoll's Betio.

With insufficient hydrological data, the Marines went ashore in the early-morning hours of November 20, 1943. Many drowned under the weight of their gear as their landing craft scraped and got stuck on underwater reefs well offshore; many more were gunned down as they waded the shallow stretches between reefs and beach. Nearly one thousand Marines died at Tarawa and more than two thousand others were wounded.

Amphibious operations are by their very nature risky and

costly, but accurate hydrographic intelligence could reduce risk and save lives. It was clear that the Navy needed men to go in ahead of the invasion forces to survey the landing beaches, and demolish obstacles and reefs that blocked Allied landing raft. There was a war on; these men had to be found and quickly trained for this important task. Soon, to accomplish this work, the Navy turned to naval officers like the guiding force of the Pacific UDTs, Lieutenant Commander John T. Koehler, who commanded UDT-2. Koehler set up the new UDT base at Maui, and developed and oversaw the needed comprehensive training programs.

Another man the Navy turned to was Draper Kauffman. He proved to be an ideal man for the job. The origins of the Navy "frogman"* can be illustrated by the life of the charismatic Kauffman. Kauffman graduated from the U.S. Naval Academy in 1933, but because of poor vision was unable to pass the commissioning physical. So he entered the ambulance service in France just in time to see its army overrun by the Germans in 1940. After a brief stint as a POW he went to England, where he promptly joined the Royal Navy. Midway through his training to become a British naval officer he volunteered for ordnance disposal work. Soon Sub-Lieutenant Kauffman was

---

* According to SEAL historian Tom Hawkins, "The term 'frogmen' originates with the British, who were (except for the Italians) the first combat divers. They wore protective dress made from green rubber and were hence labeled 'frogmen' in the British press. Once the UDTs adopted the underwater capabilities of the OSS Maritime Units after the war . . . they too began exploring protective dress for thermal protection. They were not really called Frogmen until after Korea, and they hated the term initially, but soon learned that it made them very popular in books, magazines, and movies." Also, see the end of this book for Hawkins's detailed account of the World War II ancestor-legacy units of the U.S. Navy SEALs, including the Naval Combat Demolition Units (NCDUs), Underwater Demolition Teams (UDTs), Amphibious Scouts and Raiders (S&R), Special Mission Naval Demolition Unit, Naval Demolition Project, Special Services Unit One (SSU-1), Sino-American Cooperative Organization (SACO), and Office of Strategic Services Maritime Unit.

crawling through the rubble of London, defusing unexploded bombs.

In 1943, Kauffman, now a U.S. naval officer, was summoned to a mosquito-infested mangrove swamp at Fort Pierce, Florida, to help oversee the training program of the new all-volunteer group called the Naval Combat Demolition Unit (NCDU), which was tasked with removing obstacles from landing beaches held by Axis forces. The NCDUs saw action in two landings in Europe, Normandy and southern France, with beach clearance being their main job, and six NCDUs remained together throughout the war in the Pacific. The training headquarters was set up in a former casino that housed the headquarters of a naval amphibious outfit called the Scouts and Raiders. Their training called for an intensive eight-week physical training regimen.

The Scouts and Raiders staged an extraordinary training exercise in mid-1943, an operation that featured nothing less than a simulated, real-world commando raid on South Florida. "Our mission was to capture several military installations and vital national security areas," recalled U.S. Navy Captain Howard Moore. "In executing it, one of our teams captured the DuPont Building [in Miami], which housed the 7th Naval District Headquarters. Not only did they take the Marine guard in custody and 'knock out' its communications center, they bodily carried out the admiral commanding. My team was taken to within a couple thousand yards off Ft. Lauderdale. After paddling rubber boats ashore we got onto the highway several miles from our objective, the Port Everglades docks and oil terminals. We were black-faced, in black jumpsuits, with camouflaged helmets on, and we stopped the first vehicle that came along, a Greyhound bus with a few passengers. We told the driver to turn around and take us to Port Everglades. He complied with our 'request.' We ran through the gates as the guards tried to wave us down. Our leader, Ensign Ray G. Walter, told the driver not to pay any attention to them. We kept going for about a half mile and told the driver to let us off near a swampy area. We disappeared into the brush, paired off, and attached a pound or so of modeling clay 'plastic explosive' to each storage unit, with dummy blasting caps and fuses. Part of the team also 'blew up' the unloading terminal's structures and pipeline."

No doubt impressed by the Scouts and Raiders' capabilities, Draper Kauffman asked the Scouts and Raiders if they could compress the highlights of their training program into a single week. It quickly became known as Hell Week. And that's what a critical part of Navy SEAL training is still known as today. "Hell Week isn't designed to kill you," wrote modern-day SEAL Rorke Denver. "It's designed to make you wish you were dead—or at least to push you to the edge of physical and mental endurance to see how you react. While the demands are mostly physical, the journey through them is all about mental attitude."

Kauffman and the officers went through the first Hell Week with their enlisted trainees. That established a precedent that continues to this day; officers and enlisted men endure training side by side during the arduous week. Those who survived Hell Week were then trained in demolitions, beach reconnaissance, and hydrographic survey work. Then, as now, they trained in boat crews of six to eight men with an officer in charge. The crews worked as teams during training and in combat, just as SEALs do today.

Kauffman also set the tone for a special bond between officers and enlisted men. Beginning with the first class, he brought the volunteers into a room, officers on one side and the enlisted men on the other. To the enlisted he said, "I will do everything in my power to see that no officer graduates from this school under whom I would not be happy to go into combat." To the officers he said, "I will do everything in my power to see that no enlisted man graduates from this school whom I would not want to lead in combat." The officers and enlisted men then shared alike in the miseries of Fort Pierce and NCDU training. The carnage suffered by the Marines at Tarawa added urgency to the pace of their training, and the need to get them into action in both the Pacific and European combat zones.

After being transferred to the UDT training base at Maui, Hawaii, Commander Kauffman was called into the Pearl Harbor office of Admiral Richmond Kelly Turner, head of the Fifth Amphibious Force of Admiral Raymond Spruance's Fifth Fleet. "We don't want another blunder like the one at Tarawa," announced Admiral Turner, referring to the costly landings four months earlier when nearly one thousand U.S. Marines were killed in part because Navy planners didn't have detailed data on the water depths in the landing zones.

Kauffman watched Turner trace his finger on a map of Saipan, an island that measured fourteen miles long by five miles wide. "Here," said Turner, "are the beaches on which we plan to land. And here is a coral reef protecting them. At the north end, this reef is about one mile offshore. Down here, about half a mile.

"Now," said the admiral, "the first and most important thing is reconnaissance to determine the depth of water. I'm thinking of having you go in and reconnoiter around eight."

"Well, Admiral," said Kauffman, thinking his superior was using civilian rather than military time, "it depends on the phase of the moon."

"Moon?" snapped Turner. "What in the hell has that to do with it? Obviously by eight o'clock I mean 0800."

Kauffman was stunned. The UDTs had conducted smaller-scale daylight reconnaissance missions earlier in the year, like their combat debut at the island of Kwajalein on January 31, 1944, as part of Operation Flintlock in the Marshall Islands, during which two UDT men, Ensign Lewis E. Luehrs and Chief Petty Officer Bill Acheson of UDT-1, spontaneously decided to conduct the first American swimming reconnaissance of an enemy beach. But the Saipan plan would put hundreds of UDT personnel in extended, point-blank daylight range of enemy gunners.

Kauffman marveled, "In broad daylight—onto somebody else's beach in broad daylight, Admiral?"

"Absolutely," said his superior. "We'll have lots of fire support to cover you."

"I just don't see how you can do it in broad daylight," said Kauffman despairingly.

Turner cut off the objections by declaring a simple truth: "The main reason is you can see in the daytime and you can't see at night." When he got back to the Maui UDT training base, Kauffman oversaw a crash program in daylight reconnaissance, and pushed up the swimming requirement for a UDT man to swim a minimum of two miles. Until now, long-distance swim training wasn't part of the UDT toolkit, but it quickly became hugely important, just as it is for today's SEALs.

The core unit of the UDTs became the classic two-man team of "swim buddies," who trained together and stuck together in combat at all costs, always looking out for each other, ready to tow the other man if he became wounded or exhausted. Seventy years later, the swim buddy tradition is still going strong with today's SEALs. As one modern-day SEAL explained to us: "A swim buddy is the man you look after, and that man looks after you. No matter where you go or what you do on an operation or exercise, out of the water or in, that swim buddy is with you. You never, ever, leave your swim buddy. That rule is number one in the Teams. The swim buddy rule especially holds true when you're operating in the field. If you're in the water or in enemy territory, whatever you're in, wherever you are, you take care of each other. You make sure nothing happens to him and he makes sure nothing happens to you. And that basic integrity goes through the whole group. You always take care of your swim buddy."

Now, on the morning of the Saipan reconnaissance, the admiral's prediction came true. The UDT men enjoyed excellent visibility on this clear morning. The problem was, so did the Japanese. And they were raking the demolitioneers with 3-inch and 5-inch guns and 88 mm mortar fire. One mortar shell detonated underwater and blew a UDT man clear above the surface, but he maintained his swim stroke before falling back into the water and continuing his work.

Draper Kauffman maneuvered his "mattress" to an anchor spot three hundred yards off the beach and waited for the heavy air support that was promised at 10 A.M. "Not one plane appeared," recalled Kauffman in a letter to his father the next day. "I got to about 100 yards from the beach and even with my bad eyes could see the Japs." He continued, "I set up my radio and called for the damned aviators, but the aerial was shot away while I was using it."

The mattresses, which Kauffman hoped would help him and his team leaders maintain control and communications during the operation, were instead so conspicuous they were acting as magnets for bullets and mortar fire. One of the mattress-riding UDT men was killed by a sniper. When another UDT man's mattress was punctured by a Japanese bullet and Kauffman offered him a lift, the man waved him off, saying, "Get that

damned thing out of here!" It was the first and only time the
mattresses were used in combat.

Watching his men methodically go about their work, Kauffman was amazed. "Every single man," he recalled, "was calmly
and slowly continuing his search and marking his slate with stuff
dropping all around. They didn't appear one tenth as scared as
I was. I would not have been so amazed if ninety percent of the
men had done so well, but to have a cold one hundred percent
go in through the rain of fire was almost unbelievable."

For his own part, Kauffman was also a study in courage
that morning, as the commander of a nearby ship described:
"Learning that two of his men had been left on the reef, [he]
returned to the beach and personally rescued his men under
extremely heavy rifle and machine gun fire." For this action,
Kauffman was later awarded the Navy Cross.

When their job was complete, the UDT men collected their
data, withdrew en masse to their landing craft, and made it back
to their mother ship, the *Gilmer,* to review their charts with
Navy planners. "How we got back with the loss of only one
man and seven injured," marveled Kauffman, "I don't know."

The UDTs were ordered to lay explosives to blast open a
path through the coral reef for the Marines' landing craft the
next day, June 15, which was the invasion's D-Day, and to do it
before dawn. But the job was so complex that it took them until
10 A.M. to be ready to detonate their charges. Kauffman himself
pulled the nine fuses, set for ten minutes, and the demolitioneers
swam to safety as fast as they could. The teams placed so many
explosives that they had no idea what the blast would look or
feel like. Kauffman later explained that the UDTs "were not
skilled artists in the use of explosives," and "we always used far
more explosive than we really needed." The resulting detonation was so powerful it threw a surge of black water up a quar-

ter of a mile before engulfing several American landing ships, and Kauffman later said the blast was comparable to what he witnessed at the nuclear underwater test at Bikini Atoll.

After the Marines had landed and secured a beachhead, the UDT men followed them ashore for additional demolition work. When Kauffman and another UDT man walked onto the beach, which was under heavy fire, they cut such exotic figures in their swim trunks, baby-blue sneakers, and body paint that one Marine, so the story goes, said, "Christ, I've seen everything. We ain't even got the beach yet and the tourists are here already." By the end of the day, twenty thousand U.S. Marines were on Saipan.

Over the course of two days, the UDT men used more than 100,000 pounds of explosives to slice landing paths through the reef and lagoon on the southwestern side of the island, enabling U.S. Marine and Army forces to push in and capture Saipan after more than three weeks of heavy combat. From here American bombers could attack Tokyo itself. In Tokyo, Hideki Tojo was forced to resign his post as Japan's prime minister. It was a critical turning point in the war.

Japan's defensive wall was cracked open, thanks in part to the demolitioneers of UDTs 5, 6, and 7, three of whom died in the operation. Draper Kauffman later sent his Navy Cross to the mother of one of the UDT men who died in the Battle of Saipan, a popular UDT-5 team member named Bob Christianson. "He deserves it far more than I do," wrote Kauffman.

AT THE AMERICAN LANDINGS on Guam in late July 1944, UDTs 3, 4, and 6 played a critical role in reconnoitering and blasting open channels for U.S. Marines and vehicles to pour across the beaches.

Days before the invasion, the demolitioneers paddled toward the beach in small rubber craft stuffed with explosives, then slid into the water towing twenty-pound packs of tetrytol. After tying in the packs with detonation cord on the coral reef and Japanese obstacles, everyone but two "fuse men" swam back to the boats. The fuse men cut fuses long enough to let them swim as fast as they could to safety before the detonating cord blasted the obstacles sky-high. The UDTs joked that the fuse men were the fastest swimmers on earth.

The UDTs worked for three days and nights blowing up the beach obstacles on the beaches of Guam. "150 obstacles [were] removed using 3,000 pounds Tetrytol," read a UDT after-action report. "The enemy had placed obstacles in an almost continuous front along the reef. These obstacles were piles of coral rock inside a wire frame made of heavy wire net."

At one primary landing spot near the little town of Agat, the night before the Marines were scheduled to storm ashore a team of demolitioneers slipped onto the enemy-held White Beach and playfully erected a five-by-two-foot wooden sign, carefully lettered with black paint and facing the ocean, then slipped back into the water. The sign read:

WELCOME MARINES
AGAT USO TWO BLOCKS
COURTESY UDT 4

As the war in the Pacific ground on, every landing beach was different and each presented its own unique challenges. So these first UDT demolitioneers became adept at improvisation. As the problems arose, they solved them. A good example is the development of the waterproof firing assembly. From the beginning, the NCDUs and UDTs were trained in the use of demolitions against natural and man-made obstacles. Beach obstacles, from man-made steel tetrahedrons to natural coral reefs, had to be blown out of the way, and that meant the reliable priming of explosive charges—underwater explosive charges. Navy scientists and engineers tried any number of ways to make a reliable waterproof initiator for submerged explosives. None of them worked. Then a bright sailor came up with the idea of using condoms and neoprene cement. It was simple, cheap, and it worked every time. The UDTs in the Pacific became a huge consumer of military-issue condoms, ordering thousands of them while the Navy supply system was trying to figure out what exactly was going on.

A few years ago, a SEAL team commanding officer stated in his standing orders: "Flexibility is found in the dictionary under Naval Special Warfare." That all started with the NCDU and UDT demolitioneers of World War II. The conditions were ideal for innovation and spontaneity. All the men selected for this new naval specialty were volunteers, carefully selected and screened. They were then subjected to a physical regime that further cut their numbers, often dramatically. Then they trained as teams, in a competitive environment and with officers and enlisted men sharing the same miserable conditions and dangers. This produced a tightly bonded group of men who were smart, tough, and adaptive. There were procedures for handling explosives, but given the conditions under which these first demolitioneers practiced their trade, they developed the procedures and wrote most of the first manuals. Finally and perhaps most important, they worked alone, with little tactical oversight. They were the first of their breed. Unlike conventional forces, there were no admirals or generals who had experience in this form of warfare. Basically, Admiral Ernest J. King, then chief of naval operations, gave the order to "do it," and the teams got the job done. This way of doing business became a part of the NCDU-UDT culture and has carried forward to today's SEALs—to the SEALs now serving around the world. Indeed, an oft-heard command within our deployed SEAL platoons is "Okay, guys, make it happen," and the job gets done.

Today's SEALs are trained to operate from submerged submarines, but this was unheard-of seventy years ago. During World War II, UDT men were never launched underwater, and only once from the decks of a surfaced submarine, which culminated in the tragedy of the *Burrfish* operation detailed on the following pages. The marriage of UDT diver and submarine was first tried in the late 1940s and made an operational tool in the 1950s. Then, as now, most submarines were only equipped with escape trunks used to "lock out" men trapped underwater in a crippled sub. The locking out and recovering of submerged divers was, and still is, a highly choreographed underwater ballet. A great deal of coordination was needed between the UDT swimmers and submarine sailors. The early lessons and procedures validated by the postwar UDTs are in use today as nuclear submarine crews often train to routinely launch and recover SEALs and their minisubs. The protocols and procedures that drive these complex operations were pioneered by the UDTs.

Getting UDT men to the job site was one matter; picking them up was another. In World War II, they were often recovered by a rubber lasso of sorts. A speeding small craft with an inflatable Zodiac-type boat tied alongside would race down a line of swimmers. A rubber loop secured to the speeding boat by a bungee cord would be dropped over the swimmer's raised arm, and he would be flipped into the inflatable as it sped past. Starting in 1947, the UDTs began to experiment with helicop-

ters. Swimmers were cast or dropped from helicopters and re-
trieved as the helo flew past towing a ladder across the top of
the waves. This procedure is still used today, but only when
the presence of a slow-moving helicopter offshore is compatible
with the mission. Cast-and-recover by helo is still a procedure-
driven business; communication between the aircrew and the
swimmers is essential. In fact, the last SEAL fatality in Vietnam
was the result of a failed jump from a helicopter.

WHEN OSAMA BIN LADEN was killed in May 2011, the world
gained a glimpse into the shadows of the strong partnership
between the SEALs and the Central Intelligence Agency. But
what few people realize is that the relationship stretches back
all the way to the summer of 1943, when the CIA's predecessor agency, the Office of Strategic Services, or OSS, formed its
own Maritime Unit of spies, boatmen, saboteurs, swimmers,
and demolitioneers.

Although the maverick OSS chief General "Wild Bill" Don-
ovan was often the loser in bureaucratic turf battles with the
regular military and the FBI, he did manage to create a maritime force that saw action during World War II on the coasts
and rivers of Burma, India, Thailand, China, and Europe. The
mission of the Maritime Unit was defined officially as "infiltration of agents and operatives by sea, the waterborne supply
of resistance groups, execution of maritime sabotage, and the
development of special equipment and devices."

Working out of secret training bases in the Caribbean and
California (some of the OSS swimmers were former Santa
Monica lifeguards), the OSS Maritime Unit helped pioneer
several of the techniques and technologies that flowed into the
toolkits of the postwar UDTs and are still used by the SEALs

of today. They included face masks, flexible swim fins, limpet mines, waterproof watches and compasses, fast patrol boats, swimmer submersible craft, a closed-circuit, pure-oxygen re-breathing apparatus called the Lambertsen Amphibious Respiratory Unit (LARU), which was very handy since it let you swim thirty feet down without leaving a trail of air bubbles for the enemy to spot. "The gadgets that OSS Maritime developed were along the lines of capabilities to do their mission of sabotage or get to the shoreline," explained SEAL historian Tom Hawkins. "They adopted the first usable submersible from the British, which was called 'Sleeping Beauty,' and it was a submersible canoe. It was a one-man vessel that could be propelled on the surface and then submerged for the attack. They developed a floating mattress that was powered by a 12-volt battery to propel one or two people through the water." Hawkins sees the pioneering work of the OSS Maritime Unit as establishing early legacy capabilities still seen today in the U.S. Navy's Special Boat Teams.

The story of one legendary OSS maritime operative offers a good picture of what amazing work they did. His name was Walter L. Mess. He played pro football and got his law degree before blazing a trail through the China-Burma-India Theater of Operation. As an OSS patrol-and-rescue-boat skipper, Walter Mess reported having conducted thirty-six operations in the Bay of Bengal, picked up scores of downed Allied pilots on the Burma coast, and made a series of parachute jumps leading teams of Burmese forces to clear seven landing strips. He recalled ferrying swimmers and spies fifty to seventy miles into enemy territory, quietly slipping through narrow channels from where he could see enemy campfires. "Shooting wasn't our mission," he told espionage historian Patrick K. O'Donnell. "Our mission was taxi driver, our mission was not to fight, but we were prepared to do it." He described it as "a river war like the movie *Apocalypse Now*."

ON THE NIGHT OF August 18, 1944, a UDT special mission group that included volunteers from UDT-10 and OSS Maritime Swimmers assigned to the UDT-10 set off in a rubber raft from the submarine *Burrfish* toward the island of Yap, in the Caroline Islands of the western Pacific. It was the first submarine-borne operation in Naval Special Warfare history. Their mission was to conduct a reconnaissance survey of the beaches for a possible amphibious landing. On the second night of the operation, three men, Howard L. Roeder, John C. MacMahon, and Robert A. Black, became separated from the others, missed their post-midnight rendezvous, and were never seen by Americans again. They were captured and executed by Japanese forces.

The reality of UDT operations in the Pacific was one of constant danger and routine courage, as UDT-10's Robert Kenworthy described when recalling his first mission off the coast of Angaur Island in September 1944: "I jumped up like on a diving board, curled my body, and dove [from the boat] into the water. This was in broad daylight; we were at least 300 yards from the beach, all the while avoiding getting shot. As we were approaching the beach, we were expecting them to open fire but they were waiting for us to get closer. You are looking at the beach expecting to see a flash. We were perfectly at home in the water, if it was two or three miles out, it wouldn't make a difference. There were four landing craft. I was with Platoon Number 3. I'm looking out at my 500 yards of beach. The water was mighty cold but crystal clear. But we were used to it. Fifty-four-degree water after several hours becomes very untenable.

Your testicles climb up inside, it's later when they come down that it is not very nice.

"On the left of the section I had to cover a concrete pillbox," recalled Kenworthy. "Just remembering it makes the hair stand up on my arms. The Japs knew that this was the best beach for a landing and accordingly set up a pillbox. We were about 75 to 125 yards away from it when all hell broke loose. I turned my head and from the right end of the beach I saw three Jap soldiers push palm fronds aside and open fire. We were caught right between the two machine guns." Several American planes accidentally opened fire on the UDT men. "Bullets were hitting the water all around us," according to Kenworthy. "Our CO broke radio silence and told the admiral, 'Get your goddamn cowboys out of there!' Luckily, they broke off the attack and none of our guys were killed."

When the demolitioneers returned to clear a path for landing craft through the coral reef with C-2 explosive charges, Kenworthy remembered, "I held my breath over two minutes so we could go down and stay down and set the charge. Boom! We detonated it. Coral shot into the air." On D-Day, Kenworthy helped guide the landing craft in passages through the remaining coral. He remembered watching the Marines as their craft passed by: "This was a powerful thing as you looked at the clenched faces of these 18- and 20-year-olds and in another 15 or 20 minutes they were dead. It's a visual thing you carry with you all your life."

At the amphibious invasion in late 1944 of Leyte, the first big island in the Philippines to be recaptured by the Allies, UDT demolitioneers conducted surveys and laid charges to clear beach obstacles while under fire from Japanese machine-gun and sniper fire. A UDT-10 man later described the scene on October 19, the day before the invasion, "At about 400 yards we dropped off the side of the boat and loaded up with the amount of tetrytol that we anticipated we would need to level the beach [obstructions] so the LSTs could land, open their doors, and tanks could roll out. As we swam forward the water around us was being peppered with machine-gun, rifle, and mortar fire. Water was splashing up around me from the rounds. I noticed that the Japanese had fish traps in the water in front of the beach. They turned out to be markers that allowed them to direct their mortar and cannon fire."

Having witnessed the UDTs in action in the Philippine campaign, the commander of the Amphibious Forces of the Seventh Fleet, Vice Admiral Daniel Barbey, marveled, "The results achieved by these UDTs are far above anything one might imagine. It seems incredible that men in small boats and men swimming should be able to close a heavily defended, hostile beach in broad daylight to almost the high-water mark without receiving such severe damage as to make their operations a failure."

On October 20, 1944, General Douglas MacArthur, fulfilling his 1942 promise to the Philippine people that "I shall return," strode onto a beach on Leyte that had been surveyed by UDT personnel, and the liberation of the Philippines began. The American and Filipino forces made tough but steady progress until the last pockets of organized Japanese resistance on the islands surrendered the following August.

ON THE MORNING OF February 16, 1945, some four hundred Underwater Demolition Team men staged another daring broad-daylight reconnaissance operation, this one on the beaches of the Japanese-held island of Iwo Jima, a key strategic stepping-stone on the path to mainland Japan. Their mission was to survey the landing approaches that Marines would storm through two days later, and to retrieve soil samples from the beach to help planners figure out how landing craft would perform.

One of the demolitioneers recalled, "We were rigged in just swim trunks, swim fins, a face mask, knife, several mine detonators, and a lead weight with line for determining depth, but beads of sweat took the place of goose bumps. And instead of having choppy water as we had expected and wished for, we had a sea as calm as a mill pond." Calm seas meant they were easier to spot by enemy gunners.

The wave of approaching UDT landing craft must have looked like the start of an actual invasion to Japanese forces dug into fortified positions in caves and cliffs on the island, and in response they let loose a terrifying barrage. When the landing craft reached 1,500 yards offshore, the Japanese unleashed a torrent of machine-gun and mortar fire.

As the UDT swimmers launched themselves into the cold water close to the Iwo Jima beach, they were backed up with steady fire from their landing craft and a picket line of destroyers, cruisers, and battleships farther offshore, plus rocket-firing aircraft. Underwater, they could see shrapnel and bullets floating down around them, in the words of one UDT man, "as thick as snowflakes." Some swimmers crawled onto the beach and scooped up samples of black sand into pouches and slipped back into the water. When they returned to their command ship, the USS *Gilmer,* they enjoyed some soothing shots of brandy. While drinking aboard ship was against Navy regulations, brandy for "medicinal purposes" was permitted because of the cold water.

The UDT teams reported encouraging news for the upcoming invasion: few mines or obstacles, no coral reefs, deep-enough water for the landing ships. However, Navy analysts misinterpreted the soil samples, which seemed packed hard enough to support vehicles with tires like armored cars and jeeps. In fact, the powdery volcanic sand a few feet inland of the beach was as loose and slippery as ball bearings, and only tracked vehicles could drive over it. This caused a traffic jam when the invasion of Iwo Jima began two days later. The landings at Iwo were initially unopposed but after the Marines crowded onto the landing beaches, the Japanese opened fire. A UDT-14 demolitioneer named Jack Basham recalled the "extremely hairy" experience of combat at Iwo Jima: "I can remember, very vividly our cover ship being sunk before we got into the water to swim, the mortar fire from the island, shelling falling short from our own gunners. I can also recall those machine gun bullets hitting the water over me and the bullets settling down in front of me, the smoke shells and a lot of other things. Three of us decided to go ashore at Iwo after we had gotten our swimming work done. We wanted to take in some of the land fighting. Of course we had absolutely no business doing it. They were still fighting on the beach. We didn't have any weapons to defend ourselves with and finally picked up carbines from dead marines on the beach. The Japanese snipers would shoot at us and we would run and jump into shell holes for protection. We worked our way up to the edge of an airstrip and found seventy-five or more marines laying dead and stripped of their uniforms."

Tragically, on the same day the invasion of Iwo Jima began, February 18, 1945, a 500-pound bomb dropped by a Japanese "Betty" twin-engine bomber fell through the stack of the USS *Blessman* and detonated in the mess hall, killing forty men, including eighteen sailors from UDT-15.

On the morning of February 23, the UDT men paused from their work to let out a cheer when they spotted the American flag being hoisted atop Mount Suribachi. But the battle was far from over. Altogether it took the American Marines, Army, and Navy forces eighty-two days to wrest Iwo Jima from over 100,000 Japanese troops who were dug into the hills of the island.

AT 3:33 P.M. ON March 29, 1945, Ed Higgins of UDT-11 was swimming in cool water toward the beach of Okinawa, trying to figure out why his body was pounding so severely.

"Behind us every ship in the fleet thundered, blasting the beach and shore line with thousands of tons of hot steel," Higgins recalled. "Overhead, fighters and dive bombers from the fleet carriers wheeled and dived, with their blazing guns and smoking rockets bombing and strafing every Jap position they could locate or even suspect." Like NCDU man Ken Reynolds at Omaha Beach the year before, Higgins felt he was in the middle of an epic scene: "It was the most magnificent and awe-inspiring spectacle I ever saw or expect to see or hear."

Higgins knew he was absorbing the rhythmic slamming of the U.S. Navy guns pasting the shoreline with supporting fire as he and his fellow UDT men got ready to go to work, but this feeling was different. The vibration was so strong that Higgins figured there must be a heavy machine gun somehow following him close by. Then he realized it wasn't a gun that was creating the jackhammer effect on his body. It was his own teeth. They were vibrating so violently from chattering in the frigid water.

Higgins was taking part in one of the biggest formations of men and ships of the Pacific War: including nearly 1,000 UDT demolitioneers, comprising the largest UDT operation of World War II. They were charged with reconnoitering, surveying, and clearing the landing beaches for D-Day on April 1, when the first waves of nearly 450,000 U.S. troops from four divisions of the U.S. Tenth Army (the 7th, 27th, 77th, and 96th) and two

Marine divisions (the 1st and 6th) would take on 100,000 Japanese forces dug into the island. The Americans needed a big base to strike from that was close to the main Japanese islands, and Okinawa fit the bill perfectly. It was just 340 miles south of Kyushu, and would be the essential final piece of the Allies' long island-hopping campaign.

In the waters off Okinawa, Higgins and his UDT colleagues got to work dropping weighted fishing lines to check the water depth, measuring the surf, checking for mines and other obstacles, and writing their data on waterproof slates. They were fifty to sixty yards offshore and Japanese gunners were opening up with sniper and machine-gun fire. In response, U.S. landing craft fired 3-inch guns and 20 mm and 40 mm artillery toward the shore over the bobbing heads of the UDT men.

UDT member Edwin R. Ashby, a boatswain's mate, second class, reported, "The ship wasn't my blanket, the water was my blanket. As soon as I got into the water, things were all right. Everything seemed to calm down and I could concentrate much better on what I was supposed to do. The first thing you would notice, especially off of Okinawa, was that the water was more than a little cool. That shock brought you to your senses pretty quick. Then you and your swim partner would take a look and make sure everyone was in line before striking out for the beach. Moving on to the beach, we would take our soundings and make notes on our pads. . . . As soon as the stuff started flying, the whole situation started to seem a little like a dream. It was happening all around you, but it didn't seem real. You would psych yourself up and even the sound of the shells and rifle fire seemed to get less. They were kind of muffled, though you could still hear everything. But you just kept going, did your job, and turned back out to sea, for pickup."

The waters off Okinawa were so cold that the UDTs worked

at an increasingly frantic speed as they felt their limbs go limp from numbness and severe cramps. They finally made it back to their ships for a warm brandy, a hot shower, and intensive debriefings. They came back with no casualties and a wealth of detailed information. The UDT's survey had revealed a giant underwater field of pointed Japanese pole obstacles, as many as three thousand of them, laced with barbed wire and some tipped with mines, blocking the planned landing paths to the beach. Based on the data, American planners decided the UDT men would return the next day to stage a demolition raid to remove them.

At 9:30 A.M. on March 30, UDTs 11 and 16 were sent in to blow up the pole obstacles on Beaches Red 3 and Blue 1 and 2. "As we went in," wrote Edward Higgins, "the fire from the fleet increased until it reached a crescendo that threatened to split the very air and water around us. Straight ahead we went until the boats were within 400 yards of the obstacles in the surf. Then the demolition packs went over the side and after them the swimmers." Many of the UDT swimmers were towing five packs of 25-pound explosive charges. The demolitioneers came to fifty yards off the beach, within close range of the Japanese pillboxes. Splashes of automatic weapons fire closed in on Higgins as he zigzagged in the surf.

Higgins, who was wearing highly visible long john underwear in a vain attempt to fight the cold, swam toward one of his buddies, who yelled furiously at him, "You son of a bitch, get away from here with that goddamn white sweatshirt! Do you want to get us all killed?"

Higgins recalled that the carrier-borne American fighter planes and torpedo bombers "added their own individual tones to the murderous symphony, loosing their bombs, rockets and machine guns barely above the heads of the entrenched enemy . . . To avoid fire from the shore, all crossing from post to post was done underwater. Swimmers came up to breathe only when they were safely behind a post. The pattern had been drilled into us by many months of rehearsal: dive to the bottom of the post, fix the charge with the soft metal wire twisted around the post, surface behind the post with the prima-cord lead, tie the lead into the trunk line, dive under-water to the next post and repeat, repeat until all the posts were tied and all charges connected to the trunk line."

Just minutes after the teams began placing the charges, something mysterious happened. The men of UDT-16 abruptly pulled away from the scene. Something, thought the nearby UDT-11's Higgins, must have gone radically wrong, but he couldn't imagine what it was.

When the explosives were detonated at 10:43 A.M., spotters concluded that all the targets in UDT-11's area were cleared, but few in UDT-16's zone were. Late that afternoon, the UDT-11 men were stunned to learn they were going back in at 9:00 A.M. the next day to finish UDT-16's aborted mission. "Our sympathy for UDT 16 hit a zero reading at that point," Higgins later wrote. "Going in on the same beaches for the third straight day was asking for it, and we knew it."

The exact sequence of events that befell UDT-16 and triggered the failure of their first mission will probably never be known, but at least some of the men may have withdrawn too early when Japanese snipers opened fire on them. Petty Officer First Class John A. Devine of UDT-16 believed that the failure of the team's explosives was the product of wave action that severed the connecting wires. He later reported that "approximately fifteen men and a few officers from our team volunteered to swim back out in the afternoon, to wipe the remaining obstacles out. I was one of the men that swam back in, after the tide had receded and without any gunfire support. With the Japanese firing at us, we crawled on our bellies across the coral to get to the obstacles. We did blow some of them out, but again left some still standing—for whatever reason, only God knows."

Whatever the truth was, the men of UDT-11 had to finish the job on March 31, a day prior to D-Day. They spent three hours in the water, rigging up 2.5-pound charges to each pointed stake and connecting them with primacord. "As on the previous day, the barrage from the ships and carrier planes was tremendous," recalled Edward Higgins. "Around me heads were bobbing and ducking in the water as the men dived and surfaced in evasive action against the Jap gunners firing from the trees and cliffs on the shore."

In the landing craft right behind them, officers of UDT-16 acted as spotters and guides for the UDT-11 men. Higgins noted, "We had to admit that the Team 16 officers, having fouled out on their own time at bat, were doing all in their power to help us finish the job."

On board a vessel approaching Okinawa on the morning of the invasion, Higgins spoke with a group of Marines destined for the battle. "They considered all of us as crazy as they had ever seen," he reported. "They thought the idea of swimming in to the beaches almost naked was insane and they wouldn't have our jobs for anything." The Japanese contested the American beach reconnaissance and obstacle clearance at Okinawa, and again struck hard once the Americans had moved inland.

The eighty-two-day-long campaign turned into the bloodiest battle of the Pacific War. The U.S. Navy alone suffered its worst losses of the war, with 5,000 killed and 29 ships sunk, much of the damage inflicted by swarms of Japanese suicide plane attacks. "I was never so happy to leave a place as I was to leave Okinawa," remembered Draper Kauffman, "and those terrible kamikazes."

With the capture of Okinawa, the Americans finally had a huge naval and air base close to the heart of Japan. In August 1945, all twenty-eight UDTs were sent to Oceanside, California, for cold-water training to prepare for a planned November attack on Japanese beaches for the final invasion, of Japan itself.

That invasion never came, as the atomic bombs detonated over Hiroshima and Nagasaki that August forced Japan's surrender. The American B-29 Superfortresses that dropped the weapons flew out of bases on islands previously held by the Japanese and had been captured with the critical help of the UDTs.

The history books record that the Japanese Empire surrendered to General Douglas MacArthur and the Allies aboard the battleship *Missouri* in Tokyo Bay on September 2, 1945. But there was at least one earlier surrender encounter of Japanese military personnel to American forces on the Japanese Home Islands. On August 28, 1945, a Japanese Army Coast Artillery major formally presented his sword to Lieutenant Commander Edward Porter Clayton, USN, of Underwater Demolition Team 21. This impromptu ceremony was held on the beach near a small fort near the entrance to Tokyo Bay and at least one photograph was taken of the event.

The World War II demolition men were definitely a breed apart from the regular Navy. "We didn't look very much like any sailors that had been seen before and that rankled some people in command," remembered UDT man Edwin R. Ashby. "Some admiral made a comment to Kauffman that he considered us 'the most unruly bunch of Navy men' he'd ever seen in his life and he didn't know what he would ever do with us. And Kauffman answered that officer with, 'Yes, sir, but they got the job done.' 'Yes,' the admiral said, 'I hate to admit it, but they did.' So even in those early days we were not accepted well by the regular Navy. When we went on board our ships, the APDs, we went around in our shorts. The regular crew had to keep their uniforms and hats on as per regulations. We just didn't comply with that sort of thing very much. That did raise some resentment among the rest of the Navy."

And as UDT Commander Francis Douglas Fane wrote, "The UDTs were always the despair of more conventional Navy officers. The demolitioneers were, almost to a man, Reserves. They sometimes made mistakes of administration or discipline or form; but their very unconventionality and originality worked amazingly well in the pinches." He added that the demolitioneers found that "there is no place for epaulets on a wet, sunburned shoulder, but there is plenty of room for mutual confidence and genuine discipline when officer and enlisted man alike know that the other will get every man back, or drown trying."

A total of some 3,500 UDT sailors served in the UDTs in World War II, and they took part in nearly every major amphibious operation in the Pacific, including Eniwetok, Saipan, Guam, Tinian, Angaur, Ulithi, Peleliu, Leyte, Lingayen Gulf, Zambales, Iwo Jima, Okinawa, Labuan, Brunei Bay, and Borneo. Eighty-three of them died. They were one of the most heavily decorated American combat units in the war, and their recognition included 750 Bronze Stars, 150 Silver Stars, a Navy Cross, and several Presidential Unit Citations.

The distant forefathers of the U.S. Navy SEALs helped pave the way to the liberation of Asia and the Pacific and the Allied victory of World War II, but like the SEALs, they did their work in a veil of secrecy. They sought no publicity and during the war they were mostly unknown outside the U.S. military. As the U.S. commander of amphibious forces in the Pacific, Admiral Richmond Kelly Turner, put it: "owing to the classified nature of their work," the UDTs "were unknown to the public." He added, "Their work greatly eased the landing of troops and cargo and reduced casualties, making them invaluable to the amphibious forces. And they never let us down."

In the thick of battle, the UDT and NCDU demolitioneers, Scouts and Raiders, and OSS Operational Swimmers laid the earliest foundations for what would become one of the most legendary special operations forces in military history: the U.S. Navy SEALs.

CHAPTER 3

HOT WAR, COLD WATER

WONSAN HARBOR, NORTH KOREA, MARCH 1952

THE FORCE:

One UDT-5 demolitioneer and 1 U.S. Navy bomb disposal
expert

THE ENEMY:

North Korean coastal sentries

THE MISSION:

Locate, disable, and recover Soviet-made mine

There was a bomb ten inches from Lieutenant Dick Lyon's face.

The Underwater Demolition Team-5 sailor was eight feet
underwater and one hundred yards off North Korean territory, and he was staring at a horned object the size of a large
beach ball; it carried a payload equivalent to forty-four pounds
of high explosive. This was enough firepower to blow a hole
in a medium-sized steel-hulled warship. It was a Soviet-made
prototype RMYaM contact mine designed to cripple incoming

landing craft, and Lyon was swimming in a submerged forest of the devices.

The mine was live. If he knocked one of the mine's protruding contact horns, or if a tidal surge pushed him against it, Lyon told us, "I was going to say my prayers very rapidly, because I was going straight to heaven, or wherever it is Navy frogmen go."

Dick Lyon was carrying no weapons or tools other than a Ka-Bar knife strapped to his ankle and a pair of twenty-four-inch bolt cutters in his hands. He had no formal training in mine handling and recovery. He wasn't wearing scuba gear, and no protection other than a face mask and flimsy green dry suit that offered little protection against the near-freezing water. He recalled, "I went down a couple of times always to get the layout of the area and to make sure the current would not take me into the mine."

A few yards away, crouched down in a highly visible small yellow rubber boat, was a U.S. Navy EOD (Explosive Ordnance Disposal) expert named Dick Edwards. The mission was for Lyon to swim down eight feet to cut the mine loose from the mooring cables that held it to the ocean floor, and guide it to the surface. Then and he and Edwards would gently tow it to their host ship and then to a nearby Allied-controlled island to be defused and analyzed, to improve the chances that U.S. and South Korean forces could land on the beaches of strategic Wonsan Harbor at some point in the future and try to complete the liberation of the Korean Peninsula.

Three weeks earlier, at the American base at Camp McGill in nearby Japan, which hosted UDT-5, Lieutenant Lyon was called into the office of Lieutenant Commander Louis A. States, a veteran of World War II service with UDT-11 in Okinawa and elsewhere.

"I want to let you know," said the commander, a southern gentleman with a heavy North Carolina accent, "that you're the strongest swimmer we have on the team." This was an understatement. Before joining the joint Navy-Army Scouts and Raiders force in World War II, Lyon was captain of the Yale championship swimming team of 1943, and was a world record holder in the four-man 100-meter freestyle relay.

"Sure, skipper," said Lyon of the compliment after a wary pause. "What are you leading up to?"

His commander replied, "We've got intelligence with regard to a new small, shallow water anti-amphibious assault mine which is planted inside Wonsan Harbor, which is a huge harbor on the east coast of the Korean Peninsula. What we need is for somebody to go in and get 'em. They'll take bolt cutters, go down under the mine, cut the mine mooring cable and attach a towing line to it and with the help of the EOD officer, tow it to one of the little islands and render it safe. Then we'll ultimately transport it back to Indian Head, Maryland," to the headquarters of the Navy's mine planning and analysis efforts.

The North Korean communist forces held the harbor of Wonsan and the land around it, but American and South Korean forces held the waters off the harbor in a tight blockade, and controlled several nearby islands. Navy minesweepers and UDT teams had conducted minesweeping operations around Wonsan since the early days of the war, but this new intelligence suggested the North Koreans had planted a new, highly compact mine close to shore that was harder to spot and could play havoc both with minesweepers and assault craft attempting to land.

"We had control of that harbor so that any shipping of armament and supplies coming out of Wonsan, which is a pretty good-sized city, were not being made," recalled Lyon. "We controlled the harbor itself. That's one of the reasons that we had a

Republic of Korea [military] detachment along with our Marine Corps detachment on the island of Yodo. We felt relatively secure where we were on those islands, as they were under Allied control. How smart were the North Koreans? Not very damn smart. They could have made it very difficult for friendly (locals) to be out there on those little islands. They could have made trouble for them all the time but they did not."

Now, after pinpointing the location of the mines from a helicopter, Lyon was underwater, and face-to-face with his prey.

He dove and surfaced several times to make sure he had lined up the delicate operation perfectly. Finally he dove fully under the mine and got to work trying to sever the thick mooring cable that anchored the device to the ocean floor. He was about eight feet below the surface, and the mine was at about six feet underwater.

But suddenly Lieutenant Lyon noticed impact trails of bubbles shooting down from the water surface above him. That could only mean one thing: North Korean troops had spotted him from the shoreline, and they were opening fire. The next time he came up for air, he would be in their sights.

Then he sensed something else—his fingers and limbs were slowly locking up from the shock of the frigid 36-degree water he had been submerged in for almost twenty minutes. Very soon, he realized, the onset of hypothermia would immobilize him completely, and he would be helpless if the ocean current pushed him into the mine.

If he didn't surface in the next few seconds, he would drown.

"Why am I really doing this?" Lyon thought. "What in the world has brought me to this?"

AFTER WORLD WAR II and the massive peacetime demobilization of the U.S. military, the combat strength of the Underwater

Demolition Teams was cut by almost 95 percent. The remaining Pacific Fleet UDTs 1 and 3 were based at Coronado Amphibious Base, near San Diego, and the Atlantic Fleet UDTs 2 and 4 were based at the Little Creek Amphibious base, near Norfolk, Virginia.

When the Korean War erupted in June 1950, there were only eleven UDT men available in the region, a training detachment from UDT-3, based in Japan. Eventually, three UDT teams with a total strength of fewer than three hundred men joined the fight, but this would be an entirely different war than what they had been trained for, calling for new tactics, new skills, and new weaponry. The UDTs made things up as they went along, found new missions, and improvised their way into the next stage in the evolution of Naval Special Warfare. As UDT Lieutenant Ted Fielding explained, "We were ready to do what nobody else could do, and nobody else wanted to do."

Beginning in August 1950 and continuing off and on through late 1952, U.S. Navy UDT personnel conducted onshore raids on the Korean mainland to harass the North Korean war machine by blowing up railroad facilities, capturing prisoners, and harassing coastal targets. These were the first true commando-style operations by the UDTs, who until this point were primarily naval beach reconnaissance specialists and shallow-water demolitioneers. In these early "over the beach" operations, the UDTs teamed up with CIA personnel, South Korean naval commandos, U.S. Marine reconnaissance experts, and British Royal Navy commandos.

The very first raid, on the night of August 5, did not go well. That night, a UDT-3 detachment led by Lieutenant George Atcheson left the USS *Diachenko* (also known as APD-123; "APD" stood for "Amphibious Personnel Destroyer") in an inflatable boat to attack a railroad bridge and tunnel near

Yosu with explosives. Before they could plant their standard Mark-135 satchel charges containing 20 pounds of C-3 plastic explosive, ten North Korean soldiers appeared out of the tunnel riding a handcar, their guns blazing. Boatswain's Mate Third Class Warren "Fins" Foley was wounded, becoming the first Navy casualty of the Korean War. Several well-thrown hand grenades held back the enemy long enough for the UDT men to scale down the seawall and escape to their inflatable and reach the safety of their mother ship, the *Diachenko*. "Heading back to the beach," recalled Atcheson, "one of my own men shot my hat off as I approached [the boat] on the run, mistaking me for the enemy in the dark." He continued, "Very soon after that first mission, UDT-1 arrived in Japan along with a platoon of Marines from the First Marine Division Reconnaissance Company to act as backup. I joined up with them and we went on to do some fairly respectable operations that worked out considerably better than that first one."

A typical UDT raid on a Korean target would begin after dark and originate from one of four high-speed transport APDs that rotated through Yokosuka Naval Base, Japan: the *Horace A. Bass* (APD-124), *Begor* (APD-127), *Diachenko* (APD-123), and *Wantuck* (APD-125). The APDs were World War II–era vessels that were ideally suited for amphibious operations, as they were highly maneuverable and had shallow draughts that let them come close to shore. The APD would stand a few thousand yards off the beach, and launch a landing craft that towed a rubber boat filled with the UDT men to a point some five hundred yards from land. From there, the raiders would paddle in to about 250 yards and launch scout swimmers, who would reconnoiter the landing zone and flash back the "all clear" with an infrared light.

Outside of small arms and grenades, the UDT raiders were

not heavily equipped for sustained combat. Their mission was to hit, run, and swim away. In three more operations against railroad bridges and tunnels in mid-August 1950, beach security was provided by Marines under the command of Major Edward P. Dupras, who recalled, "The hardest part of my job was continually to impress the boys that our job was demolition, not fighting. If possible, we tried to avoid any firefights. If there was any interference, or if our party was detected, we withdrew and hit 'em someplace else."

Korea was a confined, regional engagement with none of the massive amphibious operations of the previous world war. Yet there were the administrative landings at P'ohang, and MacArthur's dramatic invasion at Inchon, dubbed Operation Chromite. There was little need for obstacle clearance at Inchon because the North Koreans felt the thirty-foot tides there would make a landing impossible, but UDT-1 and UDT-3 personnel did serve in a recon role and acted as wave guides to help steer landing craft to the right beach. The surprise Inchon landing on September 15, 1950, was a triumph for MacArthur and the United Nations forces. It helped turn the tide from total defeat to what for a time appeared to be imminent victory in a dash north to the Yalu River, which served as the border of North Korea and China; ultimately, however, the war culminated in stalemate.

On Christmas Eve of 1950, as communist forces closed in and the support ship USS *Begore* (APD-127) fired rounds from its 5-inch guns overhead, a U.S. Navy UDT detachment wired up a vast arsenal of explosives and primacord fuse around the harbor area of the port of Hungnam on Korea's east coast, now part of North Korea. Weeks earlier, a massive Chinese intervention suddenly threw back UN forces from the mountainous northern frontier of Korea. UN forces were completing an amphibious evacuation of some 100,000 allied troops and over

90,000 Korean refugees, and Allied war planners did not want the harbor facilities to fall into the enemy's hands intact. The demolitioneers activated the delayed fuse, scrambled back to the *Begor,* and watched the entire harbor erupt in a deafening wall of fire and smoke. It was the biggest blast of the Korean War and the largest nonnuclear explosion since World War II.

In the Korean War, the cooperation between the UDTs and America's spy agency, which had its origins in similar work in World War II, intensified into full-scale joint guerrilla operations with local forces. "In 1951," recalled UDT-1's George Atcheson, "I was again assigned to a CIA clandestine program. My part involved recon swimming, demolitions, and small unit tactics, about which I knew almost nothing. Nevertheless, we formed [a] Special Missions Group [SMG] of about 30 men. They were all North Koreans who had fled south at the time of the initial NK attack, and been recruited by a South Korean Army captain, who was himself then recruited by the Agency. It was from this cadre of highly motivated North Koreans that the E and E [escape and evasion] and SMG volunteers were drawn. Over time I took part in a dozen or so SMG landings."

In the combat zone, some UDT men even managed to mix business with pleasure. "In July 1952 we were working with UDT-5 on a beach survey near the island of Cheju-do southwest of Pusan," recalled one of their officers. "Here our froggies soon discovered that someone else was in the water with them, bare-breasted female Korean pearl divers! In a remarkable display of United Nations teamwork the UDT began diving with their newfound 'friends,' helping them recover pearls until we left the island a few short days later. UDT-5 always had high morale." We don't know if the UDT men challenged the pearl divers to a free-diving contest, but the local women probably would have won by a comfortable margin.

On January 19, 1951, the UDTs suffered their only two

combat fatalities of the Korean War, when a UDT-1 beach re-connaissance team was attacked shortly after a night landing near Popsong-ni, on the west coast of what is now South Korea. The firefight was detailed in an after-action report: "About ten [North Korean] men came over the dune line, assumed prone firing positions and commenced firing at the beach party. Immediately all of the [beach party] took to the water and commenced swimming with the rubber boat. . . . Lt (jg) Edward Ivan Frey was swimming to [a towline] when he was hit twice in the head. . . . Lt (jg) Pope and QM2 Boswell attempted to keep the body afloat but, due to the strong current, they were dragged under the LCPR [landing craft, personnel-ramped] and were forced to let go. The body of Lt (jg) Frey was never again seen [Authors' note: Frey's body was, in fact, later recovered]. Due to the extreme cold, the swimmers were unable to help [pull other swimmers aboard]. . . . Lt (jg) Paul Vernon Satterfield was boosted to the gunwale where he was shot in the back and died immediately. During this action, the coxswain was shot in the left knee but continued to man his station. He finally collapsed and his job was assumed by a UDT-1 man. The boat's radioman was shot through the left elbow as he helped to pull Satterfield aboard." In the vast scheme of the war, two fatalities was not a big number, but it hit the UDT community hard.

One year later, on the night of January 25, 1952, the UDT-CIA Special Missions Group conducted one of its most effective hit-and-run attacks. Leaving from the Amphibious Personnel Destroyer *Wantuck*, the commandos struck a train parked between two tunnels near Songjin. They knocked the train off the track, destroyed a railroad trestle, and captured eleven North Korean soldiers.

Through the first half of 1952, the joint UDT–CIA–South Korean guerrilla teams launched a series of daring hit-and-run raids on North Korean railroads and villages, landing in rubber boats stuffed with explosive charges and penetrating inland to capture prisoners, ammunition, and records. They were sometimes thwarted by high surf and counterattacks by enemy troops, but they did inflict damage to the North Korean war effort. "We landed North Koreans, who had been trained in the south as guerrillas, on the east coast of Korea up within sixty miles of [the Soviet port at] Vladivostok," explained UDT Commander Francis Douglas Fane. "Using the techniques of the UDT, we landed upwards of fifty a night for a couple of nights, from rubber boats, at two or three in the morning. We'd lie in the rocks while the Chinese passed by twenty or thirty feet away and wait until the coast was clear. They advanced some thirty or forty miles into the mountains, and I went over on a C-47 and dropped rice and explosives for them." In July through September 1952, UDT-3 and UDT-5 also participated in Operation FISHNET (also known as SEANET), an effort to damage the North Korean military's food supply by cutting fishing nets and sinking sampans in the Sea of Japan, to the north of Wonsan, up to the Russian border.

The UDT's work in Korea tapered off in the final months of the war, a bloody and bleak confrontation that saw some 54,000 American combat deaths and hundreds of thousands of civilian fatalities. The naval historian David Winkler summed up how his fellow historians viewed the Korean War in three simple sentences: "It opened with a North Korean drive that was checked at Pusan and countered at Inchon. Then a U.N. counterthrust was met by a blow, delivered by the Chinese, that sent the allies reeling back behind Seoul. U.N. counterattacks left the two sides fighting at the 38th parallel when a truce came into effect in July 1953." In other words, it was a draw.

The Korean War may have been inconclusive in its battlefield outcome, but it did save the people of South Korea from the medieval barbarity of the Kim family, whose nightmarish dictatorship over North Korea continues to this day. And while the UDTs' contribution to the war effort could not be considered decisive to the outcome, the Korean conflict saw the UDTs migrate from their strictly marine habitat onto land for the first time. The conflict also provided glimpses of skills and techniques that would later be adopted by the U.S. Navy SEALs, including commando training, blowing up land targets, and the use of helicopters for spotting targets and delivering personnel to the target zone. Still, the UDTs in Korea kept their feet largely in the water.

In the decade following the Korean War, the evolution of the UDTs was primarily underwater. Advances in radar and sonar meant that rubber boats and even surface swimmers could be vulnerable to detection. This meant developing the capacity to approach an enemy beach or harbor without being seen or heard. This required an underwater approach. The aqualung was a huge step in taking men under the sea, but had its limits as a tactical diving apparatus. There were the telltale bubbles rising to the surface and the aqualung had limited underwater duration. While the aqualung was simple and reliable, a better tactical device was needed. During World War II, Dr. Christian Lambertsen developed a closed-cycle, oxygen rebreather for use by the OSS Maritime Unit. In 1947 this apparatus, the Lambertsen Amphibious Respiratory Unit, or LARU, was adopted by the UDTs. This self-contained underwater breathing apparatus or SCUBA (a term Lambertsen coined) consisted of an oxygen bottle, a breathing bag, and a canister of soda lime. The diver's breathing medium, pure oxygen, was recirculated within the system, with oxygen added as needed and the carbon dioxide scrubbed out by the soda lime. The standard tactical rig in SEAL teams today is the Draeger LAR-V rebreather, a highly refined version of Lambertsen's gear.

IN THE WATERS OFF Wonsan Harbor in March 1952, UDT-5 demolitioneer Lieutenant Dick Lyon struggled to the surface and called out to his teammate and Navy explosives expert Dick Edwards who was still hunkered down in the little rubber boat the two of them had paddled close to the North Korean shoreline.

"Dick—I can hardly move!"

Lyon had just successfully snapped the mine's mooring cable and guided the device to the surface, but he was on the verge of total paralysis from the cold. Edwards pulled him into the raft and the two of them paddled back to their host ship while dodging enemy small-arms fire and towing away the mine. Luckily for the Americans, recalled Lyon, these North Koreans "were rotten shots."

Later, when the mine was defused and opened up, Lyon and Edwards were amazed to find a warehouse packing slip inside, written in Russian. "Clearly," remembered Lyon, "the Russians were making the mines, getting them to China, and from China to North Korea. Talk about an oxymoron, putting a packing slip inside of a mine!" It was an important piece of intelligence, but also a sensitive one, given the precarious state of U.S.-Soviet relations at the time.

Lyon was told by his commanding officer that he would receive an award for the action. But soon he reversed himself, telling Lyon, "We're going to play this down. I'm not going to be able to write you up at this time, but I will."

"You're the skipper," said Lyon. The award never came. It didn't seem to bother him much. "For most of our operations," he said, "nobody was writing up awards." The hoped-for Allied amphibious landings at Wonsan and elsewhere in North Korea didn't materialize, and the harbor remains in North Korean hands to this day.

Six decades after the end of the Korean War, on the other side of the Pacific Ocean, ninety-one-year-old former UDT officer Dick Lyon reports twice a week to Naval Amphibious Base Coronado, across the bay from San Diego, California. It's been more than seventy years since he joined the Scouts and Raiders in World War II. He qualified to be a Navy SEAL, and in 1974, while on active reserve service, he was promoted to rear admiral. He went on to become a two-term mayor of Oceanside, California, and founder of Children's Hospital of Orange County.

Today, former frogman Dick Lyon is helping to train the next generation of Navy SEALs, by giving lectures on the history of Naval Special Warfare and acting as a mentor to the new SEAL officers in training.

This latest class of SEAL trainees, he told us, "are about the finest bunch I've ever seen."

CHAPTER 4

THE BIRTH OF THE SEALS

DECEMBER 23, 1963, 2:30 A.M.
OFF THE COAST OF THE
ISLE OF PINES, CUBA

THE FORCE:
One U.S. Navy SEAL, 10 Cuban exile frogmen

THE MISSION:
Observe Cuban exiles attack Soviet-made missile boats

Bill Bruhmuller could see the lights of Cuba glowing on the horizon.

The sky was pitch-dark, the water calm and warm. It was a perfect night for an attack. He slipped off his face mask and took a compass bearing to make sure he was on the right course, and he felt the hum of distant land-based power generators vibrating through the water.

Spread around him was a formation of ten Cuban exile combat swimmers, or "frogmen," each wearing a dark T-shirt, swim trunks, swim fins, and a face mask. They were towing a rucksack containing a supply of large, plate-sized limpet mines, and they were all equipped with a depth gauge, compass, and CIA-issued oxygen rebreathers, which would enable them to remain submerged at the point of attack without leaving a trail of telltale bubbles. The Cubans were volunteers, eager to liberate their homeland from the communist Castro dictatorship.

Their target was four Cuban navy Komar missile boats that were moored at a dock on the Isle of Pines, an island just south of the main island of Cuba, and home to one of Cuba's biggest military and naval bases. The Komars were fast-attack and patrol boats capable of firing a radar-guided, 2,000-pound missile that could sink a full-sized warship at a range of fifteen miles. They posed a potential threat to American shipping, and they were a recent gift from the Soviet Union to its Cuban client state.

In the darkness a few thousand yards behind Bruhmuller and the Cuban frogmen was the twenty-one-foot, radar-equipped boat that had launched them into the water, with a Cuban volunteer at the helm, holding position to pick up the raiders when their operation was complete. Stowed inside the boat were a couple of Browning Automatic Rifles and .45-caliber and 9 mm handguns. On this mission Bruhmuller was to be an observer, not a participant. The attack would be made by the Cubans alone.

Several miles behind those boats, out of sight over the horizon, was their host vessel, a leaky Central Intelligence Agency spy ship named the *Rex*, disguised as a Nicaraguan civilian trawler.

Every man in the water knew that if they were caught, they could be lined up against a wall and shot for being spies and traitors to the revolution. Cuban security forces had condemned exiled Cuban fighters to death in absentia. Or if they were lucky and escaped execution, the frogmen, along with their American colleague Bill Bruhmuller, could expect to be condemned to years of misery and torture in the gulag of Cuban dictator Fidel Castro's prisons.

The frogmen were swimming toward a doorway to Hell. The Isle of Pines was home to one of the most notorious prisons on earth, the old colonial fortress of Presidio Modelo, where 10,000 Cuban political prisoners were currently being held in conditions of unspeakable cruelty. Torture and sadism were routine, common criminals were enlisted to beat anti-Castro inmates with pipes and clubs, and the complex was laced with mines to kill the prisoners if a rescue or invasion tried to free them. All told, Castro's jails held some 75,000 political prisoners, or 1 out of every 94 Cubans.

Bill Bruhmuller was a member of the very first group of U.S. Navy SEALs, a covert military unit created in January 1962. But on this night he was technically detached from the SEALs, on assignment for the CIA, as part of the Kennedy administration's anticommunist clandestine campaign of sabotage, assassination plots, and assorted psychological warfare and dirty tricks that unfolded from 1961 to late 1963, all aimed at toppling the regime of Fidel Castro.

"Operation Mongoose" was personally supervised by U.S. Attorney General Robert F. Kennedy, and was run out of the CIA's super-station in Miami, Florida, which controlled a $50 million budget, more than three hundred full-time staff, and a payroll of thousands of Cuban exiles. "My idea is to stir things up on the island with espionage, sabotage, general disorder, run and operated by the Cubans themselves," wrote the attorney general on November 7, 1961. The operation's headquarters was an office on the campus of the University of Miami that used the cover name of Zenith Technical Enterprises, Inc. The operatives also ran other properties, including merchant ships, aircraft, safe houses, marinas, hunting camps, and exile-operated publishing outfits. What very few people knew was that the U.S. Navy's Underwater Demolition Teams and SEALs played a role in the secret wars against Fidel Castro, especially in training Cuban exile frogmen, performing reconnaissance missions, and on occasion, preparing to land on the island itself.

On October 4, 1962, Attorney General Kennedy chaired a meeting of the top-secret Operation Mongoose "Special Group" steering committee, which included CIA Director John McCone. The meeting minutes revealed two astonishing passages when they were declassified more than thirty years later. The first was a probable reference to assassination plots against Fidel Castro or another senior Cuban leader, and RFK's direct knowledge of the plots: "another attempt will be made against the major target which has been the object of three unsuccessful missions, and that approximately six new ones are in the planning stage."

The second passage showed the president of the United States exerting strong pressure for sabotage attacks against Cuba, the kind Bill Bruhmuller would be involved in the following year: "The attorney general informed the group that higher authority [i.e., President John F. Kennedy] was concerned about the progress on the Mongoose program and felt that more priority should be given to trying to mount sabotage operations." In April and June 1963, after Mongoose-type activity was temporarily paused in the wake of the Cuban Missile Crisis, JFK again personally authorized continuing sabotage operations against Cuban targets.

From 1961 to early 1964, Operation Mongoose and other similar efforts by U.S. intelligence agencies and various anti-Castro Cuban exile groups included mafia-connected plots to assassinate Fidel Castro with a high-powered rifle or an exploding cigar; attacking an oil refinery, a molasses storage vessel, an electric power plant, a sugar mill, and a railway bridge; stashing weapons caches all over the island for use in a hoped-for popular uprising; and a wide range of attempted clandestine landings on the island by CIA and exile sabotage teams. At least two teams of Cuban frogmen were trained by CIA, UDT, and SEAL experts in underwater demolition and other techniques. SEAL historian Tom Hawkins noted, "Personnel from SEAL Team ONE and SEAL Team TWO participated in much of the 'unconventional' planning and worked directly with the CIA to establish and operate a series of 'safe houses' in and around Miami. SEAL Team personnel trained Cuban commando teams in small boat operations, beach reconnaissance, and combat swimmer methods. Much of this training was accomplished in austere base situations focused in and around the Florida Keys." The Mongoose and post-Mongoose anti-Castro campaigns continued after the Cuban Missile Crisis of October 1962, and for a brief time after the assassination of President Kennedy on November 22, 1963. It was such a chaotic stew of tangled plots, quixotic operations, and sometimes hare-brained schemes that Kennedy's secretary of defense, Robert McNamara, would later say, "the whole Mongoose thing was insane."

ON MAY 25, 1961, five weeks after the disastrous CIA-backed Cuban exile amphibious invasion at the Bay of Pigs, and a year and a half before the Cuban Missile Crisis, President John F. Kennedy gave a speech before a joint session of Congress that helped launch the U.S. Navy SEALs.

One line in the address assumed an exalted place in world history when he declared that the United States should commit itself to "landing a man on the moon and returning him safely to the earth" before the end of the 1960s. Elsewhere in the speech, though, were two sentences in dull bureaucratese that have led some to pinpoint the birth of the SEALs to this precise moment: "I am directing the secretary of defense to expand rapidly and substantially, in cooperation with our allies, the orientation of existing forces for the conduct of non-nuclear war, paramilitary operations, and sub-limited or unconventional war. In addition, our special forces and unconventional warfare units will be increased and reoriented."

With this order, Kennedy encouraged the Pentagon to beef up counterinsurgency and special operations forces like the SEALs, the Army's Green Berets, and the Marine Corps Force Reconnaissance Units. JFK was no stranger to non-conventional naval tactics himself; as a young U.S. Navy lieutenant j.g. serving in the South Pacific in 1943, he skippered PT-109, a patrol-torpedo boat that was famously cut in two by a Japanese warship, creating a legend of heroism, survival, and leadership under fire that helped launch his political career.

The full story of how the SEALs came to be created has only recently been pieced together by experts, notably by former Captain (SEAL) David Del Giudice, the first commanding officer of SEAL Team One; and by former Commander Tom Hawkins, a retired SEAL and a respected historian of the Teams. Their research reveals that the SEAL concept dated back at least to 1958, when Chief of Naval Operations (CNO) Admiral Arleigh A. Burke argued for non-conventional warfare capabilities to target the Soviet bloc, apparently in light of rising tensions in Southeast Asia. At the same time, in the post–Korean War era, the Navy's Underwater Demolition Teams, or UDTs, were experiencing a fairly quiet period of ongoing research and training. "They honed diving and submarine operational skills," wrote Hawkins, "began attending U.S. Army airborne schools, developed maritime parachuting techniques, and experimented extensively with a host of swimmer propulsion and delivery vehicles."

Hawkins added, "The changing needs for the special warfare community, and the transition from UDT to SEAL really started occurring after Korea. The one thing that President Eisenhower was very cautious about after Korea is he didn't want to tear the military apart like they did after World War II. So, he prevented that, but by the same token, he shifted the dynamic of the military to be more strategic and more deterrent-focused with nuclear weapons. Communism was expanding, and there were 'little wars' going on in Laos and they were looking at the domino effect on the Asian peninsula. So they had to find a different way to fight those wars, and so it looked like it was going to be smaller units and unconventional warfare type tactics."

In 1958, one Navy man already had a vision for a different kind of special warfare team—one that would be a blueprint for the Navy SEALs. "Arleigh Burke was the Chief of Naval Operations," SEAL Team One's first commanding officer, David Del Giudice, explained to us. "He was a very forward-looking person who felt that the services had to be alert to the changing national threat, and be able to create operations that were something less than nuclear war and would be able to give a measured response. If anyone would be considered the Papa SEAL, Arleigh Burke would be Papa SEAL."

Early in 1960, the last full year of the Eisenhower administration, Admiral Burke ordered his planners to identify Navy units that could be geared to small-scale warfare, in contrast to the mega-conventional and nuclear orientation of most of the military at the time. His staff came up with an ideal candidate who could be transformed to meet the mission: the men of the Underwater Demolition Teams. They were a ready-made commando force with strong talents for speed, mobility, sabotage, clandestine infiltration, and small-team tactics, all talents that were ideal for the new mission.

A key "birth document" dated March 10, 1961, was sent to Admiral Burke by Rear Admiral William E. Gentner, director of the Navy's Strategic Plans Division, in which he proposed an improved "Naval Guerrilla/Counter-guerrilla Warfare" capability. He laid out the specifics, which soon became the foundation of the SEALs and Naval Special Warfare that endured for the next fifty years and beyond: "One unit each is proposed under the Pacific and Atlantic amphibious commanders and will represent a center or focal point through which all elements of this specialized Navy capability (naval guerrilla warfare) would be channeled." Later in the memo, the new force was given its name: "An appropriate name for such units could be 'SEAL' units, SEAL being a contraction of SEA, AIR, LAND, and thereby, indicating an all-around, universal capability."

On December 11, 1961, a letter was issued from the office of the Chief of Naval Operations officially establishing SEAL Teams in the Pacific and Atlantic Fleets. SEAL Team One was established on January 1, 1962 at Coronado, California, with Lieutenant David Del Giudice from UDT-12 as commanding officer and SEAL Team Two was established on January 6, 1962 at Little Creek, Virginia, with Lieutenant John Callahan from UDT-11 as commanding officer. Each team had just ten officers and fifty enlisted operators.

A little more than seven months after JFK's May 1961 speech, SEAL Teams One and Two were established. "We were only ten officers and fifty enlisted at that time," recalled David Del Giudice. "We didn't even have a building to work out of. We were working out of a single office in Underwater Demolition Team 12's space. We had to start from scratch and get everything organized, not only equipment, but a place to call home. I had almost no guidance at the beginning of SEAL Team One. It was a question of trying to learn as we went along, how best to fulfill the mission."

Most of those first SEALs, like Bill Bruhmuller, were pulled from the Underwater Demolition Teams and today are called "plank-owners," an exalted group in the SEAL pantheon. But you could also consider Admiral Arleigh Burke to be an honorary plank-owner. "Little did these men know," reflected Tom Hawkins, "that they were creating a Naval Special Warfare community that would eventually promote many officers to the rank of admiral—including the two four-star SEAL admirals [Admiral Eric T. Olson and Admiral William McRaven] who commanded the 67,000 members of the U.S. Special Operations Command." In its first half century of existence, this once little-known Navy unit evolved into one of the world's most celebrated forces of combat arms.

The new teams took up residence at the naval amphibious bases in Coronado, California, and Little Creek, Virginia, respectively, where they reside today. Personnel for the teams were drawn from UDTs, but the men were to have expanded mission responsibilities that included airborne and land operations as well as traditional maritime activities. Almost immediately the new teams began to train for direct-action and reconnaissance missions on land, coming from on or under the sea or from the air.

The new "SEAL training" was an evolutionary, dynamic process. There were no SEAL training manuals. These new SEALs trained their own. Early on, SEALs adapted the UDT training they had undergone, and to this day the SEALs selection course is known as Basic Underwater Demolition/SEALs Training, or BUD/S. The rigorous conditioning and the notorious Hell Week remained much the same as it had been during the time of NCDU pioneer Draper Kauffman and the UDT men of World War II. Once U.S. involvement in Vietnam was under way, SEALs fresh from combat deployment became cadre instructors and trained those SEALs headed for Vietnam. Today, basic and advanced training for a Navy SEAL takes close to a full year. Another eighteen months of training with a SEAL team is now normal before a new SEAL makes his first operational deployment. Of all special operations ground combat components, Navy SEAL training is the longest and arguably the most difficult. With the exception of the aviation components, it certainly is the most expensive.

Perhaps the single most enduring characteristic of BUD/S training is the high attrition rate. Historically, five good men have to begin the process in order to get one qualified, deployable Navy SEAL. A great deal of time, effort, study, and testing has been devoted to this subject, but little has been done over time to make it more efficient. The physical characteristics of those who make it and those who don't are strikingly similar. Those who successfully complete BUD/S training seem to stand higher in terms of leadership, self-confidence, self-discipline, self-esteem, and intelligence. They also come from families who have high expectations of their sons.

Training is long, rigorous, and painful. Recently, careful attention to recruiting the right men and more sophisticated conditioning methods have resulted in a higher percentage of candidates getting through this difficult training. Yet, until there is a test for heart or some way to measure who will and will not quit under stress, there will always be a Hell Week and the physical, mental, and emotional crucible that is BUD/S training.

"Most SEALs, I think, maximize their God-given ability," explained Tom McGrath, former commander of SEAL Team

Four. "Quitting is very, very, selected against. Our training is spent in the water, cold water, and you can quit anytime. I mean, it's absolutely easy to quit, but it is irreversible."

Training is literally a life-and-death matter, noted former SEAL and retired Vice Admiral Joseph Maguire: "Look at Section 60 in Arlington National Cemetery, it's full of SEALs: men who've sacrificed and given their lives. The enemy gets a vote and nobody's immortal. SEALs are the best there is, but they're not perfect and they're not immortal. And that's why they train so hard. They are brought to death's door."

BILL BRUHMULLER WAS A powerfully built, soft-spoken man who had joined the Navy in 1953, at the tail end of the Korean War. In 1954 he volunteered for the Underwater Demolition Teams and was immediately assigned to UDT-22 at Little Creek, Virginia. "When I was 18 years old," he recalled, "I went into UDT and I was fortunate to work for a lot of the older World War II guys who were divers and I learned a lot about underwater work from these old-timers that really served me well throughout my Navy career." When the U.S. Navy SEALs were formed in January 1962, Bruhmuller was assigned to the new unit.

Bruhmuller recalled of the earliest days of the SEALs, "I think I attended something like 36 schools. I went to Navy survival school, Air Force survival school, Marine Corps survival school, radio school and free-fall parachute school at Fort Bragg, North Carolina, language school, patrolling school in Camp Lejeune, North Carolina, jungle warfare school down in Panama, weapons training, parachuting, and all kinds of sneaky stuff like kitchen demolition, where I learned how to use small explosives to do big jobs, from kitchen materials like flour and bleach."

The veterans from the UDTs quickly went to work outfitting

the new SEAL teams. They immediately saw the need for light-weight weapons and used team operational funds to purchase AR-15 rifles. The new rifle, the forerunner of the M-16, was the best gun for the new maritime commandos. They also began experimenting with new parachutes. The UDTs were past masters in scrounging useful equipment from military salvage depots; the new SEALs were even better.

The Teams focused on commando-style raiding while coming from the sea or through the air. Their training involved small-unit tactics for direct-action missions and behind-the-lines reconnaissance. While Vietnam loomed large in their future, some of their earliest operations were focused on what the president of the United States considered a grave security threat just ninety miles south of American shores: the pro-Soviet Castro regime in Cuba. In fact, the SEALs' immediate predecessors, the UDTs, assisted Cuban exiles in planning the failed CIA-backed invasion at the Bay of Pigs in April 1961.

Tom Hawkins traced UDT and SEAL Cuba operations in his 2012 publication for the Pritzker Military Museum and Library titled *The History and Heritage of U.S. Navy SEALs,* in which he reported that UDT personnel trained twelve Cuban exiles in swimming and demolition techniques, first at Vieques Island, Puerto Rico, then at an unused U.S. Army base south of New Orleans, Louisiana. "On the night of April 17, 1961," wrote Hawkins, "two landing craft with a CIA 'operations officer' and five UDT frogmen entered the Bay of Pigs (Bahía de Cochinos) on the southern coast of Cuba. UDT men also embarked the submarine USS *Sea Lion* (SS 315) at Mayport, Florida, and evidently were inserted near Havana to conduct harbor and beach reconnaissance. It has never been acknowledged that any U.S. advisors went ashore with their trained operatives."

In the buildup to the Cuban Missile Crisis in October 1962, the SEALs were alerted to take part in the imminent invasion of Cuba. "I was eventually ordered to command a secret SEAL detachment aboard the *Sea Lion* to 'secure the beachhead' for night-time insertion of an on-board Special Forces A detachment, partnered with a few CIA types and Cuban nationals, who would penetrate inland in Cuba and establish guerrilla activities," reported one SEAL Team One veteran. "The *Sea Lion* was called back from underwater surveillance off the southern coast of Cuba to Key West, Florida, when President Kennedy ordered a stand down." Bill Bruhmuller added, "In the Cuban Missile Crisis, we had one group that was going to parachute into the island, we had another group coming out of Key West on a submarine that was going to go in by water. I was on a group that was going in by boat to Havana harbor. We were going to shoot up the harbor. It never materialized."

The fact that the CIA engaged UDT and SEAL personnel for the Cuba operations was corroborated in detail by James Tipton, a SEAL Team Two plank-owner. "The Company—the CIA—had been using men from the UDTs in the late fifties and early sixties to do foreign training and run other operations for them," remembered Tipton to SEAL historians Kevin Dockery and Bill Fawcett. "This kind of thing went on for a number of years, with the program just kind of expanding over time. In part, this is what led to the commissioning [establishment] of the SEALs. By 1961, we had almost a permanent group of instructors stationed down in southern Florida, training Cubans and running them in and out [of Cuba] for operations." He added, "We were running people in and out of the islands on a regular basis. And there was always one or two of us on the ops. Officially, none of the instructors were to set foot on foreign soil, or at least that was always the saying down there.

It did seem that there was a time or two an instructor was away from the camp for longer than seemed necessary to just drop someone off or pick someone up."

Earlier that same year, in April 1962, according to Bill Bruhmuller, a group of seven SEALs was called into SEAL Team Two commander John Callahan's office. "There's a job that has to be done," Callahan announced. "I don't know where you're going, how long you're going to be gone, or who you're going to be working for." Bruhmuller recalled, "Naturally, everybody said 'Sure!' I was between wives at the time so it didn't make any difference to me, I was ready to go."

IN THE WATERS OFF the Isle of Pines in the early morning hours of December 23, 1963, Bill Bruhmuller and the team of anti-Castro frogmen confirmed their bearings, slipped back down underwater, and headed into hostile waters toward their target. The frogmen were about to attack a de facto enemy of the United States, in the midst of an undeclared war. Fifty years after the December 23, 1963, operation against the Komar missile boats on the Isle of Pines, Bill Bruhmuller told us the story of how it unfolded. "We went in at night," he remembered, "and I was not supposed to go in the water with them." The policy was for Americans to keep a physical distance and separation from these kinds of operations and let the Cubans do the work directly. Bruhmuller was supposed to wait out the mission on board the *Rex*, the CIA mother ship. But at the last minute, he felt the urge to swim in with the Cuban team to help them in case anything went wrong. If they were surprised by Cuban coastal patrols, for example, he could help them "evade and escape" back to safety. This was against orders, but he could get away with it, since there were no other U.S. Navy personnel anywhere near the scene: "There wasn't anybody there to watch me so I slipped into the water with these guys to kind of keep an eye on things."

Bruhmuller accompanied the Cuban team close into the target area, and at about 3 A.M. they found the Komars where their intelligence reports said they'd be, near a channel that opened to the sea. "They were tied up two abreast, two and two," he recalled, and they evidently were unmanned and unguarded except for a lone sentry. The boat crews, guessed Bruhmuller, were billeted nearby and probably fast asleep. The Cubans took the mines out of the floating satchel and went to work, as Bruhmuller observed from close by.

"Anytime you're working for CIA," Bruhmuller told us, "if you're discovered or if you're captured, they don't divulge any information of knowing you, or who you are, or how you even got there. So it behooves you to be very, very careful about where you're going, what you're doing, and how you're going to do it." He added, "I was not supposed to get in the water with these guys, but I did get in the water. I didn't personally go in and put limpet mines on the boats or anything like that but, personally, I wanted to make sure they were doing the right thing, kind of like a mother duck looking over her little ducklings.

"The limpet mine looks like a large plate," Bruhmuller explained. "Underneath, the whole circumference of the limpet mine has magnets. When you got to the [Komar] boat, you'd clean some of the marine growth off of it so you'd get good adherence. Then you'd fire your pins to make sure it wouldn't fall off. It was a stud driver, a small device that went through the limpet mine and when you ignited it, it shot a nail into the hull. It made a pretty good noise. And once you fired that, it had anti-removal devices on it, so if anybody did try to remove it, it would explode. It also had a timer on there. So they set it for about fifty minutes or an hour. They put two [limpet mines] on each boat.

"Well, there was a sentry up there that was kind of guarding everything. He heard that noise from the first mine being pinned onto a boat and we could hear him get on the radio and I guess he called up to his headquarters or someplace and he said that he had heard a noise down there and he thinks something might be going on. He apparently got a typical response, which I'd equate it to our own Navy people on a Sunday afternoon watching a football game. There's a guy down at the dock who can't see the game and tells them, 'Hey I think something's going on,' and they say, 'Hey, go jump in the lake.' The second mine was placed on the boat, the pin noise went off, and he called right back up again. They probably said, 'You're crazy, nothing's going on.' When that third one went off you could hear him running, and jump off the gunwale of the boat, up on the dock, and he took off. He wasn't sticking around to see what was going on. A couple of the Cubans that were down with me were laughing like hell."

When the last of the limpet mines were attached to the boats, the frogmen vanished in the dark water toward their pickup craft. Less than an hour later they heard and felt a series of blasts as they withdrew to the safety of the *Rex* mother ship and escaped. From various sources, Bruhmuller concluded that they sank three of the four targeted boats. The Cuban media admitted to just one boat partially destroyed, with some casualties to Cuban military personnel.

A month later, Bruhmuller was back on board the *Rex,* again approaching the waters off Cuba, this time on a reconnaissance mission. The mission was aborted at the last minute when someone on the bridge of the *Rex* monitored a startling public broadcast coming over the Radio Havana frequency, a message that referred to the only name the Cuban exiles knew Bruhmuller by.

A sailor ran down to Bruhmuller and repeated the message to him: "Welcome to Cuban shores, 'Bruh' and friends!"

The U.S. Navy SEAL was flabbergasted. He had repeatedly, and forcefully, indoctrinated the Cuban frogmen on the need for airtight security, for not talking in bars and restaurants, and for washing their own clothes and not dropping them off at laundries. But somehow, Fidel Castro's security forces had gotten hold of his name, and the exact timetable of the CIA spy ship. The *Rex* beat a hasty retreat back to American waters.

The aftermath of the Isle of Pines limpet-mine attack and accounts of the *Rex* spy ship appeared in various press accounts in 1963 and 1964. In fact, according to a declassified White House document, the operation appears to have been authorized at the top levels of the U.S. government. The operation was on a list of eleven "Proposed infiltration/exfiltration operations into Cuba during November 1963," submitted by the "Cuban affairs coordinator" to the top-level Kennedy administration steering committee "Special Group" on November 8, 1963. Identified as Operation 3117, it was described as "a UDT operation designed to sink or damage a *Kronstadt* [a Soviet-built submarine chaser and patrol ship] or other Cuban patrol craft while in anchorage in Ensenada de la Siguanea, Isle of Pines. The attack will be made by swimmer teams using limpets."

One former Cuban frogman reported decades later that through 1963, exile raiding parties were being instantly ambushed, arrested, and executed right at their Cuban landing zones. Fidel Castro's security forces seemed to have superb intelligence on many of their operations. But where the leaks came from remained unknown. The Cuban exile veteran was sure the leak came from someone in the State Department or elsewhere in Washington, D.C. In early 1964, most of the secret plots against Castro were shut down by President Lyndon B. Johnson.

Bill Bruhmuller soon resumed regular duties with SEAL Team Two, journeyed to the other side of the world to take part in the SEALs' new mission in Vietnam, and stayed in the Teams until he retired in 1978. He considers his service as a SEAL to be the most exciting and rewarding time of his life. Today, in Panama City, Florida, the former frogman enjoys life in the tropical sun along a stretch of the Gulf of Mexico due north of Cuba—just a day's cruise away.

The SEALs' operations against Cuba were conducted during the infancy of the Teams, in conditions of total secrecy and on a relatively small scale. But the skills, capabilities, and reputation of the Navy SEALs were about to take a quantum leap, as they were already gearing up to face the challenge of the global contest against communism, in the jungles of Southeast Asia.

CHAPTER 5

INTO THE JUNGLE

NOVEMBER 22, 1970, 6:25 A.M.

THE FORCE:
7 U.S. Navy SEALs, 5 South Vietnamese

THE ENEMY:
20 Viet Cong prison guards and sentries

THE MISSION:
Rescue an unknown number of communist-held POWs

Note from Dick Couch: With my coauthor's permission, I'm pleased to begin this chapter on the SEAL experience in Vietnam with an operation that took place shortly after I arrived in the combat zone. These events occurred scarcely four months after I checked in at SEAL Team One at the Naval Amphibious Base at Coronado, California. As you will see, the progression of SEALs in training to SEALs in combat was much quicker than it is today. A great many SEALs went straight from BUD/S to a SEAL Team to Vietnam in just a few short months.

"Get ready," I whispered to the SEAL next to me, "we're going to assault the camp."

The word was passed along the line of SEALs and scouts, sampan to sampan. The first rays of daylight filtered through the mangrove trees, and it looked like we were on the edge of our target.

Suspended in thick mist before us was a sight that countless American troops had dreamed of glimpsing throughout the savage, more than ten-year-long conflict known as the Vietnam War. We were on the edge of a POW camp containing prisoners of the Viet Cong. And from the outside, it looked as if we had the element of surprise. All was quiet except for the sounds of a few people snoring and coughing in their sleep. The air had a brackish smell of decay, of trees rotting and semi-tidal flush.

We could see smoke from cooking fires and a cluster of grass-roofed hooches. We didn't know if there were South Vietnamese or Americans in the camp, or how many guards there were. We just knew that if our intelligence was correct, there were prisoners in the compound a few dozen yards from the canal we were paddling down.

It was November 22, 1970. I was a U.S. Navy SEAL lieutenant who had been in Vietnam for only a week. After graduating from the U.S. Naval Academy at Annapolis, I had served as first lieutenant and antisubmarine warfare officer aboard the destroyer USS *Mansfield* (DD-728) before volunteering for SEAL duty. Following UDT/SEAL training, I made a short deployment with UDT-22 before being transferred to SEAL Team One at Coronado. I was a new SEAL, and I commanded a very inexperienced platoon of SEALs—good men all, but only three of the fourteen had combat experience. We had been in Viet-

nam for only a short while, and this was one of our first operations.

In our three sampans were six SEALs and myself from my
Whiskey Platoon, three members of the South Vietnamese "Kit
Carson" scout force, my Vietnamese army interpreter, and a
local fisherman who had guided us to the camp. Our area of
operation, or AO, was the Ca Mau Peninsula at the southern
tip of South Vietnam. The area was dominated by a vast mangrove swamp that was flooded daily by twelve-foot tides and
populated by bugs, leeches, rats, snakes, and an occasional, isolated Vietnamese fishing village. It was also a refuge for the Viet
Cong.

My platoon was working out of a base called Solid Anchor, the only Navy-controlled area of operations in Vietnam.
Solid Anchor was located in the southern portion of An Xuien
Province. If Florida were Vietnam, it was the area at the southern tip, just below and west of Miami. Most of the territory
was controlled by local-force Viet Cong guerrillas with an occasional company-sized North Vietnamese Army (NVA) unit
moving through the area. A SEAL command history from that
time described the environment like this: "exposure to almost
impenetrable mangrove swamps, mud, tidal flats, prolonged
immersions in water, and infestations of crocodiles, snakes,
and other tropical animals, insects, and diseases, in conjunction
with enemy booby-traps, punji stakes, and direct contact, have
become a matter of routine on patrols, ambushes, and listening
post operations." It was miserable, but it was equally miserable
for our enemy.

Our faces were smeared with olive green and black paint, and
we wore blue jeans. In contrast to standard-issue Navy "cam-
mies," which when wet made noise as your legs scraped together,
blue jeans were quiet when moist. Like typical SEALs on a mis-

sion, we were bristling with grenades and ammunition. I carried the SEALs' favorite weapon in Vietnam, a Stoner 63A machine gun with a short, 15.7-inch barrel. It was a limited-edition firearm that only the SEALs used routinely. We liked it because it was light, accurate, and reasonably reliable if you kept it clean. It was an early version of the modern-day SAW, or squad automatic weapon. With adjustment, you could get the Stoner up to 800 or 900 5.56 rounds per minute. It was "our gun." Two SEALs in a SEAL squad usually carried Stoner machine guns and one SEAL, a modified, short-barreled M60 machine gun that was tricked out with a flex-feed tray for fire-suppressing 7.62 rounds. The other SEALs carried M16 rifles or CAR15s with M203 grenade launchers underneath them.

This was our maiden solo mission, and it was the first operation I ever led. I did, however, have some excellent preparation for my first op. Just before we deployed to Vietnam, we had two months of intensive "cadre training" at SEAL Team One's base at Coronado. This training was conducted by team SEALs who had recently returned from Vietnam. They drilled us on what to expect, how to move, and what to watch out for in this unique world of jungle combat. They taught us what we needed to know to go to Vietnam—and nothing else. You can train in simulated situations all you want, but there's nothing like timely input from people who have just been there. Training in the SEAL teams back then was all about squad-sized operations in Vietnam. We did very little parachuting, diving, or anything else. It was all about going to Vietnam.

While most of us in Whiskey Platoon were green, we were blessed with a veteran petty officer first class named Walt Gustavel. Walt, or Gus as he was known at Team One, was on his fifth rotation to Vietnam. He was the institutional knowledge of Whiskey Platoon. It was Gus who developed the intelligence that surfaced this POW camp and found a local fisherman guide who could take us there. His skill in working with the local Vietnamese villagers and village chiefs made this mission happen.

This was not a raid that was gamed out far in advance or planned in detail. It was a pickup operation, and we had to move quickly. Gus had learned of this suspected POW camp in talking with a Vietnamese scout and two captured VC irregulars. His rapport with a local village chief produced our guide. He came to me with the information and said this fisherman could lead us to the camp.

"If this guy is telling us the truth, and I think he is," declared Gus as we huddled around a map of the AO in our Solid Anchor hooch, "There's a good chance we can get in there. Here's the camp's location. If we go in tonight, we can set up and surprise them at daylight." The suspected POW site was about twenty-six miles west of our base at Solid Anchor. It was just off a large, shallow bay called Square Bay and down a canal that meandered south from the bay. The information that Gus had come by was what today's SEALs call "actionable intelligence," and we had to move as fast as we could. POW camps were known to be moved often.

In a few hours, we worked up an operational plan and alerted other American forces in the area about the operation. We put together an extraction plan with boats and helicopters to support the mission. At 10:00 P.M. our team of seven SEALs and five Vietnamese piled into a motorized, thirty-six-foot Medium SEAL Support Craft, or MSSC, to cross Square Bay after dark and anchor near the river entrance. Accompanying the MSSC was a smaller, twenty-six-foot LSSC (Light SEAL Support Craft) and three sampans. We then transferred into the three sampans we were towing so we could make a quiet approach on the camp.

We had planned to move slowly and strike at first light, but we got lost; somehow, we had paddled down the wrong river. On learning of our mistake we quickly retraced our route, found the right canal entrance one hundred meters from the first, and softly paddled on to the target.

The South Vietnamese Kit Carson Scouts who were assigned to our platoon were a tremendous resource. The force was named after the legendary Western frontiersman and scout, and its members were drawn from former Viet Cong fighters who rallied to our side by a sanctioned amnesty program. In Vietnamese, they were called Hi Chánh Viên, which roughly translates to "members who have returned to the righteous side." SEAL platoons often operated with a half dozen or more Kit Carson Scouts. They lived with us and when in the field, they often walked on point or very close to the SEAL point man. They were officially in the South Vietnamese Army, but we paid them in cash with bonus payments for operational success. In our barracks hooch, I slept in a top bunk and one of my scouts slept in the lower bed. That's how much we trusted them.

When patrolling in hostile territory, SEALs were always concerned with booby traps, "small IEDs" before they were known as such. When a scout refused to walk down a trail and recommended an alternate route to the objective, we were only too glad to take his advice. The scouts slept, ate, and fought alongside the SEALs—we considered them brother warriors. They were an invaluable source of area knowledge and local intelligence.

In addition to our training, Walt Gustavel, and the Kit Carson Scouts, we were blessed with the Seawolves. The Seawolves were helicopter gunships from the Navy's HAL (Helicopter Assault, Light)–3 squadron. Flown by U.S. Navy pilots, they were always prepared to go into harm's way for SEALs who were on the ground. For this operation, they were standing off, ready for our signal to fly in and support us when we assaulted the POW camp. The Seawolf pilots were superb. "I don't know a single SEAL who operated in Vietnam and wasn't saved by those guys at least once," wrote veteran Vietnam-era SEAL leader Robert Gormly. "They were the best helo crews I'd ever seen. Land-based throughout the Delta and aboard LSTs (amphibious support vessels anchored at the mouths of rivers), they'd fly anywhere, any time, to support us. Night or day, good weather or bad, they were there. I can't tell you the number of times I could feel the heat from their rockets as they passed over our heads toward the enemy. Often Seawolf fire teams made dry runs on the enemy after they had expended all their ordnance in order to give our guys a chance to break contact and get the hell out. And they were just as likely to land and pick up our guys if things got really serious." SEAL veteran Tom Hawkins added, "The SEALs and the Seawolves became a natural component of each other and the SEALs set up a lot of operations with the Seawolves' support in mind. The Seawolves sometimes became Medevac helicopters. The SEALs would get in contact, the Seawolves would scramble, get out and lay down gunfire, lay down rockets, and even land to get some of the guys if they were wounded. Fabulous, fabulous organization. Great warriors, great pilots." Today, SEALs have the Army 160th Special Operations Aviation Squadron, the "Nightstalkers," but back then we had the Seawolves.

Closing on the suspected POW campsite, we quietly paddled our three sampans up to a ramshackle guard post. One of the scouts slipped into the guard shack and silently captured two enemy sentries. Through my interpreter, I asked one, "Where's the POW camp?" He refused to answer. I placed my Ka-Bar field knife at his throat and asked again. Still nothing. Now what? One of my Kit Carson Scouts offered to help, and I was delighted to step aside. The Scout bent down and addressed the Viet Cong guard in Vietnamese: "You know who I am, and what I will do if you don't talk."

Suddenly, the guard gave up the exact location: "The camp you want is one hundred meters farther down the canal." We gagged both sentries, stowed them in the third sampan, and continued gliding south on the narrow canal. But now that our target was coming into sight and dawn was breaking, I had a huge problem. Our radio was dead. I could not contact our primary support platform, the Medium SEAL Support Craft (MSSC) north of us in Square Bay.

"We are about to engage; we are about to engage!" I transmitted, hoping someone might hear me.

We had traveled outside radio range, and I had no radio contact with the support helicopters and boats. And I was scared. Today our troops in the field have individual radio headsets, secure channels, multiple backups, and satellite links for reliable communications. In Vietnam, however, we were practically in the World War II transistor age. One radioman per squad carried a heavy, old radio pack. In the dense foliage in which we operated, they were terribly unreliable.

I had no idea of the size of the guard force at our suspected POW camp. If we attacked without gunship support and were pushed back by a superior Viet Cong force, it would be extremely dangerous, not only for us but for the POWs. They could be caught in the middle of the exchange or withdrawn deep into enemy-held territory. It would be impossible to follow them. POWs are essentially hostages, subject to immediate execution by their captors at any time. If they move, you follow with great caution. In previous rescue operations, American forces acted on what seemed to be good intelligence and launched fast-reaction raids on possible POW sites, only to find the locations deserted, and in some cases, the cooking fires still warm.

But there were some shining successes in freeing Vietnamese prisoners in the South, and the U.S. Navy SEALs were often the agents of salvation. On the night of August 30, 1968, a South Vietnamese force led by an American SEAL stormed a POW compound in the Mekong Delta and liberated forty-eight prisoners. That October, a combined SEAL/South Vietnamese force inserted on Con Coc Island, seventy-seven miles southwest of Saigon, and freed twenty-four Vietnamese prisoners. On the very same day, a similar SEAL-led force freed another twenty-six Vietnamese prisoners at another location.

And on August 21, 1970, a SEAL team under the command of Louis Boink conducted a complex daylight raid on a POW camp. This action involved U.S. naval gunfire, Australian bombers, U.S. helicopter gunships, and a beach assault by Boink's SEAL team and a Vietnamese Regional Forces platoon. They found an empty compound. The guards had forced the prisoners to evacuate and flee.

As SEAL historian T. L. Bosiljevac related, the operation ended miraculously: "For two hours, the SEALs remained in hot pursuit through the swamp, following a trail of clothing and abandoned equipment. At 1245 they discovered twenty-eight Vietnamese prisoners whose guards had fled for their lives."

But not all recovery operations of that era were successful. On November 21, 1970, a joint U.S. Army–Air Force team raided a North Vietnamese POW compound at Son Tay, near the North Vietnamese capital of Hanoi, only to find the camp empty of Americans. They had been relocated to another site a full four months earlier.

It was but a day following the Son Tay raid that my small

SEAL force glided on a narrow canal to the edge of another suspected enemy POW camp. With my radio down, I was on the
verge of aborting the mission. It was a tough call, but I felt we
had come too far to turn back this close to the camp.

We were new to Vietnam, but we were aware of the Viet
Cong's reputation for combat skill and ferocity, and we had a
healthy respect for it. As SEAL Vietnam veteran Jack Rowell
put it, "Charlie [the Vietnamese communist fighters] was no
enemy to fool with or take lightly. Charlie was very professional
and acted like an animal all at the same time. We could be sly
in the Teams, but Charlie was downright sneaky. He would operate on hardly anything, little support and almost no fire support he couldn't carry with him in the Delta. But the VC were
as tough and deadly an enemy as you could face. The VC were
a lot like we were back in the days of the revolutionary war."

I passed the word along to my SEAL element: "Prepare to
assault." As I said this, I was fiddling around with one of my
pop-up signal flares, which was now my only means of communication. My top priority was to get that pop flare up into
the sky to signal my MSSC support boat out in Square Bay that
we needed help. He would call in the Seawolves and once those
choppers were overhead, I'd have an airborne relay to restore
radio communications.

It's hard to put into words the emotions I felt as a SEAL
leader coming up to that camp. I had a mission, I had a time
frame, it was starting to get light, and I didn't quite know what
I was going to get into. I had no radio communications. My
mind was trying to sort everything out. I was very much trying
to see the big picture and do the right thing. All emotion and
all fear were pushed out by two overpowering thoughts: "What
am I going to do? What's the right thing to do?"

Crouching in the boat, I fumbled the signal flare and

dropped it. It made a loud metallic clank on the floor of the sampan, like dropping an empty beer can on your back porch. Then the first shots were fired.

All hell broke loose. My Kit Carson Scouts broke from the canal bank, running and shooting in the direction of the camp. My SEALs followed them. I recovered the flare and sent it skyward, praying that the boat would spot it. The Viet Cong guards opened fire at us, and tracer rounds flew in all directions; ours were red and theirs were green.

It happened very, very quickly. It was a thirty-second gunfight. Our South Vietnamese scouts went on full automatic fire, dumped their magazines, and ran around trying to wrestle their new magazines into their weapons. The SEALs with M-60s and the Stoners were putting out a shattering volume of fire, but the SEAL riflemen were looking for targets. They didn't see too many because the bad guys shot and then they ran into the jungle. The Viet Cong guards probably figured we were a company-sized force, so they just took off. I did not fire my weapon, as I was trying to coordinate the attack and figure out what was going on and what to do next.

In less than a minute, we had overrun the camp and the shooting stopped.

In a bizarre scene straight from a Hollywood movie set, there were the POWs—a total of nineteen military-aged Vietnamese men, in four locked bamboo cages, each holding about five human beings inside. No Americans.

We stood still at the center of the POW camp, temporarily frozen by the unreality of the scene. The prisoners were in their twenties to forties, wearing T-shirts and baggy shorts, each barefoot and very thin and visibly malnourished. They were all smiles at their impending liberation, but on balance they were very stoic about it. They were subdued, probably from exhaustion and hunger, or perhaps it was just pragmatism in the face of a long war. We seemed to be much happier about this whole thing than they were.

I had a radio in one hand and a gun in the other, and my mind raced with questions. *Are the VC regrouping to counter-attack us? How fast can we get out of here? Where are the helicopters? Should I put up another flare? Where are the boats? Are there any more threats in the camp? Did we get all the bad guys or are some hiding? What's next, what's next?*

"Get out on perimeter," I told my SEALs. "We've got to protect these guys and get the hell out of here. We've got to get ready to move." It was critical that we get out fast, since we had to leave by a narrow, twelve-foot-wide canal, and the VC knew it. We didn't want to give them time to set up an ambush.

We set up a security perimeter and took stock of the camp. We learned that there had been about twenty guards. Through the interpreter I told the POWs to sit down and be quiet. The Kit Carson Scouts were starting to look through the crude hooches trying to find money. They were big looters.

"Hey, Lieutenant," said a SEAL from inside one of the hooches, "we found all kinds of shit here, documents, dossiers, ledgers, and folders." The VC were very good at keeping records. "Fine," I said, "pack it up and let's get ready to go." We scooped up all the stuff we could get our hands on and quickly prepared the documents for transport.

By now I had continuous helicopter support overhead and my radio could reach the crews. The crew of the MSSC saw my flare, and had called in a section of Seawolf gunships. Then the smaller of the SEAL support craft, the LSSC, made its way two thousand meters down the canal to our position. The officer-in-charge of my Special Boat Unit One detachment was a terrific fellow named Bob Natter, who arrived on the LSSC. Bob and I

were classmates and company mates at the Naval Academy and
had been fast friends since our plebe-midshipmen days. It was
nice to have a good buddy guarding your back. Bob would later
retire as a four-star admiral, but back then he was a special operations small-craft officer who supported SEALs.

When Bob and his boat reached the camp, we realized we
had a problem; we now had more people than the boat could
carry. In addition to the eleven of us who came in by sampan,
we had nineteen ex-POWs and a mother and daughter who had
been made to do camp chores by the now-departed Viet Cong.
And there were the two captured Viet Cong sentries.

We decided that we'd evacuate the Vietnamese by air and
the SEALs by water. Fortunately, we'd anticipated this and had
a chain saw stashed in Bob's LSSC. We cranked it up and got
busy cutting down trees and brush to create a zone for the
transport helos. The Huey slicks were able to hover low over
the mangrove stumps and ferry out the freed prisoners. It took
three lifts to get everyone out. As my SEALs and I evacuated in
the crowded but armored LSSC we took precautions against a
VC ambush on the way out. The Seawolf helicopters plastered
both banks of the canal with fire from their .50-caliber door
guns.

We slept well that night, very proud but totally exhausted.
It was Whiskey Platoon's first combat operation. The liberated
prisoners were quickly shipped out, and I forgot all about them
in the rush of new operations.

I'm often asked what I remember most about this POW
operation that took place close to forty-five years ago. What
stands out in my mind to this day is how the quality of the cadre
training at SEAL Team One and the talent of a veteran petty
officer like Walt Gustavel combined to allow an inexperienced
SEAL leader like myself to enjoy this kind of success on his first

SEAL combat operation. It was a tribute to the professional culture that was emerging in the SEAL Teams in the late 1960s and early 1970s.

Much later, I found out that we had captured one of the main Communist Party prisons in the Mekong Delta. The occupants were captive South Vietnamese soldiers and some local men who wouldn't cooperate with the VC. One of the freed captives later told military debriefers that twenty men had died of starvation in the prison in the previous year, and another sixty had been executed for a variety of "crimes."

THE NAVY SEALS WERE born of the Cold War, and they received their baptism of fire in the hot jungles of Southeast Asia. Vietnam would become the war that defined the SEALs as a modern fighting force.

David Del Giudice, SEAL Team One's first commanding officer, related to us the very earliest days of the mission: "Once SEALs were established, their first priority was Vietnam. Jon Stockholm and I received orders dated January 10, 1962, to proceed to Vietnam to find a role for SEAL involvement. Based on that survey, on March 10, two instructors, Bob Sullivan and Doc Raymond, arrived in Vietnam to begin training South Vietnamese in clandestine maritime operations. Due to their good work, SEAL Team One personnel continued to operate under CIA control until the end of 1963 when CIA relinquished support and control of most operations in the North to MACV [Military Assistance Command, Vietnam]. This operation became the maritime portion of OP-34A [Operations Plan 34, an effort to infiltrate South Vietnamese into North Vietnamese territory] under MACSOG [Studies and Observation Group, a command that focused on clandestine operations and also in-

cluded U.S. Army, Marine Corps, Air Force, and South Vietnamese personnel] operational control. The second operation
based on our survey resulted in Phil Holt, Jon Stockholm, and
nine enlisted men, two from SEAL Team Two, to deploy in
April 1962 to train selected South Vietnamese Coastal Force
personnel in reconnaissance, demolition, and prepare them to
instruct succeeding classes of South Vietnamese Biet Hai sea
commandos. A follow-on detachment deployed to Vietnam
with Al Routh as OIC [officer in charge] and George Doran
from SEAL Team Two as AOIC [assistant officer in charge]
along with eight enlisted men from SEAL Team Two."

With the landing of the Marines in 1965 and the escalations
that followed, the role of American combatants, and the Navy
SEALs, increasingly became one of direct-action combat.

Tom Hawkins has described how the SEALs' culture of
secrecy and autonomy led to an unusual reality in their early
years in action: they were, to an extent, their own bosses. "At
the time of their formation and throughout much of the Vietnam conflict, the existence of the Teams and their activities remained successfully classified outside of 'need to know' military
circles," wrote Hawkins. "Operationally, SEALs did not belong
to the Amphibious Force Commander and, in Vietnam, they
essentially reported to themselves by acting almost unilaterally
in the regions where they were assigned. While extremely successful, this led to a paradigm of suspicion that would follow
them significantly after Vietnam and throughout the Navy in
the forthcoming years." Hawkins even remembered an Army
general in Vietnam telling him, "You SEALs are assassins. I
don't want you here."

"We had no status, no standing in the regular Navy," recalled former SEAL Ted Grabowsky. "Some part of the Navy
saw us as some sort of quasi-criminal element, not a respected

profession, that should only be used in desperate circumstances. And when you were through using it, you would stop forever. Like it was some sort of immoral activity." Vice Admiral Robert Salzer, who worked with the SEALs as commander of riverine warfare in 1967–68 and again as commander of U.S. Naval Forces in Vietnam from 1971 to 1972, described his mixed opinions of the SEALs: "They were in small detachments, and we kept them on a very firm leash. SEALs are a two-edged sword. It was something like having attack-trained German shepherds: you had to keep them on a very tight leash. They did good work, but what they really wanted to do was to get out and mix it up and have a shooting match. They had some real feats of derring-do. When General [Creighton W.] Abrams [American commander in Vietnam] was having a down period, I would always try and find some particularly hair-curling things the SEALs had done, because he loved tales of personal bravery, and those guys had that."

There certainly were problems that had to be addressed. The SEALs had been established to conduct small-unit direct-action warfare in a maritime environment. Nobody in the Navy, outside of the SEALs, knew what that meant; and if they did, they didn't understand how it applied to operations in Vietnam. The other problem is one that has always plagued elite unconventional units: prejudice. Some officers of the regular Navy thought the SEALs were prima donnas.

With the exception of an ongoing advisory effort, the SEALs began operating in squads and platoons in a direct-action role in Rung Sat Special Zone, a Viet Cong–infested mangrove swamp between Saigon and the South China Sea. The Rung Sat was critical to the continuing war effort from South Vietnam. It controlled the approaches to Saigon through the Long Tao River, since Saigon is approximately fifty miles inland.

SEAL platoons began combat rotations into the Rung Sat in 1966. Many SEALs cite these early Rung Sat deployments as the first time the SEALs cut their teeth on a sustained direct-action effort. The Rung Sat presented special challenges and missions for the new SEALs. According to a 1967 command history, these operations included "harassment of the enemy, hit-and-run raids, reconnaissance patrols, intelligence collection, and curtailment of guerrilla movements through ambush and counter-ambush tactics."

The first SEALs in the Vietnam War zone were a strikingly different-looking sight than their "naked warrior" ancestors in the Underwater Demolition Teams, who were often outfitted with little more than a Ka-Bar knife and swim shorts. "The first SEALs in combat wore Marine Corps green uniforms and camouflage uniforms when they could get them," reported Tom Hawkins. "A lot of the later SEALs wore camouflage tops and Levis instead of uniformed pants. It's more comfortable. By the way, SEALs also wore pantyhose, to keep the leeches off of you when you're going through the canals. They carried as much ammo as they could. You see pictures of the guys with bandoliers of weapons crisscrossed across their chests. That's not for Hollywood. A SEAL squad in a field carried an enormous amount of firepower. If you even saw a demonstration of what they could do when seven guys unloaded, it's just unbelievable. They took everything into the field that they could."

SEALs were soon operating from riverine bases around the lower Mekong Delta. From 1966 through 1971, platoons from SEAL Teams One and Two conducted direct-action operations against the Viet Cong. The strength of the two SEAL teams grew to nearly four hundred active SEALs, but there were seldom more than 120 SEALs in Vietnam at any one time.

Most often, SEALs worked for a conventional Army, Navy,

or Marine ground-force commander. Early on in the Mekong region, SEALs learned that the key to successful operations was good intelligence. Veteran SEAL petty officers became quite adept at ferreting out information from the local sources. For the most part, they were not trained for this; these intelligence-collection skills were learned on the job to better accomplish the mission. Good intelligence led to successful missions.

When SEALs had no good targeting information, they would often go out and sit on a canal bank or a jungle trail and wait for the Viet Cong to come to them. Sometimes they sat out all night with the bugs and leeches, only to return with nothing to show for it. Even in those early days, there was no substitute for good intelligence. During the course of the Vietnam War, SEALs became good at small-unit tactics and operating at night in enemy-controlled territory. Quite often the boat-support sailors would take their SEALs close to the objective, and the SEALs would make the final journey to the target in sampans or on foot in squad file, moving through the night just like the Viet Cong. These missions were developed and launched as uni-lateral direct-action operations, but we seldom went out with-out a local guide or a contingent of Vietnamese scouts.

Invariably the most successful operations were a result of lo-cally developed intelligence on a specific target: an arms cache, an enemy base camp, or senior Viet Cong leader. Like later SEAL operations in Iraq and Afghanistan, Vietnam-era SEALs oper-ated from relatively secure bases that were under the control of a conventional sector commander. Most operations were con-ducted at night in enemy-controlled territory, but SEALs then, like now, stood ready for a quick-reaction mission to rescue a downed pilot or a POW recovery. The Underwater Demolition Teams, which continued in existence for twenty years after they spawned the SEALs in 1962, also deployed to Vietnam, but not in the combat strength of SEALs. While their combat roles were mainly restricted to reconnaissance and demolition duties, the UDTs suffered twelve killed and some forty wounded.

During the surprise enemy Tet Offensive onslaught of early 1968, according to SEAL Team Two's Command History for that year, "three SEAL [Team Two] Platoons handled themselves capably and professionally." That's quite an understatement: they took part in rolling waves of heavy, close-quarters street fighting that sometimes evoked the battle at the Alamo. According to the document, "The SEAL Platoons in Vinh Long [6th Platoon] and My Tho [7th Platoon], which were almost completely destroyed, were instrumental in thwarting the Viet Cong attempts to overtake the cities. The Eighth Platoon, in Chau Doc at the time, together with a small PRU force, succeeded in liberating that capital of that province." (Note that platoons from SEAL Team One were alphabetized, as in Whiskey Platoon, and Team Two platoons were numeric.)

At Chau Doc, a city on the Cambodian border, a detachment of SEALs assisted U.S. Army Staff Sergeant and PRU advisor Drew Dix in a successful, extremely high-risk operation to rescue an American nurse trapped deep inside the city, an operation that resulted in Dix being awarded the Medal of Honor. "Basically; the Viet Cong had overrun the entire city of Chau Doc," remembered Harry Humphries, a SEAL who participated in the operation. When Humphries arrived at the American tactical operations center, or TOC, in the city, the SEAL witnessed a sight he would never forget: "I could see an officer lying on a couch, staring up at the ceiling, with the focus of his eyes some 2,000 feet beyond it. He was a very cool and collected, experienced old Army soldier. In the background, I could hear the voices coming in over the radio, voices from soldiers at the Army Special Forces bases scattered throughout the area. And those voices were screaming about thousands—5,000 from one voice, 6,000 from another—of enemy troops crossing the Cambodian border." Humphries was amazed at how calm and cool the Army officer looked, because in a few hours, those thousands of enemy troops would be in Chau Doc, and the twenty or so Americans defending the city would probably be dead.

Humphries and Drew Dix entered a jeep to drive across the beleaguered city to attempt to rescue the nurse trapped deep behind enemy lines. SEALs Frank Thornton and Wally Schwaleberger jumped in as volunteers and the two jeeps sped off into the chaos of Chau Doc. "How we made it through those streets I don't know," recalled Humphries, who manned a heavy .50-caliber machine gun mounted in his vehicle, with Army Sergeant Dix at the wheel. "God was with us. It was just one firefight after another." The city, recalled Drew Dix, "was totally under the control of the VC."

When the team arrived at the French colonial house where they believed American nurse Maggie Higgins was trapped inside, Viet Cong fighters opened fire on them from nearby buildings. Dix called out to Higgins, "Maggie, Maggie, are you there?"

"I'm here," replied Higgins in a voice gripped with fear. "I'm under the bed, and they're inside!"

"Get down and stay down!" replied her rescuers, who could now see Viet Cong running around inside the house, which was perforated by enemy fire. Higgins could hear Viet Cong outside her bedroom door, shooting. She recalled, "I ran to the front door, which had the metal grate on it. And in doing so, the Viet Cong were running the opposite way. We were passing each other, I was looking at them and they were looking at me! They were surprised to see me there."

"Then we opened fire and just swept the area," remembered

Humphries. "We continued sweeping the area until we figured all of the VC were down or gone. We killed five or six, maybe as many as eight, inside of the house. They just piled up like cordwood right in front of us. Then things were quiet in the house."

"The key, the key, find the key!" shouted Drew Dix, who immediately realized how silly the words sounded, as the building was in shambles. Dix didn't think they could shoot the lock off, but nearby, Humphries felt they were being too polite toward private property and they could have blown the lock off the door in a second. Luckily, Higgins managed to quickly locate the key, open the gate, and link up with her rescuers. Over the next two days, the Americans and their South Vietnamese counterparts managed to take back the city of Chau Doc in a series of fierce street-by-street battles.

A Vietnam-era SEAL named Hal Kuykendall recalled another mission during the Tet Offensive that illustrated how critical SEAL training and teamwork were to surviving in combat.

"One of the hairy operations that I remember being on is one night during Tet. We were inserting on a river bank with seven SEALs in a small, fiberglass boat called a LSSC, or Light SEAL Support Craft. It was about 11 o'clock at night. Just as we were about to get off the boat, we got ambushed. There were muzzle flashes all along the riverbank. The Vietcong were sitting there waiting for us. Before each operation we informed the headquarters of the AO [Area of Operation] where we would be operating so we wouldn't be in the same area as other friendly forces. Apparently a South Vietnamese passed our insertion coordinates to the enemy."

The Viet Cong opened fire on the SEALs. Kuykendall continued: "They shot us up so bad that our boat lost steering, we were sitting in the kill zone while they shot us to pieces. Luckily, the LSSC had a .30 caliber machine gun mounted on the rear of the boat. We used it and our own machine guns to return an overwhelming amount of firepower to get the VC's heads down. So we all saved each other's life than night because we didn't panic, and instead returned fire as we had been trained. I can't believe we weren't all killed in the initial burst of fire from the VC. But somehow or another, we lived. The thing is we didn't curl up in a fetal position and hope it would go away, we all got up and returned fire systematically. We had a really good boat coxswain, who used his engines to back us out of there and out to a safe place. We were all part of a team and we all had a job to do and we didn't shoot all our bullets in the first few seconds. We took turns shooting and really worked as a team and that's how we got out of the ambush. There were many operations when we saved each other's lives by working as a team."

No discussion of SEALs in Vietnam would be complete without a mention of the SEALs' brother warriors, the boat guys. SEALs were often assisted by and worked closely with Mobile Support Teams (MSTs) from Boat Support Unit One (BSU-1) on the west coast. BSU-1 and its east coast counterpart BSU-2 were the forerunners of today's Special Boat Teams. A great many SEALs had their operational chestnuts pulled from the fire by these courageous sailors. During the tour of co-author Dick Couch's Whiskey Platoon in 1970–71, only two of the SEALs from that platoon earned Purple Hearts. Five members of the boat support detachment were wounded on that tour supporting the platoon SEALs. Then there were the SEAL advisors who helped establish the Vietnamese SEAL program, the Lien Doc Nguoi Nhia, or LDNNs. Translated literally, they were "soldiers who fight under the sea." These brave South Vietnamese soldiers, when properly trained and led, could be very effective.

Among the most successful SEAL operations in Vietnam were those conducted by the SEALs who worked with the Provincial Reconnaissance Units, the PRUs. The PRU program was a CIA-sponsored effort that later became part of the secret Phoenix Program, a CIA campaign to disrupt the Viet Cong leadership structure in the South, largely through targeted "snatch and grab" operations. After a successful raid in September 1967, one SEAL said in a rare interview with a reporter, "We like to grab people. That's of real value. Killing them does no good. Any time we make a hit we're there to take them alive. But once we're seen, we're compromised. Our primary mission ceases and we turn to our secondary mission: killing VC."

The PRUs drew their fighters from Vietnamese rural villages and Nung tribesmen of Chinese origin who lived in Vietnam. These units agreed to fight on the side of the South Vietnamese government so long as they could fight as a unit. The CIA controlled their pay. The Agency paid and they fought. Navy SEALs, along with Army Special Forces soldiers and Marines, served as PRU advisors. In the case of the SEALs, there were anywhere from 60 to 120 Nungs for every SEAL advisor or pair of advisors. It was lonely duty for a SEAL, sometimes living day in and day out with these rough men in their home villages, with only an interpreter for communication. PRU advisors were always chosen from veteran SEALs. The PRUs operated in fourteen of the sixteen provinces in IV Corps, the designated military sector in the southern part of South Vietnam. After their formation in 1967, the PRUs killed or captured thousands of suspected communist operatives.

The Phoenix Program collapsed in 1971–72 in the wake of publicity over alleged abuses, torture, and extrajudicial executions, but postwar Vietnamese communist testimony confirmed that the PRUs were the deadliest and most effective force fielded in South Vietnam. In the 1972 and 1975 communist offensives spearheaded by the North Vietnamese Army, there were surprisingly few signs of the Viet Cong leadership cadre, which had largely been decimated by Phoenix and related programs. Of the charges of brutality, one Phoenix historian, Dale Andrade, wrote, "Both SEALs and PRUs killed many VCI [Viet Cong Infrastructure, the parallel government and primary target of the SEALs] and Viet Cong guerillas, that was war. They also inevitably killed innocent civilians. That was regrettable, but inevitable when fighting an enemy that wrapped itself in the population."

DICK COUCH RECALLS HIS final days in Vietnam:

In the spring of 1971, I was a month away from finishing my SEAL deployment in Vietnam. The first half of that year was a bad time for us in SEAL Team One.

Half of the SEALs in the platoon in the neighboring province had been killed in an ambush. The other platoon operating out of Solid Anchor with me recently had six SEALs wounded, including both platoon officers. All of them had been medevaced (medically evacuated) out with combat wounds. I had the only effective SEAL platoon still operating in the lower Delta, and with the end of our tour in sight, we were being very careful. We operated mostly after dark, one squad going out every other night.

One morning I came in from patrol and found the base commander waiting for me in the platoon hooch.

"Lieutenant, the air reconnaissance people have found what looks like a trawler in a river inlet on the coast south of us. COMNAVFORV [Commander, Naval Forces, Vietnam] wants me to put someone on the ground for a firsthand look. How soon can you be ready to go?"

The base CO, the third of my tour, was a senior Navy com-

mander whose last job was commanding officer of a destroyer—
a Navy surface warship. A fair man, but he knew little of what
we were doing out there in the mangrove.

"Could you show me on the map, sir?" I replied.

He pointed to an inlet on the coast well away from the base
and in a particularly nasty area. The previous month my boat
officer, friend, and classmate, Bob Natter, had been ambushed
not far from the trawler site. The ambush killed one of our SEAL
advisors and three of his LDNNs (Vietnamese SEALs). Everyone else in the boat, including Bob, was seriously wounded. It
was reasonably safe in the daytime, if you had sufficient air
cover, but no place you wanted to go at night unless you had a
good reason to be there.

"Support?" I asked.

"All the gunships and OV-10s you need," he replied. These
OV-10s were the famous Navy Black Ponies who flew the
OV-10 Bronco close-support aircraft and often worked with
SEALs. "This one has top priority."

I knew about the priority. Over the past few weeks, strike
aircraft from the carriers on Yankee station had caught two
trawlers sneaking south loaded with arms—further evidence of
North Vietnam's continued escalation of the war in the South.
Trawlers were a hot item.

Since I had just come in from the bush and had been up
for more than twenty-four hours, I sent my chief petty officer in with the other squad. They heloed into a clearing a few
klicks from the trawler and patrolled in with helicopter gunships weaving overhead. The chief found a deserted hull well
grounded in mud. It had been there for some time, and it did
not matter whether it was an arms runner or a fishing boat; the
hulk had not seen blue-water duty in years and probably never
would again.

My chief was a good one. He took pictures, set a satchel charge on the keel to break its back, and got the hell out of there—neat, clean, no casualties.

I met him on the helo pad when he arrived back at Solid Anchor. "The thing's a derelict, boss," he reported. "Hasn't been used for months and now it never will. We busted it good."

Case closed, or so I thought. The base commander was again waiting for me when the chief and I returned to our SEAL hooch.

"You have to go back in," he told me. "COMNAVFORV wants to send a team of inspectors down to look at the craft. They'll be here tomorrow so you'll have to go in and guard it tonight. They want to make sure it's not disturbed."

"Not disturbed!" the chief exploded. "I just broke the keel of the damn thing and blew a hole in the bottom in the process. It was a worthless hulk—still is."

He handed the commander the Polaroids. "Sir, it ain't going anywhere."

"Uh, the chief's right, sir," I added, "and that's a bad area. The VC don't want us there, especially at night. Remember when Natter and Thames went down there with the LDNNs a few weeks ago."

Lieutenant Jim Thames, the LDNN advisor who had been killed, was a friend of mine. Putting him in a body bag and taking him up to the base at Binh Thuy for shipment home was very fresh in my mind.

"That may be," the base commander replied, "but those are my orders—and yours. You'll have to go back in and spend the night there." We went back and forth a short while, but the commander was firm. And so was I. Then he hit me with the line that no officer wants to hear. "Lieutenant, that's an order. Are you disobeying a direct order?"

The precursor units of the U.S. Navy SEALs were born in World War II. They include the Naval Combat Demolition Unit demolitioneers, the Scouts and Raiders, the OSS Maritime Unit swimmers, and the combat swimmers of the Underwater Demolition Teams (UDTs), here pictured in 1955 in an operation to support the evacuation of Taiwanese forces from the Tachen Islands near the Chinese mainland. Their legacy continues with the men of today's SEAL Teams. *(U.S. Navy)*

One of the first glimpses of the Scouts and Raiders, one of the earliest precursor units of the SEALs, during rubber boat training at Fort Pierce, Florida, late 1943. *(U.S. Navy)*

An Office of Strategic Services Maritime Unit diver trains with the Lambertsen Amphibious Respirator Unit, or LARU. The LARU was a pure-oxygen rebreather and first-generation SCUBA.

Fort Pierce, Florida, 1944: Lieutenant Commander Draper Kauffman (center, front) and fellow officers flank one of the first graduating classes of Naval Combat Demolition Unit demolitioneers, predecessors of the Navy SEALs. *(U.S. Navy)*

The "Naked Warriors"—early UDT members at Fort Pierce, Florida. *(U.S. Navy)*

NCDU boat artwork. *(U.S. Navy)*

Naval Combat Demolition Unit boat crew, Fort Pierce, July 1944. As SEALs do today, NCDUs trained in boat crews. *(U.S. Navy)*

Hand-to-hand combat instruction at Fort Pierce, 1944. *(U.S. Navy)*

Training at Fort Pierce, 1944. Seventy years later, such log drills are still a part of Basic Underwater Demolition/Seal training. *(U.S. Navy)*

Loading beach obstacles with explosives charges and tying into the trunk line. *(U.S. Navy)*

Surface tender at work during diver training, Fort Pierce. *(U.S. Navy)*

UDT members in beach-obstacle demolition training in Maui, Hawaii, summer 1945. *(U.S. Navy)*

German officers inspect defenses on the beaches of Normandy, 1944. NCDU members had to blow gaps through these obstacles while under fire. *(German Federal Archives)*

Nazi-installed Omaha Beach obstacles in a photo taken by a U.S. reconnaissance aircraft flying at high speed and low altitude, May 6, 1944, a month before D-Day. NCDU demolitioneer Ken Reynolds and his teammates had to clear these obstacles so the landings could proceed. *(National Archives)*

Demolitioneers train with hose charges for beach obstacle clearance. *(U.S. Navy)*

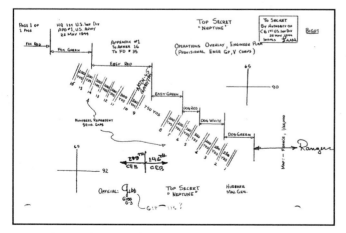

Ken Reynolds, one of the first Navy demolitioneers on Omaha Beach. *(Courtesy of Ken Reynolds)*

U.S. military planning chart for D-Day assault landings on Omaha Beach, indicating the sixteen gaps that needed to be blown open by joint Army-Navy demolition teams. *(Naval Special Warfare Command Historical Files)*

UDT-15 combat swimmers watching combat operations after completing their reconnaissance and demolition work at Balikpapan, Borneo, on July 1, 1945, one of the final UDT operations of World War II. (SEAL Museum)

An underwater demolition swimmer after setting charges off Balikpapan, 1945. (U.S. Navy)

LCVP (Landing Craft Vehicle, Personnel) with a crew of UDT demolitioneers is lowered over the side of a fast amphibious transport in the Pacific. (U.S. Navy)

Tools of the explosives trade: matériel used by NCDU and UDT personnel to demolish and clear landing zone obstacles during World War II. *(U.S. Navy)*

A Demolitioneer making up his explosive charges prior to going ashore to clear a landing beach. *(U.S. Navy)*

Wiring explosives to underwater coral growth, which posed a threat to Allied landings in the Pacific, and trapped thousands of Marines at the tragic landings at Tarawa in 1943. *(U.S. Navy)*

A typical World War II sight as demolition charges placed by Underwater Demolition Teams (UDTs) cleared a path for many Marine and Army landings in the Pacific. *(U.S. Navy)*

Beach obstacle demolition prior to landings at Guam, July 1944. *(U.S. Navy)*

On August 28, 1945, a Japanese Army Coast Artillery major formally presented his sword to Lieutenant Commander Edward Porter Clayton of UDT-21. This impromptu ceremony was held on the beach near a small fort at the entrance to Tokyo Bay and is believed to be the first such surrender ceremony on the Japanese home islands. *(National Archives)*

Friendly rivalry: Team 21 "welcomes" the U.S. Marines to Japan. *(U.S. Navy)*

Korean War, 1950: UDT frogmen in dry suits launch rubber boats and conduct mine-hunting operations in Wonsan Harbor. *(U.S. Navy)*

Helicopter used by UDTs for mine-spotting in the waters off Korea, 1952. Korea marked the first use of helicopters to support Naval Special Warfare operations, and the first limited UDT operations beyond the beach onto land warfare. *(Courtesy of Dick Lyon)*

UDT operator Dick Lyon and Navy explosives expert Dick Edwards approach an enemy surface mine marked by a helicopter-dropped signal flare in the waters off communist-held North Korea, 1952. *(Courtesy of Dick Lyon)*

UDT-5 Lieutenant Dick Lyon with the Soviet-made underwater mine he recovered under fire off Wonsan Harbor, Korea, 1952. Today, at age ninety-one, Rear Admiral Lyon (Ret.) assists in training the new generation of Navy SEALs. *(Courtesy of Dick Lyon)*

Russian packing slip found inside Soviet-made naval mine recovered by UDT-5 frogman Dick Lyon off the shore of communist-held Korea. *(Courtesy of Dick Lyon)*

UDT combat swimmers test themselves and their dry suits during polar training operations. *(U.S. Navy)*

UDT training, Little Creek, 1947. Here frogmen work to load a beach obstacle with demolitions to open a path for friendly troops and armored vehicles *(U.S. Navy)*

UDT frogmen in U.S.-occupied Japan, 1950, conducting beach survey training. *(U.S. Navy)*

UDTs train in beach obstacle demolition, Little Creek, Virginia. *(U.S. Navy)*

I considered this for a moment, but no more than that. "Yes, sir, I am." He regarded me with a cool stare, then walked out of the hooch.

There was an Underwater Demolition detachment at Solid Anchor, and though I was the senior SEAL on the base, the UDTs were a fleet detachment and did not work for me. The base commander sent them in that night, and they boarded the trawler. Morning came and nothing happened. The political implications of this new symbol of North Vietnamese aggression grew through the following day, so the next night they put in a company of ARVN (South Vietnamese) soldiers to guard the hulk. The VC did come the second night and wiped out close to half the company. After that, everyone seemed to lose interest in the trawler.

I finished my tour without incident. The base commander and I seldom spoke to each other and never about the trawler. I managed what few SEAL platoon commanders were able to do in 1970–71: I took all of my men home with me.

I've often thought about my decision not to go back in on that trawler. While the base commander took no action, he could have written me up—even court-martialed me. I did not feel right about it. My men applauded the decision, since they knew as well as I did just how foolish the mission was. When the VC came and mauled the ARVN company, it seemed that I had been vindicated. But I still knew that I had disobeyed an order—a lawful order.

Furthermore, what if they had come in the night before and taken out the UDT squad? The UDT guys were good, but they didn't have the training and operational experience of my SEALs. If they had been hit that night, their lives would have been on my conscience: they went on the mission when I refused.

I debate that decision with myself to this day. There was no question in my mind that the order was stupid and ill-conceived, one that would have put my men at needless risk. The work we did was dangerous enough without inviting disasters, and getting caught at night in the mangrove by a large VC force was just that. You either ran, fought, or died—sometimes all three. But I had sworn to obey the lawful orders of "those appointed over me" and that day I had refused.

Sometimes, on reflection, I think that I should have gone in on the trawler, then after dark, faded a hundred meters or so into the mangrove. It would have been an uncomfortable night, but we had done it many times before. We felt reasonably safe out in the swamp at night—we were Navy SEALs. And this would have kept the UDT guys out of it, perhaps even weighed against the decision to put in the ARVN company. Yet my men counted on me not to put them at risk unless it really counted. They had followed me into some hard situations that tour. I owed them a lot.

I don't really have a sure answer for this one. I didn't then and I still don't now. Had there been a Junior Officers Training Course for SEAL officers in my day, as there is now, I might have made a better decision. Or a more informed one.

I do know that in the course of a naval career, the character of a combat leader will be challenged in ways unimaginable to a midshipman or a brand-new junior officer. The nineteenth-century U.S. Navy oceanographer Matthew Fontaine Maury rightly exhorted us that "where principle is involved, be deaf to expediency." A good place to start, but I am afraid it is seldom that simple. The black-and-white is easy; the tough choices are gray. Our future leaders must take every opportunity to study the examples, as well as the mistakes, of those of us who have gone before them. It may help them to develop the strength of character they will need to make tough choices when their time comes.

THREE U.S. NAVY SEALS were awarded the Medal of Honor for their actions in Vietnam. Their stories, while exceptional, illustrate the typically overwhelming-to-impossible circumstances often faced by the Teams in that vicious conflict.

On March 14, 1969, then-twenty-five-year-old SEAL Team One Lieutenant Junior Grade Joseph "Bob" Kerrey of Lincoln, Nebraska, was leading a raid on an island in Nha Trang Bay on the South Central Coast of Vietnam.

"It was a pretty straightforward operation," Kerrey recalled more than forty years after the events. "It involved the interrogation of a Vietnamese who had got tired of it all, because the Vietnamese fought until they were tired or the war was over. He just got tired of it. He'd been doing it for four or five years, and he wanted to go home and see his family. So he swam off an island. He had told the [American] Special Forces guys that on this island was a group of North Vietnamese who were sappers, and they had been responsible for blowing up a number of mostly civilian targets in the city of Nha Trang. He agreed to lead us to where they were. And the object was to round them up. He told us they were sleeping in two different groups. So we went up the back side of the island, which was a fair amount of climbing [up a 350-foot sheer cliff]. We positioned at the first sleeping group, but at the second sleeping group we got there a bit too late. They had broke camp and were on the move. Some sort of explosive device was thrown and it started a firefight."

A grenade exploded at Kerrey's feet and propelled him back onto rocks. "I felt down where the leg was and it was mashed up pretty good and bleeding pretty good so I tied a tourniquet onto it and I tried to stand and couldn't." Despite excruciating pain, Kerrey directed fire into the enemy's compound. "There was a lot of confusion. We didn't quite know and had to figure out what's going on. You knew there were rounds coming in from two different directions so we had to reposition ourselves. We now knew it was a life-or-death situation, so were returning fire and taking fire. I didn't really think about anything other than stopping the bleeding, and trying to come out on the high end of a pretty lethal firefight that was going on."

Kerrey's SEALs managed to survive, and prevail, and capture several Viet Cong prisoners who provided valuable intelligence. Kerrey's Medal of Honor citation hailed his "courageous and inspiring leadership, valiant fighting spirit, and tenacious devotion to duty in the face of almost overwhelming opposition."

Kerrey was evacuated by helicopter to the 26th Field Hospital at Cam Ranh Bay, then on to a Navy hospital in Philadelphia, where he endured months of rehabilitation. "There are some rare people who don't appear to have any physical fear at all," he recalled. "I don't happen to be one of those. And I think most of us aren't. I think soldiers know that death doesn't come quickly, that it can be painful as can be, it can be disfiguring, so you set it aside on behalf of the guys that you're with. . . . I cared deeply about the guys I was with. I would fight for them and protect them and carry them out if necessary if they were injured. So I wouldn't have thought for a second to put myself in between live fire and one of my men to do it." As with many Medal of Honor recipients, Bob Kerrey was reluctant to receive the award for his actions at Nha Trang. He was presented the award by President Richard Nixon on May 14, 1970.

THREE YEARS AFTER KERREY'S Medal of Honor mission, on April 10–13, 1972, an operation unfolded when Lieutenant

Thomas Norris of SEAL Team Two, among the dwindling number of American advisors remaining in Vietnam in the wake of President Nixon's "Vietnamization" policy of turning the war over to local forces, volunteered to rescue two downed American aircrew personnel.

The rescue mission was triggered by the events of April 2, 1972, when an EB-66 electronic warfare aircraft was shot down by an SA-2 Soviet-made surface-to-air missile. The aircraft crashed just south of the North/South Vietnamese border—what was then known as the Demilitarized Zone, or DMZ, but it was anything but demilitarized. Of the six crewmen, only one parachuted safely and survived, USAF Lieutenant Colonel Iceal "Gene" Hambleton. USAF First Lieutenant Mark Clark was subsequently shot down in an attempt to rescue him. They were dubbed by their call signs Bat-21 Bravo and Nail-38 Bravo respectively. The American airmen had parachuted separately into an area that was surrounded by nearly thirty thousand North Vietnamese troops who were launching a ground-based offensive southward, their biggest of the war.

A series of failed rescue attempts had been made by air, killing several Americans in the process, and Thomas Norris was the downed airmen's last hope.

Lieutenant Colonel Hambleton was an Air Force ballistic missile expert with a highly compartmentalized, top-secret security clearance. His value to the patrons of the North Vietnamese regime, the Soviet Union, was inestimable; his rescue was a strategic imperative for the Americans. So began one of the longest and most costly combat search-and-rescue missions in U.S. history. Over the next week, more rescue aircraft were shot down, the total number of Americans killed reached ten, and two Americans were taken prisoner.

The two airmen were on the ground, alive and in hiding, and located about a half mile from each other. Both were in contact with orbiting American aircraft on their survival radios. And they were in the path of thousands of North Vietnamese soldiers making their way south during the 1972 Easter Offensive. The rescue had to be a ground operation, as helicopters were not going to work in the overwhelmingly North Vietnamese–controlled area. American rescue pilots and air controllers hit upon a brilliant idea to help Hambleton navigate on foot toward a rescue spot. "Hambleton was a very avid golfer," Norris told us, "particularly in Arizona. He knew the golf courses there and we knew the North Vietnamese had our radios and they were listening to what we were saying. So we utilized golf courses to work him to the river. It took him a while to understand what we were doing, but he finally got the hang of it. We'd tell him, 'You're on the 18th hole at Phoenix.' So he knew, 'Okay, I've got to hit my ball 385 yards this way and then I hook to the right and then I hit it another 285 yards this way, and I get to the green.' By golf courses, we were able to work him down to the river. It took him a couple days to get there."

On the evening of April 10, Norris led a patrol north to search for Hambleton and Clark. The five-man patrol consisted of Norris and four South Vietnamese Sea Commandos. They set out from a small outpost, heading north and dodging main-force North Vietnamese units that included tanks and motorized artillery. They located Lieutenant Clark, put him in a sampan, and the next night floated him south to a friendly outpost and safety. Nail-38 Bravo was safe; this left Bat-21 Bravo—Lieutenant Colonel Hambleton.

The rescue of Nail-38 Bravo took courage, luck, and nerves of steel as the North Vietnamese troops passed close by. But Bat-21 Bravo would prove to be more challenging. His signal was becoming faint, his physical condition was deteriorating, and his location was farther into enemy-controlled territory than that of Nail-38 Bravo. One of Norris's Sea Commandos was wounded in a North Vietnamese mortar attack on their forward operating base. Two of the remaining three refused to go back; it was simply too dangerous for them. The fourth, Petty Officer Nguyen van Kiet, volunteered to follow Norris in the attempt to save Hambleton. "I'm going with you," declared Kiet. Norris replied, "Kit, I'm not sure I'm coming back from this." Kiet said, "If you go I go."

Norris and Kiet, now disguised as fishermen, headed back north on April 12 just after dark. They hadn't much time. North Vietnamese troops were pouring into the area and Hambleton was getting weaker, barely able to speak on his survival radio. At dawn on the thirteenth, Hambleton was told to get in the river near where he was hiding and float downstream; help would be waiting for him. Hiding under a bank from enemy troops and pinned down, Norris and Kiet saw Hambleton float by but could do nothing.

Finally they were able to work their way down the fog-shrouded river, slip past sleeping troops in enemy guard posts, find the exhausted Hambleton, and get him into their sampan. Norris told us, "My concern was his health, because on his hands there were spots that looked like gangrene. He was bashed up. He'd been down there now eleven days."

Norris and Kiet hid Hambleton in the bottom of the native craft, covered him with vegetation, and pretended to tend their fishing nets, floating past whole companies of enemy troops. As they passed through enemy lines, an alarm was raised and they came under fire. Norris was able to call in an air strike on the enemy positions to cover their escape. When they returned to the outpost, a waiting medevac helo whisked Hambleton to safety—mission complete. That night their outpost again came under attack and half the garrison, including two of the Sea

Commandos, were killed. Norris and the survivors fought the enemy through the night and were lifted out by helo the following morning. Hambleton recovered, having successfully been shielded from capture by Norris and Kiet. It had been an incredibly costly rescue operation. "I had to stand by and watch six young men die trying to save my life," Lieutenant Colonel Hambleton wrote from an Air Force hospital after he was rescued. "It was a hell of a price to pay for one life. I'm very sorry."

The Medal of Honor was presented to Lieutenant Tom Norris by President Gerald Ford on March 6, 1976. Norris accepted the award with some reluctance, explaining to us years later, "I still today don't think it's a Medal of Honor mission. It's just what I do. It was my job and I was just fortunate enough to be really, really successful at it, but any other SEAL in my spot would have done the same darn thing. I'm not unique, I'm just an average guy that was pretty good at my job." He added, "To me, the true heroes of that operation were those that gave their lives in an effort to recover a fellow American. They gave everything. What more can you ask?" Norris was indeed good at his job. Having recovered the two downed pilots, he was preparing to go back after a third aviator when it was learned that this pilot had been discovered by the North Vietnamese and killed.

IN AN ASTONISHING TWIST of fate, six months after his Bat-21 rescue mission, Norris's own life was saved by yet another SEAL team member, a petty officer by the name of Michael E. Thornton, in an operation that earned Thornton the Medal of Honor.

Thornton and Lieutenant Norris were among the comparatively few American sailors left in South Vietnam in October 1972. The so-called Brown Water Navy had been "Vietnamized," and most of the remaining U.S. Navy personnel were advisors to the Vietnamese Navy (VNN). But being an advisor did not necessarily mean being out of harm's way, especially when the North Vietnamese invaded South Vietnam in force in the spring of that year.

On October 31, 1972, Norris and Thornton led a three-man South Vietnamese Navy team on a prisoner-snatch and intelligence-gathering mission behind enemy lines. They landed farther north than planned on the coast of Vietnam, and when dawn broke they realized they were on the edge of a large concentration of enemy troops near a naval base on the Cua Viet River, near the coast of Quang Tri Province, just north of the southern boundary of the Demilitarized Zone.

The North Vietnamese Easter Offensive into South Vietnam had been blunted by a generous dose of American airpower, but their forces remained massed just north of the DMZ. Senior military planners needed intelligence on North Vietnamese troop movements and concentrations. Norris sensed this would be a risky mission and felt he needed the presence of another U.S. Navy SEAL. His choices were limited, but he did know of a SEAL petty officer assigned to the LDNN training base at Thuan-an just north of Da Nang. He was from Team One and his name was Mike Thornton. Though the two had never worked together, Norris knew of Thornton's reputation as a solid operator. He sent for Thornton, who immediately volunteered to help with the mission.

Thornton, Norris, and three Vietnamese SEALs approached the coast in the South China Sea near the North/South border by fishing sampan in the early morning hours of October 31. In the shallows several hundred meters off the coast, they swam ashore. Due to imprecise navigation, they found themselves farther north than planned. Moving cautiously inland, they encountered the enemy, in force.

A North Vietnamese patrol came down toward the beach. It was the point element of a North Vietnamese Army battalion. A firefight broke out between the SEALs force of five men and several hundred enemy troops. The SEALs, as SEALs are trained to do, headed for the water. Getting back to the coast turned into a three-hour running gun battle as Norris, Thornton, and their Vietnamese teammates were just able to stay ahead of the advancing enemy.

Thornton and Norris maneuvered around the sand dunes as they fired, creating the impression of a bigger force. The superior North Vietnamese forces immediately began to conduct their own fire-and-maneuver and flanking movements. Attempting to hold back their pursuers, Norris aimed a LAW (Light Anti-armor Weapon) rocket at the biggest group of enemy soldiers he could find and got ready to pull the trigger. "I never got a shot," he explained. "A round came in and hit me in the head, right above my temple area. It just blew out a portion of my head. It just picked me off of the sand dune and dumped me on my back. I knew I'd been hit, but I didn't know how bad."

"Where's Tom?" asked Thornton of a South Vietnamese teammate who had witnessed what happened to Norris. "Mike," he replied to Thornton, "he's dead."

"Stay here," ordered Thornton, "I'll go get Tommy." Thornton recalled, "I thought he was dead, but I wasn't going to leave him behind. We never leave anybody behind. So I sure wasn't going to be the first one."

With Thornton carrying Norris, they made their way through the surf and into the open water. Along the way, Thornton took a round through his upper arm, but they kept going. In addition to Norris's devastating injury, one of the South Vietnamese had been shot through the leg and another in the butt. Over the next two hours in the water, Thornton supported Norris and the wounded Vietnamese until they were recovered by American vessels. When the five men were taken aboard, Thornton refused medical attention until Norris was attended to.

"The doctor gave him no chance at all to live," recalled Thornton. But Tom Norris refused to die. After a long ordeal of surgeries and rehabilitation, Norris recovered to the extent that he would pursue a successful new postwar career as an FBI agent.

The Medal of Honor was presented to Petty Officer Second Class Mike Thornton on October 15, 1974, by President Richard Nixon. Thornton helped smuggle his buddy Tom Norris out of a nearby naval hospital in the middle of the night to a hotel so they could attend the White House ceremony together. The hospital staff told Norris he couldn't attend, but, as Norris pointed out to us, "Of course, that's not the thing to tell a SEAL. You just don't tell a SEAL *he can't*. It's not a word in our vocabulary. Mike kind of kidnapped me out of the hospital."

THE LAST SEAL FATALITY of the Vietnam War claimed the life of Lieutenant Spence Dry. The twenty-six-year-old Dry was the SEAL element leader for a highly complex and hazardous SEAL Team One/UDT-11 mission to rendezvous with and rescue two American POWs who planned an escape from the infamous "Hanoi Hilton" prison in North Vietnam.

In May 1972 the American prisoners in the Hanoi Hilton had managed, miraculously, to open a direct channel of two-way communications to the American military. The system was neither instantaneous nor perfect, and it still is not known if it was based on electronic transmissions or human intelligence, as to this day the details of the system are classified. However they did it, the signal came out that two Americans were planning an escape, and a rescue plan, dubbed Operation Thunderhead, was hatched by the U.S. Pacific Fleet and launched from the USS *Grayback* (LPSS-574), an amphibious transport submarine that was adapted to carry four swimmer delivery vehicles, or SDVs. The SDVs were small minisubmarines with primitive navigation systems that had never been used in combat before. Tragically, two of the SDVs malfunctioned badly during Operation Thunderhead, and for one SEAL the consequences were fatal.

Lieutenant Dry and his three SEAL and UDT teammates were supposed to launch their SDV at night and make their way through poor visibility and powerful currents to a little island in the Red River to watch for a signal from the escaping POWs in a fishing boat. "The time Spence and I were to spend on the island was a minimum of 24 hours and up to 48 hours," recalled Dry's fellow SEAL Philip "Moki" Martin. "We were to look for a red light on a boat during the night and a red flag during the day." Their first reconnaissance attempt was aborted when they went off course, could not find the island, and their SDV's battery ran out.

The would-be rescuers were forced to swim out several miles offshore and tread water until they were rescued by a search-and-rescue HH-3A helicopter. They were flown to the guided-missile cruiser USS *Long Beach* (CGN-9), which was serving as the command ship for Operation Thunderhead, where plans were made to night-drop them back into the water next to the submarine *Grayback* at 11 P.M. on June 5 to resume the mission. Dry and Martin stressed to the chopper pilot that the drop would only be safe at an altitude of twenty feet or less and an airspeed of 20 knots or less. But when the helicopter pilot spotted what seemed to be the *Grayback*'s red signaling beacon atop the sub's snorkel mast, visibility was very poor, the tailwind was some 20 knots, and the craft may have been as much as fifty or sixty feet high. Many years later, Martin said, "I still think about Spence's face. I could see him in the red light of the helicopter by the door. I can still see his face reflecting in it." Dry's last words before jumping, Martin remembered, were "We gotta get back to the *Grayback*."

Martin recalled, "The problem was an extremely strong wind creating at least a 5-foot sea state, and so when we got into the water we couldn't have seen the *Grayback* anyway because it was so rough. I questioned the height of the helicopter when we went out, and I thought the helicopter was too high. Four guys went out, and the first guy was killed. The second guy suffered an injured back. I was the third guy and I went out and just about everything that was on my body was ripped off. I barely hit the water at the right angle and I still injured my knee. The fourth guy was knocked unconscious and almost drowned until I found him. Our saving grace was we all wore wetsuits under our camouflage uniform and that kept us afloat."

When Spence Dry and his colleagues jumped out of the helicopter, the impact snapped Dry's neck, killing him. The survivors, now a total of seven men, were rescued the next morning. It turned out that the POW escape attempt had already been canceled by the POW leadership inside the Hanoi Hilton, but there wasn't enough time to alert the would-be rescuers.

The details of the mission were classified for many years, thwarting the campaign of Spencer Dry's father, himself a former Navy captain, to earn his son a posthumous Purple Heart and the proper recognition for his sacrifice. The Navy officially designated it as a training accident. Ten days after the accident, the surviving men of Dry's SEAL platoon wrote a group letter to Dry's father, pledging, "His memory will remain with us so long as man values positive leadership and courage in the face of danger."

Proper recognition for Spence Dry did not come until 2005, seven years after the elder Dry's death, when two of Dry's classmates at the U.S. Naval Academy, retired Navy Captains (SEAL) Michael Slattery and Gordon Peterson (a naval aviator and Seawolf pilot in Vietnam), published a detailed account of the mission in the prestigious journal *The Naval Institute: Proceedings*. The article helped spur the 2008 award of a Bronze Star with valor to U.S. Navy SEAL Spence Dry.

DURING THIS FIRST DECADE of their history, the life of a Navy SEAL was one of continuous combat rotations to Vietnam. Officers might get in one or two combat tours, but the enlisted SEALs went back time and again. In spite of the broad direct-action warfare portfolio handed the SEALs, their training and deployments were all about operations in Vietnam. In short, SEALs became very good jungle fighters and little else. They maintained minimum qualifications in diving and parachuting but seldom practiced these in an operational scenario. Yet, within certain constraints and the guidance of area commanders, the SEALs had a free hand in choosing which missions they would undertake. With this latitude comes a great deal of responsibility. Today in Afghanistan, platoon officers, platoon chiefs, and task unit commanders have that same latitude and responsibility. While it leads to operational success, it also means these combat leaders must make these life-and-death decisions on a daily basis. It means that they have to balance the importance of the mission against the risk to their men, not easy then and not easy now.

During the late 1970s and early 1980s, the UDTs and SEAL teams shrank to pre-Vietnam levels and operating budgets were tight. A fifth UDT was commissioned in the summer of 1968 for duty in Vietnam and decommissioned in the summer of 1971. There was even talk of disbanding the SEALs and the UDTs altogether. Today there are close to 2,700 active duty SEALs; at the height of the Vietnam War there were just under 450. "What happened to the Teams after Vietnam was pretty much a mirror image of Korea except there were more Teams— UDT-22 on the east coast was immediately disestablished," according to Tom Hawkins. "The SEAL Teams were reduced to basically pre-war strength. Some SEALs either had to get out or they had to go find a place to go. Some of them went back to UDT because there were some billets available. Many went to the EOD [Explosive Ordnance Disposal] community. Many went to the diving community and those that couldn't find a diving billet of some kind had to get out of the Navy. And we lost a lot of really, really good operators as a result. But, you also have to understand that when the SEALs came back from Vietnam, they didn't have a Navy mission. What was the Navy going to do with the SEALs? We had to figure all of that out."

How did the SEALs perform during the course of the Vietnam War? On the basis of numbers, their record was impressive. For their relatively small size, the SEALs were among the highest-decorated units in the conflict. In six major POW rescues involving SEALs, some 152 Vietnamese captives were freed, accounting for 48 percent of POWs freed during the war. One SEAL historian, Dale Andrade, put it this way: "By the end of 1970 SEALs and their South Vietnamese allies had killed more than two thousand Viet Cong and captured about twenty-seven hundred, many of them important members of the political infrastructure. All this had been accomplished relatively cheaply in terms of SEAL casualties. Only three dozen or so were killed during nine years of involvement in Vietnam. In the overall conduct of the war, SEALs did not change the tide of battle. But they did illustrate that a few well-trained men using counterinsurgency tactics and specially trained allies could devastate a guerilla enemy, particularly the political infrastructure." As General William Westmoreland said, "I would like to have a thousand more like them."

There are some vets who even think that if SEALs were deployed in greater numbers, they could have turned the tide of the war. "Some people have said that if there were more SEALs or more SEAL-like activities, we could have actually won the war," said Hawkins. "I think there's probably not a SEAL alive that wouldn't tell you that. To actually fight in an unconventional warfare campaign, you have to get down where the people are, and I think the Army was still fighting a conventional war. I think the Marine Corps adapted pretty well. It took the Navy quite a while to adapt to what became a brown water Navy. It took the Navy quite a while to figure out that it needed SEALs, riverine force, and armed helicopters. Everybody eventually learned the lesson, but the difference is in the village, with the people, with their hearts and minds. Our role wasn't to win too many hearts and minds—our aim was to think like the Viet Cong and to take what he gave back to him, through unconventional warfare. But there should have probably been a lot more emphasis put on structure building, and community building."

Nevertheless, the SEAL culture and many of the skills and techniques of the modern SEAL force were pioneered in Vietnam and have had a lasting impact on modern special warfare ever since. But at the time, as former Marine and then RAND company analyst Bing West said after a 1968 visit to a SEAL platoon, the SEALs were a "tactic in search of a strategy." Another SEAL historian, T. L. Bosiljevac, put it this way: "Although they were highly successful in their own districts and provinces throughout the Delta, their full potential was never fully under-

stood or tapped. Most of their operations, especially early in
the war, were nothing more than small-unit infantry tactics in
a swamp environment." He continued, "Most of all, their full
potential in special operations was never fully integrated in the
overall military strategy and goals of the war. They were never
really viewed as anything more than a local tactical asset."

Vietnam-era SEAL veteran Bob Gormly agreed, arguing,
"For the most part, we were relegated to the Navy river patrol
forces. SEALs killed considerable numbers of the enemy, and
obtained locally important intelligence. A lot of our men were
wounded, but surprisingly few were killed. The latter statistic I
attribute to training and the fact that we called our own shots;
we simply didn't operate where or when we didn't want to. In
my view, we should have been conducting high-risk, high-gain
operations. Instead of chasing VC who harassed the river patrol
forces, we could have been applied to such vexing problems as
freeing American prisoners of war." At least one SEAL officer
proposed to the higher-ups in the chain of command that the
SEALs be unleashed in a fully coordinated program of POW
hunts and attempted raids across South Vietnam. His pleas
were ignored.

The last SEAL platoon left Vietnam on December 7, 1971,
exactly thirty years after the attack on Pearl Harbor, and the
last remaining SEAL advisors left Vietnam in March 1973. On
April 30, 1975, North Vietnamese tanks crashed through the
gates of the South Vietnamese Presidential Palace in Saigon,
bringing the war to an end.

Between 1965 and 1972, there were forty-six SEALs who
died in battle in Vietnam. Their names are etched on the Vietnam Veterans Memorial in Washington, D.C., and are also
memorialized on the Navy SEAL Memorial at the Navy SEAL
Museum in Fort Pierce, Florida.

In the Vietnam War, the Navy SEALs first forged their skills in battle, and launched a legendary reputation as direct-action warriors. It was a conflict that saw naval special warriors transform, in the words of Vietnam veteran SEAL Carl Swepston, from being "a guy in the water with fins on and a facemask and lifejacket and a Ka-Bar to a guy with AR-15 and M-16 machine guns going in and going directly against the enemy." They caused such damage to communist forces in the zones they operated in that the enemy respectfully dubbed them "The Men with Green Faces" and announced cash bounties for killing of SEALs.

The stage was set for the SEALs to face a new era, of limited wars, hostage rescues, and the dawn of global terrorism.

CHAPTER 6

TRAGEDY AND RESURRECTION: THE POST-VIETNAM YEARS

GRENADA, OCTOBER 25, 1983, 10:00 A.M.

THE ASSAULT FORCE:
U.S. Navy SEALs

THE ENEMY:
Grenadian army and militia troops backed by Cuban advisors

THE MISSION:
Support the U.S. invasion of Grenada

In fifteen seconds, I will be dead.

For U.S. Navy Lieutenant Jason Kendall, it was a reasonable assumption. He and eleven other members of a Navy SEAL assault team were soaked in the blood of wounded enemy prisoners, and trapped inside a building that was surrounded on three out of four sides and being shot to pieces. Around them were the dead bodies of nine enemy soldiers, four more on the brink of death, and fourteen other enemy POWs, eight of them wounded.

Their only escape route, out the building's back door, was a fenced-in open field that was flanked on both sides by enemy troops pouring fire into it, creating what looked to Kendall to be an amphitheater-sized shooting gallery. If they were forced to cross it, his SEALs had little chance of survival. Beyond the field outside the fence were jungle, cliffs, and the potential safety of the open waters of the Caribbean, but there seemed no chance of getting there. "I could see trucks coming up both flanks," recalled Kendall, "they unloaded guys down the fence line, and my best guess is we were outnumbered a good three to one, maybe four to one, and surrounded."

And their radios wouldn't work. One of the SEALs was frantically punching buttons on an encrypted satellite radio, trying to contact other U.S. forces invading the tiny Caribbean island of Grenada. The SATCOM 101 device was their primary radio, but it wouldn't work. The codes and frequencies in the "crypto" gear had somehow been switched in the vast chain of command, and no one had given the SEALs the new data. "How the hell would we know?" recalled Kendall. "We were already on the ground fighting, and when we tried to use our radios they were worthless."

Their backup field radios wouldn't work, either. Those radios could receive calls, but they couldn't transmit far enough. "Our tactical radios were only good for line-of-sight communication," said one of the SEALs.

"Our commanding officer's helicopter got shot up while trying to land at the Grenadian governor general's mansion and made an emergency landing on the deck of the amphibious assault ship USS *Guam* (LPH-9, Amphibious Platform, Helicopter; essentially a small helo aircraft carrier), so I had no commo with him," recalled Kendall, the assault team leader. "We had no SATCOM, no commo with the general flying in the airborne command post, or with our own commanding officer. We just didn't have the radios to reach them."

This was the SEAL team's first test in combat, and it was going badly.

The SEALs' mission seemed relatively simple. They were to capture a lightly guarded radio transmission tower and briefly hold it until U.S. Army and other American personnel could arrive and set up a broadcast for the island's Commonwealth governor general to transmit to the Grenadian people, telling them to cooperate with invading American forces to restore stability to the island, which was a member of the Commonwealth.

Grenada was a small south Caribbean island of about one hundred thousand people that had received its independence from Britain in 1974, but remained a member of the Commonwealth of Nations led by Great Britain. For the previous four years, it had fallen under the increasingly Cuban-influenced rule of Marxist prime minister Maurice Bishop. Six days before the U.S. invasion, political chaos had broken out. Bishop and several other officials were gunned down on the orders of even more radical cabinet members of Bishop's own government; martial law was declared. Hundreds of U.S. and foreign students were thought to be in danger at the local medical school. More than a thousand Cuban and Soviet bloc troops, engineers, and advisors were thought to be on the island, augmenting Soviet-bloc-trained Grenadian military forces.

Inside the Oval Office, President Ronald Reagan saw the prospect of another communist toehold in the Americas as unacceptable, and he ordered the American military to capture the island and restore constitutional democracy. The invasion was supported by other Caribbean nations and backed by a secret plea for help from the governor general of Grenada, Sir Paul Scoon, the local representative of the Commonwealth and Queen Elizabeth on the island.

The SEALs' target in these opening hours of the invasion was on a hilltop near a beach area called Cape St. George Beausejour, on the west side of the island of Grenada. This objective consisted of one small building with several rooms and a radio transmitting tower, separated by a fenced-in field that was bigger than a football field. The mission was thought to be vital to the overall American invasion of Grenada, because it would sever a major line of enemy propaganda communication with the population.

Just before the mission, a senior officer told Lieutenant Kendall, "It'll be a piece of cake. You'll be in and out in two hours." But having served in combat in Vietnam with Underwater Demolition Team 12, Kendall knew better, and always expected the worst could happen. And now, with no radio communications, few rations, low ammunition, little water, surrounded by enemy troops, and trapped in a small building being shredded by enemy fire, Kendall was in the middle of what he called a "royal shitstorm."

What Jason Kendall and his SEALs did at Cape St. George Beausejour on this day foreshadowed the words of another SEAL, commander of U.S. Special Operations Command Admiral William McRaven, when he spoke in 2014 to graduating students at the University of Texas, his alma mater. Every SEAL knows, said McRaven, that "the darkest moment of the mission" is "the time when you must be calm, composed—when all your tactical skills, your physical power and all your inner strength must be brought to bear." McRaven added, "You must be your very best in the darkest moment."

Kendall didn't have time to reflect on it then, but his fifteen years as a frogman had prepared him for this moment, beginning with his initial training in Coronado, California. As Admiral McRaven described it, "Basic SEAL training is six months of long torturous runs in the soft sand, midnight swims in the cold water off San Diego, obstacle courses, unending calisthenics, days without sleep and always being cold, wet, and miserable. It is six months of being constantly harassed by professionally trained warriors who seek to find the weak of mind and body and eliminate them from ever becoming a Navy SEAL." But, McRaven added, "the training also seeks to find those students who can lead in an environment of constant stress, chaos, failure, and hardships," and those factors were exactly what Jason Kendall and his SEALs were facing at this moment in Grenada.

"This was not an ideal mission for Navy SEALs in the first place," recalled Kendall years later. "We were a surgical military instrument, best designed for lightning strikes, not for a strike-and-hold operation. We were equipped for a quick in-and-out operation like an embassy assault or hostage rescue, not a prolonged field operation. We were not prepared to engage in a protracted battle like this; that's not what we do. The idea is to get in and hit somebody hard, and either snatch, rescue, or kill them, and then get the hell out of there. We were not equipped for a pitched battle." Since it was expected to be only a three-hour operation, the SEALs carried rifles and pistols and a limited supply of water, rations, and ammunition.

Kendall's small force was composed of two separate squads of SEALs. They had never trained together prior to the mission but the two squads were melding well. From basic small-unit tactics to urban-warfare procedures, their training was the same; they were SEALs. Now, having captured the radio station, they had set up defensive positions. Kendall again briefed his team on the rules of engagement, or ROEs, and emergency procedures in the event they had to make a hasty withdrawal. This seemed unlikely, but standard special operations doctrine calls for it—hope for the best, but plan for the worst.

Earlier that morning, at daybreak, the SEALs had landed by Black Hawk helicopter in the field that adjoined the radio transmitter at Cape St. George Beausejour, and they quickly captured the station building after a brief firefight that chased off a handful of Grenadian guards. A short time later a military truck pulled up to the station and twenty armed Grenadian soldiers in their blue field uniforms piled off. They looked like service station attendants with automatic weapons. The SEALs were on alert, concealed, and well positioned to confront them.

Kendall stepped from behind cover and, in accordance with his rules of engagement, identified himself as an American military officer. He asked them to disarm and leave the area. "We're American soldiers," he announced "We're here to liberate the island. Put down your weapons and withdraw."

Instead, the Grenadians responded by opening fire, and they paid a terrible price for it. Kendall jumped behind a tractor and the SEALs raked their opponents with automatic weapons fire for less than thirty seconds, devastating the Grenadian unit. Half were killed immediately and the rest seriously wounded. Kendall's SEALs hastily converted one of the rooms in the station to a makeshift morgue for the dead and another to an infirmary for the wounded and dying Grenadians. Then four Cuban POWs who showed up in a separate truck in the wake of the firefight were captured by the SEALs. "I directed my medical corpsman to do the best he could do with the wounded and dying," recalled Kendall, who realized that meant the SEALs would soon have no medical supplies for themselves. No Americans had yet been hurt.

Without warning, a station wagon carrying a family of

five Grenadian civilians drove right into the SEALs' perimeter. Kendall felt he had no choice but to hurry them into the radio station building to shield them from danger. "We were pretty scary looking," recalled Kendall. The family—a father, mother, and three children under twelve years old—were "absolutely terrified," especially when they grasped the bloody scene of wounded and dying soldiers inside.

The SEALs had achieved their objective by capturing the target area, but they could tell no one about it since their radios didn't work. Kendall figured that hearing nothing from the SEALs, other Americans probably would assume his team of SEALs was all dead by now.

Kendall realized that without any way of summoning help to evacuate the civilians, he'd have to set them free. This created a terrible dilemma for the SEALs, one that resembled the quandary faced by Lieutenant Michael Murphy and his SEALs in 2005 when two local Afghans wandered into their path during Operation Red Wings, a story told by Marcus Luttrell in his book *Lone Survivor*.

"If we let them go," argued one SEAL to Kendall, "they're going to give away our position!"

"We're already compromised!" replied the young lieutenant. "There's no way they'll survive a firefight inside this house."

"The hell with them, they're prisoners, they stay here! Whatever happens, happens!"

Kendall overruled the objections. He was schooled enough in the Geneva Convention to know there were certain things he couldn't do as an officer responsible for the safety of civilians, and keeping the family detained in those circumstances was one of them. He escorted the family to their car, pointed them in what he thought was a safe direction, and told them to go. Kendall never forgot the look on the faces of the mother and father, a mixture of extreme gratitude, terror, and jubilation. Before they left, the children hugged Kendall's legs so hard he had to pry them loose.

The SEALs redistributed ammunition, went to their defensive positions, and held fast. Kendall scaled the radio tower with his backup transceiver, desperately trying to make contact with the American forces coming onto the island. Still no luck.

"Holy crap!" yelled a SEAL from the roof. "We've got trucks coming on our left flank, an APC [armored personnel carrier] on the right. This is it; they're here!" The Grenadians were closing in for a major assault not long after the family escaped—though the enemy's appearance was probably only coincidental, Kendall thought.

In front of the house where the SEALs had sought refuge, a Soviet-made BTR-60 armored personnel carrier (APC) pulled up to the entrance and opened fire with a heavy machine gun, blasting off pieces of the building. The trucks stopped and each deployed a dozen or more armed men. It was clear that they had come in force to retake the radio station.

Kendall quickly pulled his men back from the perimeter, intending to carry out a defensive action from the main station building. The Grenadians flanked the structure and opened fire, while the APC fired rounds point-blank. Up close and personal, a 20 mm cannon is a devastating weapon. The APC's turret swung back and forth, punching holes in the walls.

To counter the APC, the SEALs would need antitank weapons. They had none. "The cannon was just ripping away at the house," according to Kendall, "and they were also raking it with small arms. The house was coming apart like paper. The floor of the house was awash in blood. We were all covered in blood from tending to enemy wounded from the previous assault. We won that firefight, but we were getting the worst of this one.

This was a close-quarter battle. We were fighting it out at ten feet. The Grenadians were shooting up the entire building."

The SEALs could hold their own with the Grenadian infantry, but the armored vehicle with its cannon was another matter. With the building about to come down on their heads, one of the SEALs got a clear shot at the APC with a bullet-trap grenade and managed to jam the turret. The APC could still shoot, but the gunner was now unable to traverse the turret. This gave Kendall and his SEALs a breather, but their situation was still precarious in the extreme.

The Grenadians were well armed with good reserves of ammunition. They were now pouring heavy automatic weapons fire into the building. Inside, the walls were exploding, bullets splashing everywhere. When bullets pass close by, they carry a sonic wave and produce a distinctive snap. "They were essentially blowing us out of the building," recalled Kendall, who was now increasingly hearing the sonic *snap-snap* of rounds breaking close over his head. If the 20 mm came back on line, they had no chance.

Behind the radio station was a broad meadow leading to a path that cut between the cliffs to the beach. This was their preplanned escape and evasion route. When SEALs plan their first training missions in BUD/S, they include alternative escape routes and emergency procedures. Clearly, if Kendall and his men remained to defend the radio station, they would all be killed. The APC surely had a radio and more soldiers could arrive at any moment. Kendall gave the order to pull out. He told his SEALs to redistribute their remaining ammunition and prepare to leapfrog across the meadow for the beach. "When we reviewed the escape-and-evasion plan before the operation started," Kendall explained, "I told my guys if things go to shit, we'll head for the water. If we can get to the sea, we'll try to steal a boat or something and get away from the coast. They had us surrounded on three sides, and we had to do something. We decided to fight our way out and make for the water. Because in SEAL training, when you're in that kind of situation, you're taught to go to the water. We're good in the water."

Kendall had no option but to lead his men across the field and down a steep slope that led to the beach. It was a dramatic scene—but this wasn't the movies. Twelve Americans had every reason to fear they were going to die in that open field. In life-and-death situations, mortal danger can cause men to freeze, totally immobilizing them. Often, only the confidence instilled by repetition and drill can get them moving. Often, there is a fine line between preparation and bravery.

"I'm going first, I'm going out the door," Kendall said to the second of his two squads lining up behind him as they got ready to try to "leapfrog" through the kill zone. "When you see us go down, you follow." Fire and maneuver is a standard infantry tactic in which one element moves position while the second element provides covering fire. The SEALs had performed this countless times in training; now they would do it in a desperate effort to save their lives.

Kendall later said, "I'll remember to my dying day everybody stacking up behind me lining up to go out the door. We were used to doing assaults through doors, lining up on the outside to go in. Now we were lined up inside to go out into a three-way crossfire."

Looking out the window, Kendall could see bullets shredding a nearby wall. He thought, "God, I'm not going to make it two steps out of this door. I'm going out this door and I'm probably going to be dead within fifteen seconds. But I gotta do this."

"Here we go!" he announced.

The SEALs burst out of the rear of the house and started leapfrogging down the sloping open field. It was about 2:30 P.M. The SEALs needed no direction; they had done this many times, beginning at BUD/S, where they learned basic squad tactics. The open area behind the station was the size of a football field. They would be terribly exposed, but escape was their only hope.

"Go, go!" Kendall yelled as he and his squad bolted from the radio station toward the base of the transmitter antenna. They laid down covering fire while his second squad sprinted into the field. Grenadian troops were moving along the chain-link fence on both sides. Thirty yards into the field, using the antenna's cement anchors for cover, the second squad went down and began to return fire sparingly, using single shots to conserve ammunition.

Jason Kendall was knocked down three times running across the field—once when the heel of his boot was shot off, and another when a round glanced off an ammunition magazine strapped to his torso. The third time, a bullet destroyed his right elbow, flipped him into a somersault, and caused him to lose his rifle.

"I was trying to figure out how the hell we'd get out of there," recalled Kendall. "On our left and right flank, enemy troops were following us down the fence line shooting the living daylights out of us. Halfway down the field a bullet went through my elbow and practically took my arm off. I was sure I had lost my arm. I managed to pull off my knee pad and stick it in my arm as a bandage. I thought I was going to bleed to death."

Kendall paused to get a quick count. A SEAL team leader, just like a boat-crew leader in BUD/S training, must always account for his men. Kendall was a man short. Back in the field, his wounded radioman was making his way across the field, dragging the useless radio. While the SEALs laid down a base of fire, Kendall screamed for his wounded man to abandon the radio. The young man pulled his 9 mm pistol and destroyed the SATCOM radio with its classified encryption components. As the SEALs expended the last of their ammunition, the final member of their team rejoined the others.

At the end of the field, the SEALs were trapped by a high wire fence. "By the time I got to the fence, everybody was kind of bunched up, taking rounds and trying to suppress fire," recalled Kendall. "They looked at me and said, *Holy shit*. My arm was flapping around and there was blood all over me. We couldn't go over the fence because it was too high and it had wire on top.

"We gotta cut the fence," said Kendall. His SEALs looked at him. Their faces registered a vivid impression to him, a look that said, "Now what—we're screwed!" One SEAL said, stating the obvious, "We don't have any wire cutters!"

"I gotta pair," Kendall said. He was losing blood and struggling to think clearly. Navigating through his bloodstained pocket, he produced the tool. "Now cut the damn wire!"

The Americans sliced through the fence and hauled off toward the trees. Once in the dense brush behind the field, they had a brief respite from their pursuers. Yet their prospects were anything but good; they were outnumbered, had ammunition only for their pistols, and they had no communications. No one else in the American military knew where they were or if they were still alive.

Kendall remembered thinking, "We're all going to get whacked for sure."

In the late afternoon, Lieutenant Kendall and his group of eleven SEALs were moving quickly through the cover of thick jungle, bracing for an expected final ambush by enemy troops. But the Grenadians had paused their attack, probably to regroup with reinforcements, and probably dealing with a lot of wounded soldiers.

The SEALs kept heading for the open water. On reaching the shore, they descended the path to the beach and waded out into the water. The shoreline arced in a shallow crescent that formed a scenic bay surrounded by rocky cliffs. The SEALs began swimming, but they knew it was a temporary sanctuary. It was clear that if they kept swimming close to shore, they would be sitting ducks for the Grenadians on the cliffs. Kendall told them to ditch all their equipment except sidearms and signal flares, and to swim parallel to the beach. A short way along the shoreline, they came back into a rocky portion of the beach and made their way up into the cliffs, where they were now protected from above by overhanging ledges and vegetation.

More Grenadians arrived and searched along the shore and high on the cliffs until nightfall. Kendall and his men could hear them talking as they searched above and around them, but the SEALs remained undetected. As dusk approached, the Grenadians finally pulled back to the radio station.

"We were out of ammunition," recalled Kendall. "We were down to our pistols and knives and a few signaling devices spread out among the guys so everyone had something to fight with and signal with." They had been battling all day with little food or water, and between gearing up and rehearsing for the invasion, they hadn't slept for days.

A series of deafening explosions shattered the nearby meadow, and the SEALs realized they could be killed any second by something they hadn't expected: American fighter-bombers strafing nearby Grenadian positions. "We had our own damn Navy put five air strikes on top of us trying to get the bad guys.

We were pretty rattled. Having escaped a superior force of Grenadians, we were about to get bombed by our own Navy."

As darkness fell, Kendall sent two pairs of SEALs to swim across the bay to steal a few of the small fishing boats they'd spotted earlier, so the whole group could make it out into the open sea. He told the swimmers, "If something happens and you can't get the boats, you just swim out to sea and listen for the rescue aircraft." They never came back. "We waited and waited for those swim pairs," Kendall remembered. "After a few hours nothing happened. We never heard any gunfire, so we just assumed the boats were gone or they couldn't get to them." It turned out that the boats were snagged to the bottom by their fishing nets and couldn't be freed, so the SEALs just headed out into the water, as Kendall told them to do.

Soon after dark, two U.S. Hughes 500D observation helos, or "Little Birds," made a pass over the nearby radio station. The SEALs heard the choppers roar in over the beach and assumed they were looking for them, but the men huddled in the side of the cliff could do nothing, as they didn't want to alert enemy forces who could be nearby. Kendall, in consultation with his senior petty officers, decided to wait until after midnight before trying to swim out to sea. His wounded arm was throbbing and he had lost all feeling below the elbow. Another SEAL suffered from a wound in his upper leg. The SEALs hunkered down, but just before ten o'clock they again came under fire.

Unknown to Kendall, the Little Birds had taken fire from the Grenadians at the radio station and a nearby antiaircraft battery. Since nothing had been heard from the SEALs and the Grenadians held the radio station, the U.S. force commander assumed they had been killed and sent an air strike against the radio station. While the SEALs burrowed into the rocks and vegetation, a squadron of Navy A-7 attack jets made several strafing runs on the radio station and surrounding area. Again the SEALs were on the wrong end of friendly fire, this time from the A-7s' Vulcan gun pods—20 mm rounds at seven thousand rounds per minute. Stray rounds splashed around them, chipping at rocks and bringing down tree limbs.

After the A-7s left, Kendall's chief petty officer turned to him and said, "Sir, maybe it's time we got the hell out of here." Kendall agreed. The SEALs had had enough friendly fire. Descending the rocky cliff would have been dangerous in the dark, but there was an outcropping from which they could jump. With a strong leap, they could clear the rock face and make the water. Kendall's right arm was useless and he was in incredible pain. The SEALs had pain drugs in their medical kit, but Kendall feared the side effects; he was still in command. Unsure if he had the strength to make the leap from the cliff, he had two of his SEALs throw him off. The remaining ten of them made the water and began to swim seaward. Kendall had to drag his useless arm through the water; the other wounded had to swim as best they could. But the SEALs were well prepared for this. In BUD/S training, the trainees are bound, hands and feet, and made to swim this way. They call it "drown-proofing."

"We were several miles out in the open ocean," Kendall later explained. "We could barely see the outline of Grenada, though we could hear the Marines conducting combat operations on the island. We were trying to swim as far away from that damn island as we could because we couldn't be close to the shore when the sun came up." He added, "We were hoping against hope that that SAR bird [search-and-rescue plane] was up and would spot us. We knew there were some ships out there but we didn't know where." The SEALs were now five pairs of bobbing heads in the vast, dark ocean, and the probability of being rescued was, in Kendall's words, "infinitesimally small."

Hours passed. "My biggest concern," recalled Kendall, "was that from spending all day fighting, sweating and not drinking water, and then spending all that time in salt water, we'd get dehydrated very quickly. I was really weak, and my swim buddy had taken a round through the back of the leg."

Then, just before sunrise, the SEALs heard the sound of an approaching aircraft. It sounded like a C-130. "I hoped to God it was that search-and-rescue bird," recalled Kendall, who fired up a couple of precious signal flares. Then a fireball erupted in the sky. It was a gigantic illumination parachute flare dropping slowly down from the C-130. "It was like the sun dropping down on us," recalled Kendall.

The overjoyed SEALs looked around the bright water and realized that incredibly, all of the previously separated SEALs had wound up in the same small patch of ocean, now including the two men who had gone on the aborted attempt to get boats. The C-130 found the SEALs in the water with its powerful searchlight, and vectored a Navy ship to their position. They'd been in the water for close to five hours when they were rescued.

By this time, Kendall had been awake for over forty-eight hours. The last time he had been this beat up and sleep-deprived was during his Hell Week with BUD/S Class 52. Once on the deck of the USS *Caron,* he again counted his men. During every BUD/S Hell Week, exhausted, half-dead officers and petty officers again and again count their men. BUD/S instructors do unspeakable things to leaders who lose track of their men. So Kendall counted his men. Once the count was right and he knew his men were safely aboard, he passed out. When he awoke a day later in the hospital at the Bethesda Naval Hospital in Maryland, his first question was "Where are my men?"

U.S. Navy SEAL Lieutenant Jason Kendall was awarded a Silver Star for his actions in Grenada, the citation for which reads, in part: "Determined to hold his position, he twice engaged the enemy and eliminated their combat effectiveness, taking 10 wounded prisoners of war without casualty to his assault element. Administering to the enemy wounded, he again established a defensive perimeter. Engaged a third time by a numerically superior force, his position came under heavy automatic weapons, RPG-7, and 20-mm. cannon fire. With complete disregard for his personal safety, he directed fire and maneuver tactics which allowed his force to take up new positions. Although painfully wounded himself and closely pursued by a large enemy force, he courageously directed his men in evasion and escape maneuvers which resulted in the safe extraction of his entire force."

All twelve SEALs who assaulted the radio Grenada tower on October 25, 1983, are alive today. Jason Kendall's shattered arm almost forced him to be medically retired, but he recovered sufficiently to complete a full career as a Navy SEAL, including participating in Operation Assured Response in 1996, when SEALs and other U.S. military forces rescued and evacuated over 2,100 people, including 435 Americans, from war-torn Liberia.

"We should have all died," said Kendall, recalling his Grenadian ordeal. "More than once that day I thought we were finished. It's a frigging miracle that we all lived."*

THE GRENADA INVASION MARKED a sea change for the SEALs, for American special operations, and for the U.S. military. It

---

* Mark Adkin, author of a definitive history on the Grenada invasion, criticized this mission on pages 174–175 of his book *Urgent Fury* (1989), asserting that the SEALs' target was a long-range transmitter used primarily by the Bishop government for broadcasts throughout the Caribbean, while the key Radio Free Grenada transmitter used to transmit inside the country itself was at another location on the island. In other words, incomplete intelligence led the SEALs to a target that was not critical to the success of the invasion.

marked a shift from America's historical reliance on warfighting dominated by conventional forces to a new world where special operations units like the SEALs played an increasingly critical role in fighting threats and conflicts small and large.

The U.S. Navy SEALs were experiencing a difficult time in their own history. Funding in the Navy budget for Naval Special Warfare dried up in the 1970s, and while training continued at Little Creek and Coronado, and Cold War–style exercises were held with foreign partners in Europe and elsewhere, actual operations were rare.

According to one SEAL who joined in 1975, "I can remember being issued an M-16 and cleaning it one day and looking down the barrel and not seeing any rifling. Basically it was a smooth-bore weapon. It had so many rounds fired through the barrel that it was absolutely worn-out."

At the same time the SEALs were enduring their severe post-Vietnam drawdown, their popular image was enjoying a tremendous boost from an unexpected place: Hollywood, California. "It seemed like half the tough guys on 1970s and '80s TV— Lieutenant Commander Steve McGarrett in *Hawaii Five-O,* the Tom Selleck character in *Magnum, P.I.,* and on and on— were SEALs or ex-SEALs," wrote former SEAL Rorke Denver. "Network scriptwriters," he added, "seemed convinced that SEALs were the toughest, shrewdest, most devious, most physical, most expertly trained warriors around, a breed apart from any other commandos you'd want to stack them up against." In fact, there was an earlier burst of screen-generated interest in Naval Special Warfare when some 1950s-era UDT members and 1960s-era SEALs were inspired to join after watching the 1956 movie *The Frogmen,* starring Richard Widmark, and the 1960s TV series *Sea Hunt* starring Lloyd Bridges.

But despite the SEALs' growing mythic reputation in pop

culture, the reality of the SEALs' first major post-Vietnam com-bat operation was one of tremendous difficulty.

One U.S. Navy SEAL described the Grenada operation, code-named Operation Urgent Fury, as "one screw-up after another—nothing seemed to be going our way." Another SEAL recalled, "Our Intel had been atrocious. Nobody knew really what we were going to be facing." An Army special operator recalled, "We had no decent maps. We were able to get our hands on a Michelin guide to the Windward Islands with a somewhat usable chart of Grenada. This allowed us to get a basic feel for the layout of the island." The *Wall Street Journal* reported, "When the battle was under way, frustrated commanders ashore could see the Navy ships at sea, but they couldn't reach them by radio. The Navy couldn't talk to the Army. The Air Force couldn't talk to the Marines." Many American troops, already groaning with heavy equipment, wore all-weather, polyester combat outfits that were unsuited to a tropical environment like Grenada. "We were like slow-moving turtles, my rucksack weighed 120 pounds," said one American trooper. "I would get up and rush for 10 yards, throw myself down for 10 or 15 minutes [to recover]."

One SEAL recalled how the hurried planning for the Gre-nada operation caused different SEAL small-unit assault teams to be mixed together at the last minute. "A lot of our tactics, techniques, and procedures worked differently, and mixing units on the eve of an operation can be catastrophic, partic-ularly when you don't have communications, and you're not used to working with the same people. We violated some of the things we should never violate. Part of the reason that this mis-sion is so sensitive is because of all the screw-ups that were done in haste to get into battle." SEAL commander Robert Gormly recalled, "I inherited a command that we all—the members of the command as well as myself—learned wasn't ready to go into combat. We were lacking some training, and we certainly lacked equipment. The boats at the time were horrendous, they were in terrible shape." Gormly had less than three days to plan his operations in Grenada.

The SEALs had four main missions in the Grenada invasion: to help the Air Force place beacons at the Point Salines airfield on the southwestern tip of Grenada to guide in troop-carrying transport aircraft; to scout a beach on the northeastern coast of the island for a possible Marine landing; to rescue and protect the senior Commonwealth official on the island, Governor General Scoon; and to secure the radio tower that was several miles north of Scoon's residence. For the latter two operations, the SEALs were supposed to be relieved within a few hours by other American forces. Few of these missions went off as planned; the first mission, which was the first major known SEAL combat operation since the Vietnam War, was a tragedy. It was a chilling echo of the fatal aerial drop of Spence Dry in 1973 during Operation Thunderhead, only this time, four SEALs were lost.

On the night of October 23 and early morning of October 24, 1983, twelve SEALs were supposed to be dropped into the ocean along with their assault boats from low-flying C-130s, rendezvous with the destroyer USS *Caron,* then cover miles of open water to perform a reconnaissance on Point Salines Airfield, in advance of a planned airborne assault by the 75th Ranger Regiment. "At 1800 we listened on the SATCOM radio as the planes reported their drop runs," remembered Gormly. "My guys on the ship sent a radio report that they were ready and the weather was okay. The planes turned final and dropped." Then things went bad. Tropical squalls can arise without warning, and the seas suddenly became windblown and choppy. It was pitch-black, instead of the planned-for partial light of dusk.

The C-130 dropped the men too far apart. And the SEALs had not recently trained for such a complicated drop in these severe conditions. "I didn't know it at the time," admitted Gormly, who had taken over command of the unit only earlier that year, "but they had never done a night boat drop—or any night water parachuting, for that matter."

Gormly was shattered by the accident: "Four good SEALS drowned, and one of the two boats capsized, apparently also because of the squall. I was devastated. I blamed myself (and still do) because I had done nothing to prevent it." SEALs Machinist Mate First Class Kenneth Butcher, Quartermaster First Class Kevin Lundberg, Hull Technician First Class Stephen Morris, and Senior Chief Engineman Robert Schamberger were never found. The surviving SEALs tried to complete the mission, but the rough seas threatened to swamp their remaining inflatable boats. Gormly recalled bitterly, "The damn boats weren't capable of doing what we needed to get done. They weren't seaworthy." On the night of October 24, frogmen from SEAL Team Four successfully conducted a classic UDT-style night mission to check the condition of a potential Marine landing beach on northeast Grenada, an amphibious landing that was called off when the SEALs reported unfavorable conditions.

Just before daybreak on October 25, Bob Gormly was aboard a Black Hawk helicopter leading the SEAL mission to rescue and protect the governor general of Grenada, Sir Paul Scoon, his family, and several aides. All were being held under house arrest at the Commonwealth governor general's mansion on the outskirts of the capital, St. George's. Gormly's assault team leader and Vietnam veteran SEAL Lieutenant Wellington "Duke" Leonard remembered the approach to the target: "That helo ride was absolutely fantastic for me. We flew treetop level all the way into the target zone, then popped up as we approached the mansion. The birds were crowded. I had to squat for the whole sixty-one-minute flight. Nobody could move. We had fifteen guys in the bird—all combat troops—and everybody was jammed in place."

Leonard and twenty-one SEALs managed to successfully exit their Black Hawk under fire by fast-roping through trees and brush onto the residence's grounds. But as Bob Gormly prepared to exit his command helicopter, it was hit by an anti-aircraft weapon and at least forty-six rounds of ground fire, and the chopper had to abort from the mission. The wounded helicopter took the SEALs' SATCOM radio with it and was forced to make an emergency landing on the deck of an American warship offshore.

Hearing the sounds of the firefight outside and not knowing what was going on, Sir Paul Scoon, his wife, and aides took refuge in the basement. They heard footsteps above them in the main reception room and voices calling urgently, "Is anyone here? Mr. Scoon, Mr. Scoon?" Scoon's wife wondered, "Suppose they are Russians?" Her husband replied, "No, those voices have American accents, and they must be here for our protection." One of Scoon's guards opened the door and beheld a Navy SEAL pointing his gun directly at him. "We are here to protect the governor general and not to harm anyone," came the announcement, and the relieved Grenadians were moved to the mansion's dining room, deemed by the SEALs as the most defensible spot in the house against heavy fire.

The SEALs thought the mission would last forty-five minutes. Instead, the encounter lasted twenty-six hours. At the same time, Lieutenant Jason Kendall and his SEAL assault team were fighting for their lives at the Grenada radio transmission tower; elsewhere, thousands of U.S Army troops and Marines were pouring into different spots around Grenada.

As the sun came up, soldiers from the pro-Marxist Grenadian People's Revolutionary Army and militia launched a rolling wave of attacks on the governor general's compound with AK-47s, rocket-propelled grenades, and Soviet-made BTR-60 armored personnel carriers. "We were constantly under attack from the arsenal of arms and ammunition in the [nearby] Prime Minister's residence," remembered Sir Scoon. "For the next twenty-six hours, the dining room was our dormitory without food, without water, and without the necessities for a comfortable rest. In fact, there was no sleep during the long and perilous night that followed the dismal and dreadful day. As the sounds of gunfire resounded in our ears, the portraits of members of the Royal Family past and present looked down solemnly upon us as we quietly and humbly lay on the bare hard wooden floor."

At one point, a pro-Marxist Grenadian police official got a call through to the house and told Mrs. Scoon he would send some of his troops over to "protect" them. The quick-thinking Mrs. Scoon sweetly turned him down, explaining that he needn't bother, since they were already being guarded by "a large number of extremely well-armed men." As the battle intensified, Mrs. Scoon broke down and wept. "Suppose we were to die?" she asked. "Is it really worth it?" Her husband replied that "if it was the Lord's will that we should die, then I truly believed that we would be dying for the sake of our country in which common humanity, love, and freedom would hopefully prevail thereafter."

"I don't care if I die now," said a nearby Grenadian police corporal who was loyal to Scoon and stayed by his side during the ordeal. "I am happy that these people [the SEALs] have come to our rescue. They should have come long before now." His words were punctuated by an incoming explosion that struck a bay window in the next room. "The Commander of the SEALs performed superbly throughout the siege," explained Sir Scoon years later. "He was never too far from my wife and me and his ever-watchful eye over us helped to embolden our spirit. He appeared not to be ruffled. From time to time he would enquire about our health, always reassuring us that all would be well."

Without their SATCOM satellite radios, the SEALs had only limited-range MX-360 handheld radios with a short battery life, and they had to patch together a tenuous radio relay system through nearby U.S. Army radio posts to call for air support. Suddenly a trio of Soviet-made Grenadian BTR-60 armored personnel carriers appeared ready to storm up to the residence. "I got real worried," recalled SEAL commander Gormly, who at this point was coordinating support for his team from the USS *Guam*. "We had enough men in the mansion to resist a good-sized infantry force, but they didn't have the weapons to deal with BTR-60 APCs." He summoned an Air Force AC-130 gunship to fly over the mansion. "The BTRs were now inside the gate, headed slowly for the house, as if they weren't sure what to do," Gormly wrote. "The first one got nailed by 20mm Vulcan cannons from the AC-130 just as he was swinging his turret toward the mansion. The next two were hit immediately afterward."

Once the BTRs were destroyed, Gormly radioed to Leonard that he would keep an AC-130 constantly overhead for protection, and a reinforced U.S. Marine company would make an amphibious landing that night and patrol to the mansion by early the next morning to relieve the SEALs. Leonard replied with a laconic "No sweat." Gormly later wrote, "At this point I was really proud of Duke. He had seen action in Vietnam and had been decorated for bravery, but in this situation he'd been more than brave—he'd been smart and cool."

When the Marines finally arrived at the mansion on the

morning of October 26, the SEALs had only a few rounds of ammunition left. Scoon, a courtly, highly distinguished civil servant, made a point of thanking the SEALs, who were, he said, "perfect gentlemen." From his first interactions with the SEALs onward through the difficult ordeal that followed, Scoon said he knew he and his wife would be safe.

Days after the invasion of Grenada, in an appearance on *Meet the Press,* then–Chairman of the Joint Chiefs of Staff General John Vessey candidly summarized the episode: "We planned the operation in a very short period of time—in about 48 hours. We planned it with insufficient intelligence for the type of operation we wanted to conduct. As a result we probably used more force than we needed to do the job, but the operation went reasonably well." General Colin Powell, then assistant to Secretary of Defense Caspar Weinberger, saw some hollowness in the victory, saying, "The operation demonstrated how far cooperation among the services still had to go. The invasion of Grenada succeeded, but it was a sloppy success."

Retired U.S. Air Force Colonel John T. Carney Jr., a veteran of the failed Desert One operation in Iran, analyzed the operation with much more brutal candor: "We achieved our mission, but took heavy casualties. Nineteen men were killed in action and 123 wounded. The enemy was a hastily organized force of about 50 Cuban military advisers, over 700 Cuban construction workers, and one thousand two hundred members of Grenada's People's Revolutionary Army. Many of the casualties were from friendly fire. To this day, I doubt that any one person knows how ineptly Urgent Fury was planned and executed. However, the operation proved a defining moment for special operations, for it led directly to the creation, by Congressional mandate [the Goldwater-Nichols DOD Reorganization Act of 1986], three years later, of the U.S. Special Operations Command."

However controversial the overall operation was, at least one Grenadian insider saw the invasion as a symbolic first domino in the imminent global collapse of Soviet Marxism. "It is in Grenada that the fall of communism began," wrote Sir Paul Scoon. "Since then the world saw the dramatic dismantling of the Berlin Wall and the gale force wind of change which knocked down the prevailing political system in the Soviet Union and opened up the way for democracy and personal liberty." Grenada, he asserted, "could justifiably claim to be the first country to have escaped from communist domination and immediately revert to democracy and freedom." Although some nations condemned the invasion at the time, many Grenadians welcomed the Americans as liberators and agents of stability, and the invasion is today celebrated in Grenada every October twenty-fifth as a national holiday, called Thanksgiving Day. The SEALs and their fellow American military personnel helped return Grenada to a constitutional democracy.

The success of the SEAL mission to rescue Governor General Scoon was critical to bringing the whole invasion to a fairly quick, successful conclusion, since Scoon represented the last vestige of legality and continuity to the island's government. It was Scoon, safely delivered from danger by the SEALs, who soon ordered the People's Revolutionary Army to lay down its weapons, and it was Scoon who rapidly assembled a new government, ushering in an era of stability that endures on the island to this day.

For the U.S. Navy SEALs, Grenada was a story of triumph and tragedy, of lessons learned, and of characteristic courage under fire.

One SEAL veteran of Grenada had this to say of the tough lessons learned from the operation: "I think we learned a lot about ourselves. We were living for a long time on our Vietnam legacy. As we tried to break free of the whole stigma of Vietnam we became a little overconfident in our ability. We had guys who were tremendous operators and we had great resources that we'd never had before. But we had a lot of hubris that was nearly our undoing. We thought we were so good that we put together this marvelous force and we had all these great tactics, training, techniques and equipment, but Grenada brought us down a notch. We were lucky that it did, because it told us this stuff is harder than you think. The irony is that in Grenada we went back to fighting the kind of war we fought in Vietnam, and we weren't very damn good at it. No matter how good you think you are, some Third World guy with a gun can take you out in a heartbeat. Here we were the premier force in the world, and we saw a ragtag bunch of Grenadians surround us at the radio station and nearly take us all out. It was a wake-up call, and it was a good thing. It was a horrible lesson because we lost people, but in terms of the growing up in the real world it was very valuable."

ON THE NIGHT OF October 10, 1985, two years after the Grenada operation, a force of eighty-three U.S. Navy SEALs, led by Grenada veteran Robert Gormly, faced off against some 1,600 Italian troops and military police on the tarmac of the NATO base at Sigonella, Sicily.

In an unusual twist of history, the troops of two allied NATO nations were in a guns-drawn showdown with each other, as Italian and American diplomats and military officials frantically negotiated over who would take custody of five terrorists, who had been forced to land at the NATO base.

The SEALs had surrounded an EgyptAir Boeing 737 airliner containing the pro-Palestinian terrorists who had hijacked

the Italian cruise ship *Achille Lauro*. They seized the ship for
three days, holding four hundred passengers and crew hostage.
During the siege, the terrorists shot and killed the wheelchair-
bound sixty-nine-year-old Leon Klinghoffer and pushed his
body overboard. After several days of negotiations, the hijack-
ers agreed to abandon the ship and surrender to the Egyptians
in exchange for safe passage to aircraft passage to Tunisia. En
route, American warplanes forced the plane to land at Sigonella
on the orders of President Ronald Reagan, and the SEALs were
preparing to storm it and capture the terrorists.

The SEALs faced overwhelming odds, but Bob Gormly,
their commander on the ground, was confident. They had
sealed off their target, the jet, and the terrorists were inside
it. "No problem—the 737 isn't going anywhere," Gormly said
by radio to another American. He had sent Bob "Bobby Lew"
Lewis, a trusted Grenada veteran SEAL, to block the front of
the 737 with a truck. Bobby Lew assured Gormly, "Don't sweat
it, Skipper."

The Italians were furious. "I could understand how they
felt," remembered Gormly. "Suppose the Italians landed unan-
nounced at one of our airfields and held our forces at gunpoint.
We'd be pissed too."

"Hey, boss, you'd better get over here, the Italians are about
to assault my position," said Gormly's executive officer, who
was stationed in a blocking position with several other SEALs
at the base of the aircraft's stairs. A furious Italian officer declared that he and his men were boarding the plane. Gormly
refused to allow the boarding until an agreement was reached.
They stared each other down until the Italian agreed not to
force his way onto the aircraft. When Gormly heard a loud
"bang" as Italian armored vehicles approached, he immediately
thought "shot fired." Then SEAL Bobby Lew Lewis radioed
that he shouldn't worry, it was an engine backfire.

After a five-hour standoff, an agreement was reached that resolved the crisis, with the Italians taking custody of four of the terrorists and eventually convicting and imprisoning them. The mastermind, the infamous terrorist known as Abu Abbas, was allowed to escape by the Italians. He made his way to Baghdad, where he was captured by American forces in 2003. He died in American custody the following year. According to Gormly, his SEAL team was awarded the Joint Meritorious Unit Award for their actions at Sigonella. The *Achille Lauro* episode and the SEALs' participation in the multinational peacekeeping force in Lebanon in the early 1980s were vivid introductions to the conflicts and terrorism endemic to the Middle East. In the years ahead, this theater of conflict would increasingly dominate the destiny of the U.S. Navy SEALs, and it was a challenge for which the SEALs would prove ideally prepared.

IN 1989, A YOUNG U.S. Navy SEAL was taken captive as a de facto POW, along with his own wife. What happened to them next helped convince the president of the United States to order the full-scale invasion of another nation by nearly twenty-six thousand combat troops.

It was six years after the Grenada invasion when SEAL Teams were called into another Caribbean operation—this time in Panama. Their mission was to topple and capture dictator Manuel Noriega, who had been indicted on drug trafficking charges in the United States, and was also accused of endangering some thirty-five thousand Americans living in Panama, who were being increasingly harassed by Noriega's security forces.

What few knew was that it was the Panamanian Defense Forces' treatment of the wife of a Navy SEAL and her husband stationed in Panama that would help spur President George H. W. Bush to unleash the actual invasion of that nation.

It was just before Christmas 1989 when the wife of SEAL Lieutenant Adam Curtis came to Panama to visit her husband. "We were going to go out to dinner and celebrate our reunion and went to downtown Panama City," Curtis explained to us. "We finished dinner in early evening. It was dark and I realized I was going into a bad part of town. I was not very far from the Bridge of the Americas to get back to base. So my plan was at the next intersection, *I'll take a right-hand turn and I'll be back on base in under five minutes.* At the next right-hand turn, the next intersection was a roadblock, so we got stopped there. I told my wife that this was going to take a while. They're going to ask us a whole bunch of questions then they're going to get somebody with a higher rank, and he's going to ask more questions and eventually the second or third or fourth guy up will let us go when he decides we've been harassed enough." As they were being questioned, Panamanian forces opened fire on another car containing several American military officers, and Marine First Lieutenant Robert Paz was dead by the time they reached the hospital.

Now, instead of being released, Navy SEAL Adam Curtis and his twenty-two-year-old wife were seized and brought to a police station, then to a Panamanian military base for interrogation. The couple was soon face-to-face with a man who seemed to be a commander. Curtis recalled the scene vividly: "My wife and I were on a bench against the wall. He [the officer] stood right in front of me and I was waiting for the set of questions that I'm pretty sure were coming, and instead he just hauled off and belted me in the chin, and kicked me in the groin. Then he pulled his Browning 9 mm from his shirt and put it right in my nose. So my wife was getting a little upset at this point. I was a little worried. I should mention he was stumbling drunk. So I had a drunk with a pistol pointed at me, not a real comfortable feeling.

"They blindfolded and handcuffed us," Curtis recalled. "That was a trying moment for my wife. Blindfolding us, they were wrapping my head with medical tape. She thought they were doing it to hold my head together when they shot me. They were taping my head and she was thinking that it's because they're about to blow it off with a machine gun, and she started to scream. It's the only time that she really lost it. There was a soldier nearby who told her in Spanish, *Shut up!* Then she had a feeling as if she heard the voice of God saying *Be quiet, I got it*. After that she was very calm and peaceful the whole night and she just felt God's presence the whole way.

"Once they separated us," Curtis continued, "they threatened my wife with a lot of very lewd things and thankfully didn't do any of them, but they made her life pretty miserable. I was blindfolded, my hands were behind my back, and so they kept asking me question after question. They were starting to focus on things that I know I can't tell them. I was clearly in a POW-type situation now. But every time I either refused, or didn't give them an answer, or if I gave them an answer they didn't like, they kicked me in the groin, beat on my feet with a hammer, [and] if they really didn't like it, then they'd rifle butt me in the head."

"We think you're a spy!" the captors declared. "You're planning something! We think you're CIA, you're Special Forces! If you don't answer we're going to kill you."

"This is a military guy's worst nightmare—to be a prisoner," Curtis admitted, "until someone adds into your nightmare that they've got your wife in the other room. I had a mantra going in my head and it was, 'Stay in the game, Curtis, stay in the game.' Was it from SEAL training? That's definitely part of it. I'm a man of faith and that was a prayer for me. I had to shove away any idea of what they might be doing to my wife. It's still painful to think what might have happened. I felt terrible about it happening to my new young bride, believe me. Particularly for the young guy who gets lost coming back from dinner. So she doesn't always trust my directions.

"Then they took me outside blindfolded," the former SEAL told us, "put me up against a wall and said, *Okay, now we really are gonna kill you.* I could hear they had other people around. I started hearing bolts cycle on AK-47s, the whole *ready, aim, click* thing." Still, Curtis refused to talk.

After several terrible hours as prisoners, the SEAL and his wife were released. But for President George H. W. Bush, it was the last of many straws. Days later, he launched "Operation Just Cause" to depose Manuel Noriega, an operation that had been in the planning stages for several months. At the White House, Bush announced publicly in his characteristically fractured syntax, "Look, if an American Marine is killed, if they kill an American Marine—that's real bad. And if they threaten and brutalize the wife of an American citizen, sexually threatening the lieutenant's wife while kicking him in the groin over and over again, then, [Soviet leader] Mr. Gorbachev, please understand, this president is going to do something about it!"

"My wife is my hero," Adam Curtis told us a quarter century after their ordeal. "She's a tough lady. We had been married a year and a half at this point so she had a sense of the things I didn't tell people naturally [as a SEAL]. She was amazing through the whole thing. She had a pretty good bump on her head from rough treatment but she was in good shape. We had some challenges after the fact that were pretty tough for both of us, particularly for her. Now we can see it was clearly PTSD. We couldn't spell those letters at that point. We didn't get counseling. We were very young and just not informed at all. But throughout the whole thing she was just amazing and when the chips were down in the middle of it she truly just did everything she needed to do. She kept her wits about her, said the right things. She was my hero. My wife was a junior in college when I married her at twenty-one so at that point she was twenty-two. She didn't have the stress inoculation that you get in SEAL training, though she had been around the world a bit as a Navy brat. She's pretty sharp and pretty tough so by the grace of God she knew naturally what not to say."

The invasion of Panama, launched in the early morning hours of December 20, 1989, was the first combat test of the U.S. Special Operations Command, or SOCOM, which was created in 1988 in part as a reaction to the interservice planning and operations failures highlighted by the Grenada invasion.

The SEALs had two major combat missions in Panama, both scheduled for the early morning darkness of December 20, 1989. The first was to disable Noriega's potential getaway plane, a Learjet, at Paitilla Airport near Panama City. The mission was a near disaster in which, as in Grenada, four SEALs lost their lives. The second operation, to disable Noriega's potential getaway boat, went off flawlessly.

Soon after forty-eight operators from SEAL Team Four and members of an Air Force Combat Control Team exited their black rubber raiding craft and raced to the Paitilla Airport target area after midnight on December 20, things started going wrong. They were dangerously exposed. The area was illuminated with city lights and landing-strip beacons, and there was little cover. Gunfire noise from other American units around the capital city was quickly waking up the guards at the airport, and the element of surprise was lost. Compared to a basic SEAL operation, which was typically structured around one or two squads of a sixteen-man platoon and a minimum of moving parts, this was an unusually large and unwieldy force based on more than three platoons.

As the SEALs approached, a voice came from the hangar demanding they surrender. "Drop your weapons!" shouted the voice in Spanish. "Drop them or we will shoot!"

"No!" replied a Spanish-speaking SEAL. "You drop *your* weapons!"

The SEALs were caught in the open by an unknown number of Panamanian snipers. Gunfire erupted from multiple directions, and soon four SEALs were dead and seven wounded, the worst casualty numbers of any SEAL operation up to that date. One of the SEALs, Isaac G. Rodriguez, reportedly bled to death while waiting for a medevac helicopter that was delayed by operational mix-ups.

"We've got heavy wounded!" shouted squad leader Lieutenant (jg) Thomas W. Casey into a radio. Nearby, SEAL Lieutenant Pat Toohey calmly reported their plight by radio to a general hovering overhead, "Two KIA . . . three KIA . . . seven WIA . . . need a helicopter." An officer listening in on the line marveled at Toohey's serenity under fire, and later told author Orr Kelly, "what I heard in those radio transmissions bespoke a very brave man." When the general asked Toohey if he wanted to withdraw, the SEAL replied, "Sir, my orders were to seize the airfield and hold it until relieved and those remain my intentions, over."

"Where's the Spectre?" yelled one of the SEALs, referring to an Air Force AC-130 gunship that was three thousand feet overhead to provide air support. "Where the f— is that gunship?" But radio communications between the Air Force combat control team on the ground and the Spectre were inexplicably dead.

Inside the circling Spectre, the fire-control officer, who initially couldn't figure out why no one had asked for fire support, could see the wounded SEALs lying so close to the hangar that he realized that if the AC-130 opened fire, they would risk hitting the wounded. In the hangar, a SEAL fired an AT-4 anti-tank rocket at Noriega's Learjet, and scored a direct hit on the forward fuselage, triggering a fireball. After some fifteen minutes of combat, the Panamanians withdrew and the SEALs were in control of the hangar and the airfield. The operation was supposed to last four hours, but the SEALs held the airfield for thirty-seven hours before they were relieved.

Two Navy Crosses were awarded for the action, one post-humously, and the citations offer a glimpse of the ferocity of the brief encounter. The citation for Lieutenant (jg) Thomas Casey, Commander, Golf Platoon, SEAL Team Four, reads: "As the firefight intensified and with nearby aircraft explod-ing in flames, he placed himself in front of the wounded and delivered devastating covering fire, neutralizing the enemy forces and enabling the wounded to be evacuated." That for the late Chief Petty Officer Donald McFaul, Platoon Chief, Golf Platoon, SEAL Team Four, states: "He left the relative safety of his own position in order to assist the wounded ly-ing helplessly exposed. Under heavy enemy fire and with to-tal disregard for his personal safety, McFaul moved forward into the kill zone and began carrying a seriously wounded platoon member to safety. . . . He was mortally wounded by enemy fire."

The mission was accomplished, but at the cost of four SEALs' lives. Debates over the operation have raged in the SEAL community ever since. Some SEALs figured it just shouldn't have been a SEAL mission in the first place; but fore-most a job instead for either a larger conventional force or a smaller special operations team. "If the mission was to take and hold the airfield, Army Rangers or Marines are better-equipped for the job," said one anonymous SEAL to a reporter shortly after the event. "Taking out the planes was a standoff operation, a job for a three-man team equipped with AT-4s and machine guns," he argued. "If the job was to deny entry and exit to the airfield, a single team spotting for naval gunfire or using the AC-130 gunship overhead could have done the job. There were alternatives," he declared. Another SEAL later argued, "In Panama we violated our own doctrine, we tried to act as light infantry, or a Ranger force, which we were never trained to do. But when wars happen, you don't want to be left out, that's sort of the thinking, and everybody wants to get in the game."

One former SEAL, Bob Schoultz, said of the Paitilla Airfield operation, "They overplanned this operation to where every time they went through it, another contingency was thought up and they put more pieces into it to cover those contingencies until it got to be so big and so complicated that it was not flexible enough to respond quickly to changes. That whole thing could have been handled by four to six people. One of the things I think the SEAL community did badly is there was never a 'hot wash' to sort it out. I was in the Navy for another fifteen years after the Panama event and I never saw an after-action review that laid out for people on active duty here's what we learned, here's where we made mistakes, and here's what we want to make sure we never do again. That I think is a real crime, a shame, I'm not sure why it didn't happen."

Commander Gary Stubblefield, a Vietnam veteran and respected former commander of SEAL Team Three, wrote a highly critical letter about the Paitilla Airfield operation to his superiors on January 7, 1990, soon after the invasion concluded. "The objective, no matter how stated," the letter stated, "was to prevent General Noriega from using the airfield for evacuating the country. This could easily have been accomplished with a small number of SEALs using some of

the advanced weapons and technology we have been spending large amounts of money to develop and procure over the
past two decades. Instead, our leaders sent too many troops,
who are not accustomed to working in larger numbers, against
the defended position when it was absolutely unnecessary in
order to achieve our objective. These leaders must be held ac-
countable and not allowed to lead our fine young SEALs into
such unwarranted and costly scenarios again rather than given
praise for a job well done."

Stubblefield's comments generated pushback from senior
SEALs in the Naval Special Warfare chain of command, and a
lot of controversy. Yet it is noteworthy that in this first operation following the establishment of the U.S. Special Operations
Command, operational SEALs were the first to stand up and
criticize an operation. It was the mark of an increasingly professional standard that was emerging within the SEAL Teams
and indeed, all of American special operations. "We learned a
whole heck of a lot," concluded former SEAL and Vice Admiral
Joseph Maguire. "You have to get better and you have to improve because they bury the guy who comes in second."

In sharp contrast to the Paitilla Airfield operation, the simultaneous SEAL mission to disable Noriega's potential getaway patrol boat *Presidente Porras* went off without a hitch, and it was
the first publicly identified SEAL "combat swimmer" demolition
attack. At about the same time their fellow SEALs were assault-
ing the airfield, four SEALs from "Task Unit Whiskey" were
swimming under the waters of heavily defended Balboa Harbor.
Using Draeger LAR-V oxygen rebreathing devices that left no air-
bubble trail, they attached satchels full of C-4 explosive on the
patrol boat, and silently slipped away to their extraction point.
As one SEAL reported, at exactly 1 A.M. on December 20, the
sixty-five-foot *Presidente Porras* blew up "ass-end destroyed, the

engine vaporized as it went straight up and then straight down into the harbor." Another of the SEALs on the operation, Randy Lee Beausoleil, later recalled, "my dive buddy was Chris Dye, the most calm, cool, and collected cucumber you could ever find to dive with. . . . All in all, the operation probably took us about five hours, in and out. It was a long op, but it was standard. There was nothing we did that any other SEAL Team couldn't have done. We were just lucky enough that our platoon was there. And I feel that we were the most prepared for that particular job. The dive went flawlessly." Other SEAL missions in Panama included working with Army Special Forces to track down Manuel Noriega, and raiding several islands believed to house PDF troops.

Major combat operations in Panama were largely wrapped up within days of the invasion, and Manuel Noriega was captured on January 3 after taking refuge in the Vatican embassy. He was flown to the United States, convicted of drug trafficking, money laundering, and racketeering, then extradited to France, where he was convicted of money laundering. Eventually he was extradited back to his home country, where he remains in prison. Twenty-three American service personnel died during the invasion, along with several hundred civilians. After the removal of Noriega, Panama returned to a democratic government, and today it has one of the fastest-growing economies in Central America.

"THE GROUND WAR STARTS at 0400 hours," said Lieutenant Tom Dietz. "Let's go in and blow the shit out of the beach!"

In the early morning hours of February 24, 1991, hours before the first Gulf War began, a small team of U.S. Navy frogmen from SEAL Team Five's Foxtrot Platoon pulled off an audacious stunt at Iraqi-held Kuwait's Mina Saud beach that may have helped save thousands of Iraqi and American troops from dying in the desert.

In one of the cleverest "head fakes" of modern warfare, they tricked Iraqi troops into thinking a massive amphibious assault by seventeen thousand U.S. Marines was being launched in the dark waters off Kuwait. But the Iraqis had no idea that instead of two U.S. Marine divisions, they were facing only fifteen lightly armed Navy SEALs carrying 160 pounds of C-4 explosives, machine guns, and grenade launchers.

The Persian Gulf was familiar territory for the SEALs. In the late 1980s they performed a number of operations to help protect international shipping in the oil-rich region during the Iran-Iraq War, including capturing oil platforms and intercepting ships in "visit, board, search, and seizure" operations. But when American military planners prepared to enforce UN Security Council resolutions and liberate Kuwait from Iraqi occupation in early 1991, the SEALs were almost nowhere to be seen in the order of battle. "We didn't have a major role" in the war, said Captain Walter S. Pullar III, a SEAL and commander of Naval Special Warfare Group Three. "We weren't part of the strategic picture. We were part of the tactical picture—a small one."

General H. Norman Schwarzkopf, the Allied commander, was said to favor conventional forces over special operations units like the SEALs. *Newsweek* magazine reported, "The movies might glamorize secret commandos like . . . the Navy SEALs, but to an old foot soldier like Schwarzkopf they were nothing but trouble—weirdos and 'snake-eaters' who had to be rescued by the regular grunts when their harebrained operations went awry." The SEALs, however, were eager to pitch in, and they came up with a potentially brilliant idea to help kick off the Allied ground invasion scheduled to launch in the early morning hours of February 24. Schwarzkopf listened to the plan, and approved it.

At about 10:15 P.M. on February 23, platoon commander Lieutenant Tom Dietz and his fifteen SEALs quietly approached Mina Saud beach in Iraqi-held Kuwait in three eighteen-foot rubber Zodiac 450 Combat Rubber Raiding Craft or CRRCs, stopping less than a thousand yards off the beach. The SEALs knew the target well, having secretly scouted the area in re-connaissance missions on two previous nights. The ground war was scheduled to begin in less than six hours, and what the SEALs were about to attempt could significantly affect the outcome. From intelligence reports and his own observations, Dietz understood there to be as many as 2,500 Iraqi troops dug into bunkers around the area.

A highly choreographed sequence of maneuvers now un-folded, all designed to fake Saddam Hussein and his generals into switching thousands of his troops away from the Saudi-Kuwait border, where American and allied forces were poised to punch through and around their defensive lines, and toward the beach to block a nonexistent amphibious assault.

It looked a lot like the kind of job the UDTs performed in World War II and Korea: a small team of frogmen approaches an enemy beachhead—and sets off demolitions.

Six of the SEALs climbed out of the boats and began swim-ming gently on the surface of the water toward the beach. Each man wore a wet suit for protection against the cold 54-degree water, gloves, fins, pocket lights, a life vest, an emergency three-minute SCUBA bottle in case they had to escape underwater, a pistol, and a Heckler & Koch MP-5 submachine gun or M-16 rifle fitted with a grenade launcher in case a shoot-out broke out on the beach. Their faces were smeared with black camouflage paint, and they had knives strapped on their legs in case they got snagged in seaweed or barbed wire. Dietz had picked up his own knife at a San Diego dive shop.

Each SEAL pushed a flotation bag containing a haversack filled with twenty pounds of C-4 explosive, and one of a series of four-foot-wide orange channel buoys to be strung out as signal markers to simulate an imminent amphibious landing. As was routine in a SEAL operation, they had planned for unexpected contingencies and "what-ifs" by bringing multiple backups: backup timers for the charges, backup lights, backup knives, even a backup Zodiac CRRC. The six SEALs approached the shoreline in a horizontal line that fanned out to cover 250 yards of beach.

The assault leader, twenty-nine-year-old Tom Dietz, was a compact, highly athletic New Jersey–born Naval Academy graduate who joined the SEALs in 1986. He had planned this night's deception operation with Captain Ray Smith, the commander of Naval Special Warfare Task Group, Central, who was commanding SEAL operations in the Middle East. Their plan called for the charges to be set in shallow water at 11 P.M., to detonate two hours later at precisely 1:00 A.M. on Sunday, February 24, when the receding tide would lower the C-4 directly onto the beach, three hours before the allied ground forces began punching across the border of Kuwait. Twenty-four hours earlier, as part of the deception, U.S. military aircraft and naval artillery abruptly stopped their relentless bombardment of the area around Mina Saud beach, creating an ominous silence intended to goad the Iraqis into believing that something big was about to happen.

Working in shallow water just east of the beach's edge, the SEALs positioned the haversacks on the ocean floor, pulled the timer pins, and swam back into the dark sea to rendezvous with the Zodiacs and their host speedboats, both manned by the nine other SEALs in the platoon.

The fireworks began at 12:30 A.M. and lasted for a solid thirty minutes. As an opening act, the SEALs' speedboats moved toward the shoreline and began strafing the beach with .50-caliber machine-gun fire, .762 chain guns, and 40 mm grenades for fifteen minutes, to throw the Iraqi coastal defenders out of bed and alert them the "invasion" was on. For extra effect after the strafing, ten 4-pound charges of C-4 were tossed into the water, exploding over the next ten minutes. Then at exactly 1:00 A.M. the six main charges began detonating along the beach, creating tremendous fireball explosions that could be felt for miles away. Any Iraqi soldier poking his head out toward the mayhem would come to one deeply unsettling conclusion: *Here come the Marines.* The SEALs escaped to their boats, and back to their quarters at the Saudi naval base at Ras al-Mishab. Hours later, Lieutenant Dietz got word of the mission's impact through a cable from Captain Ray Smith, the SEAL commander in the Persian Gulf. The cable read, "Your mission was a success. Elements of two separate Iraqi divisions moved to the beach immediately after your operation. Pass it on to your men. Job well done."

"It worked!" thought Dietz.

The SEAL officer later learned that as many as several thousand Iraqi troops reacted to the deception, were pulled off the Saudi-Kuwaiti border, and were sent toward the coast to block the phantom amphibious invasion, likely allowing the allied land invasion to proceed with less difficulty and fewer casualties. Dietz was quietly proud to have played a small but important role in the liberation of Kuwait. "Naval Special Warfare went over there with 275 personnel," he remembered, "and we returned with 275 personnel. When everybody comes back and the task is accomplished, it is a success by every measure of the word."

DESERT ONE AND GRENADA marked the beginning of a turning point, a boundary in SEAL history. The SEALs had always been tough guys who were smart, brave, and could improvise, but now they were becoming even more professional, well-drilled, experienced operators. After Desert One, Grenada, and the establishment of the U.S. Special Operations Command in 1987, they morphed into professional, well-drilled, experienced, responsible operators with a strong organization framework to include better screening, expanded training, dedicated mission sets, and forward-deployable command and control. Flexible, but with a strong measure of interoperability and professionalism. They honed a set of "best practices," like other warfare communities in the Army, Navy, and Air Force.

Grenada, Panama, and the Gulf War all saw SEALs deployed in direct-action, special-reconnaissance, or search-and-rescue roles. In most of these operations their work was maritime related, and in support of conventional battle plans or expeditionary warfare objectives. And in each of these conflicts, SEALs worked largely alone, or as a diversion to main force activity. Through the 1990s, there were isolated engagements with the emerging threat that could be categorized as terrorism.

As the threat of war between the Soviet Union and the United States waned with the easing of the Cold War and the collapse of the Soviet Union, a new threat was on the rise: al-Qaeda. In its first attack on America, the terrorist organization bombed New York's World Trade Center in February 1993, killing six and wounding one thousand. This was the same year that Osama bin Laden urged his followers to kill American soldiers stationed in Somalia as part of a United Nations humanitarian mission. Bin Laden provided military training to Somali tribes opposed to the UN's intervention.

Rick Kaiser and a small detachment of fellow SEAL operators were sent that same year to Somalia's capital, Mogadishu, a city that U.S. General Tom Montgomery, deputy commander of the UN force there, called the "Temple of Doom."

"My first actual combat mission was in Somalia in 1993," Kaiser explained to us. "I was a member of Task Force Ranger, which was a joint special operations task force that went overseas to Somalia to capture Mohamed Farrah Aidid, who happened to be one of the warlords in control of the area at the time. They were taking control of the food, which was causing famine for a lot of people. Innocent civilians were dying; before we had actually deployed over there, they had actually killed a group of Pakistani soldiers and massacred them. So, our job was to go in there and try to capture him. I was part of a small SEAL sniper team of four guys, very close-knit, we had worked together for a long period of time. Our specialty was sniping. We thought that that's the skill set they needed in Somalia. When we got on the ground, though, it was a different story. The Army was in charge, rightfully so. We were only four SEALs and they decided to use their guys in those [sniper] roles. So we just took it upon ourselves to find a job. You know, that's what SEALs do. We weren't just going to sit on the cots at the airport."

Kaiser continued, "Before the big Battle of Mogadishu on October third, we had already conducted six other missions, all of which gave us, I think, overconfidence that we could do whatever we wanted in the city, that the enemy was not that fierce. But unfortunately, as events unfolded on October third, when we were doing another typical mission to go into the city, to a hotel in the heart of the bad-guy territory, one of our helicopters got shot down." The plan, wrote Calvin Woodward of the Associated Press, was that "U.S. soldiers would drop down ropes from Black Hawk and Little Bird helicopters, onto streets so narrow the rotors barely fit between buildings, so dusty the pilots could hardly see. They would snatch militia members and spirit them away in a convoy of vehicles that was to meet the choppers at the scene." The reality unfolded over seventeen hours of brutal combat that saw ninety-nine U.S. servicemen stranded in the middle of a hostile city: "a successful roundup, a sudden blizzard of opposing fire, one Black Hawk shot down, then another during a frantic rescue attempt, combat and confusion that stretched through the night, [and] the bodies of two of the 18 dead Americans dragged through the streets." One Army Ranger staff sergeant said, "I had the distinct impression that everyone in this task force was going to die." The operation was memorialized in the book and movie *Black Hawk Down,* and few know that a small team of Navy SEALs worked to help rescue the downed Americans.

Rick Kaiser remembered, "We were in a gun battle from about noon that day until about noon the next day. The SEAL Utility Vehicle was our transportation, even though it was not armored at all. It was very dangerous. So anyway, we went in to reload our magazines, get some water, and get ready to go back out. I went to the bathroom and when I came back, all the guys were in the vehicle already, ready to go except for one place: the driving seat. And I looked at them and said, *You bastards!* Because the worst place to be is in the driver's seat, because you can't shoot, you've got to just drive, especially since you've got no door and no armor. They all looked at me and a couple of guys were laughing at me! I thought, *Man, it didn't pay to go to the bathroom.* Back on the streets we took wounded guys in and went back out and fought some more, took some more wounded back in, and then we went out a third time to rescue the guys in the helicopter. And we did. We finally got 'em out."

While eighteen Americans died in the fiercest firefight since Vietnam, every SEAL who was in Mogadishu earned a Silver Star for valor in combat. But the brutality of the battle was broadcast and had consequences on future U.S. foreign policy. President Clinton soon ordered American forces out of Somalia. The warlord Aidid was never captured and was killed by a rival militia faction in 1996. Known as the "Mogadishu Effect," fear of public humiliation underscored many future American military decisions. Kaiser noted, "What we found out later is that this was really a test for al-Qaeda and other Islamic militants for the future, because what they saw us do was when the going got tough and Americans got killed, we left. So, it really gave them the courage to carry on and fight us, all the way up to 9/11."

In the late 1990s, several press accounts linked the SEALs to operations in Bosnia, offering possible glimpses of missions that are still classified, and probably will remain so for many years to come. On July 6, 1998, *U.S. News & World Report* ran a major report of what it called "secret missions" to hunt "persons indicted for war crimes" in northern Bosnia. The article, written by Richard J. Newman and titled "Hunting war criminals: The first account of secret U.S. missions in Bosnia," claimed that about sixty-five SEAL commandos were hidden inside eight-foot-high metal containers placed inside the hull of a C-17 cargo jet, and shipped to the U.S. base in Tuzla, Bosnia, in December 1997, as part of a $50 million, 300-person multinational task force assigned to apprehend five suspected war criminals. This SEAL operation was canceled, according to the report, when General Eric Shinseki decided there wasn't enough accurate intelligence to launch one of the planned raids, for which the target may also have been tipped off. The SEALs went home. Not long after the aborted raid, according to the *U.S. News* report, the SEALs returned to Bosnia, and this time

A visibly impressed President John F. Kennedy, a former naval officer, inspects SEAL Team Two in diving gear at Norfolk, Virginia, April 13, 1962. The SEAL teams were less than four months old. *(John F. Kennedy Presidential Library, SEAL Museum)*

SEAL Team One founding members, or "plank-owners," early 1960s. *(U.S. Navy)*

SEAL Team Two Executive Officer Roy Boehm inspects team members mobilized for the Cuban Missile Crisis. *(Courtesy of Tom Hawkins)*

Lieutenant David Del Giudice, first commanding officer of SEAL Team One. *(Courtesy of Dennis McCormack)*

Members of SEAL Team Two, en route to winter training in Maine, 1965. Bill Bruhmuller is fifth from the left, top row. *(Courtesy of Bill Bruhmuller)*

Hell Week, 1969. The "Sugar Cookie": soaking-wet frogmen-trainees douse themselves in sand. *(U.S. Navy)*

UDT training, 1961: diving into a mud pit. *(U.S. Navy)*

UDT obstacle course training at Coronado, early 1960s. *(U.S. Navy)*

Training, St. Thomas, 1960s. *(U.S. Navy)*

BUD/S trainees enter the water in preparation for a beach survey exercise. *(U.S. Navy)*

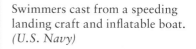

Swimmers cast from a speeding landing craft and inflatable boat. *(U.S. Navy)*

An early version of what was to become the SEAL Delivery Vehicle (SDV). *(U.S. Navy)*

UDT-11 frogmen with the Apollo 11 capsule after the first manned moon landing,
July 27, 1969. Navy frogmen supported NASA missions through the 1960s and early 1970s.
(U.S. Navy)

Apollo Recovery Team, UDTs 11 and 12. *(U.S. Navy)*

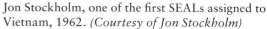

Jon Stockholm, one of the first SEALs assigned to Vietnam, 1962. *(Courtesy of Jon Stockholm)*

SEAL Team One's Dennis McCormack (left) training a South Vietnamese soldier in the use of demolition in Da Nang, Vietnam, c. 1964. *(Courtesy of Dennis McCormack)*

Mel Pearson of Team One on a surface craft, South Vietnam. *(Courtesy of Mel Pearson)*

SEAL Moki Martin with a favorite Vietnam-era weapon of the SEALs: the Stoner light machine gun. When Martin was eight years old, he saw Navy frogmen training on the beach of his native Hawaii, and he decided that this would be his destiny. *(U.S. Navy)*

Sea Float/Solid Anchor SEAL/UDT base anchored in Cua Lon River, 1969. The floating base (later moved ashore and called Solid Anchor) was a focal point for SEAL/UDT operations in Vietnam. *(U.S. Navy)*

Navy frogmen and local allies review maps before conducting a joint combat mission. *(U.S. Navy)*

SEAL leaving assault boat, Vietnam, 1968. *(U.S. Navy)*

SEALs in SEAL Team Assault Boat (STAB) move down the Bassac River during operations along the river south of Saigon, 1967. *(National Archives)*

UDT-12 sailors and South Vietnamese forces launch a small boat operation. *(U.S. Navy)*

SEALs and the South Vietnamese POWs they liberated. The SEALs conducted a number of successful operations to rescue allied prisoners in Vietnam. *(U.S. Navy)*

BUD/S or Basic Underwater Demolition/ SEAL Class 45, East Coast, 1969. Dick Couch is lower front left. Future Medal of Honor recipient Thomas Norris is lower front right. *(U.S. Navy)*

Michael E. Thornton. Thornton received the Medal of Honor for helping rescue severely injured fellow SEAL (and future fellow MoH recipient) Thomas Norris during an operation in fall 1972. *(U.S. Navy)*

SEAL and Provisional Reconstruction Unit (PRU) advisor Brian Rand with a few of his local operatives. *(U.S. Navy)*

SEALs prepare to raid a suspected enemy village, Operation Crimson Tide, 1967. *(U.S. Navy)*

Tired SEAL after Vietnam operation. *(U.S. Navy)*

SEAL squad in Vietnam going out heavy. Note the three Stoner light machine guns and two modified M-60 machine guns. *(U.S. Navy)*

December 19, 1968: SEAL Team One, Alfa Platoon, approaches a Viet Cong target on a combat mission in the Nam Can district, Ca Mau province, Vietnam. The following five pages of photographs document this single mission. Above: SEALs in the door of insertion Huey. *(U.S. Navy photo by Donald P. "Chip" Maury)*

The target is spotted.
*(U.S. Navy photo by
Donald P. "Chip" Maury)*

Safely bringing in a Huey. Note
SEAL on security at the left of
the photo. *(U.S. Navy photo by
Donald P. "Chip" Maury)*

Insertion on the edge of the target. *(U.S. Navy photo by Donald P. "Chip" Maury)*

U.S. Navy QM2 Robert M. Beanan along with other members of SEAL Team One, Alfa Platoon, enters the village. *(U.S. Navy photo by Donald P. "Chip" Maury)*

Barry W. Enoch, SEAL Team One, Alfa Platoon, takes cover in an open field while a UH-1 Huey helicopter comes in for a landing. The SEALs and the photographer were under fire from Vietcong forces during this operation. *(U.S. Navy photo by Donald P. "Chip" Maury)*

U.S. Navy ETNSN Steven P. Frisk fires a XM203 40mm grenade launcher into a suspected Vietcong hooch. *(U.S. Navy photo by Donald P. "Chip" Maury)*

U.S. Navy ETNSN Steven P. Frisk, right, fires a M72 light anti-armor weapon into the water at two Vietcong soldiers as QM2 Robert M. Beanan stands security armed with a M60 machine gun. *(U.S. Navy photo by Donald P. "Chip" Maury)*

U.S. Navy GMG1 Barry W. Enoch, with SEAL Team One, Alfa Platoon, evacuates a Vietnamese child to safety. *(U.S. Navy photo by Donald P. "Chip" Maury)*

Members of SEAL Team One, Alfa Platoon, aboard a swift boat, returning to the USS *Terrell County* (LST 1157). *(U.S. Navy photo by Donald P. "Chip" Maury)*

Members of SEAL Team One, Alfa Platoon, pose for with a captured Vietcong flag aboard the USS *Terrell County* (LST 1157), after the mission. Back row, left: Lt. (j.g.) George R. Bliss, WO Scott R. Lyon, ETNSN Steven P. Frisk, SFP2 David G. Gardner, HM2 Larry A. Hubbard, SN Donald C. Crawford and PH1 Donald P. "Chip" Maury. Front row, left: Lt. (j.g.) Dale Moses, QM2 Robert M. Beanan, AN John M. Ware, SM1 David Wilson and GMG1 Barry W. Enoch. *(U.S. Navy, courtesy Donald P. "Chip" Maury)*

SEAL Team One is presented with a Presidential Unit Citation by Lyndon Johnson for its actions in Vietnam. *(White House Photo)*

To U.S. Navy Seal Team One
with appreciation
Lyndon B Johnson

President Richard Nixon presents Lieutenant (j.g.) Bob Kerrey, U.S. Navy SEAL, with the Medal of Honor, May 1970. *(U.S. Navy)*

President Gerald Ford presents Lieutenant Thomas Norris, U.S. Navy SEAL, with the Medal of Honor, March 1976. *(U.S. Navy)*

Admiral Elmo Zumwalt confers with SEALs in 1971. A champion of the SEALs, some credit Zumwalt with saving the Teams from the bureaucratic chopping block in the severe drawdown of the post-Vietnam years. *(U.S. Navy)*

they scored a victory, taking three war crimes suspects into custody. "One suspect named Miroslav Tadic," the article reported, "was physically tackled by SEALs."

In 1997, veteran *New York Times* correspondent David Binder reported on "credible information" of a joint Navy SEAL–British SAS operation that killed Serbian war crimes suspect Simo Drljaca near Prijedor, Bosnia, on July 10 of that year. According to the reporter, President Bill Clinton personally signed off on the operation. On May 7, 2010, the British paper the *Daily Mail* reported that Radislav Krstic, an imprisoned former Serb general convicted of Europe's worst massacre since World War II, had his throat slashed by three Muslim prisoners in a British jail. The paper reported that Krstic, who was linked to the massacre of more than eight thousand Bosnian Muslim men and boys near Srebrenica in July 1995, was originally arrested "in a daring joint SAS and U.S. Navy SEAL snatch in Bosnia in December 1998." He survived the prison attack.

In the wake of al-Qaeda's bombing of the World Trade Center in 1993, the two U.S. embassies in Africa in 1998, and the USS *Cole,* something rather unusual was unfolding with the SEALs and other special operations forces. They weren't being used much. According to Richard H. Schultz Jr., the director of the International Security Studies Program at Tufts University, they "were never used even once to track down terrorists who had taken American lives." Schultz was told by General Peter Schoomaker, head of the Special Operations Command in the late 1990s, that "it was like having a brand-new Ferrari in the garage, and nobody wants to race it because you might dent the fender."

For most Americans, the war on terrorism began on September 11, 2001, the day Islamist terrorists attacked the United States. Those in the intelligence business and those who studied terrorists prior to 9/11 knew differently. But to have a war, there must be two combatants, and prior to the attacks of September 11, there had been only one. During the last two decades of the twentieth century, "they" killed more than 350 of our citizens in and around the Middle East and in the United States, even though most Americans believed we were living in a period of peace. As a result of the first attack in 1993 on the Twin Towers in New York City, six Americans died. Around the world, hundreds of foreign nationals also lost their lives, and hundreds more of our citizens were wounded. These attacks, even though they were organized, coordinated, and directed by Islamist terrorists, were treated as criminal acts, not acts of war. We had simply become accustomed to a periodic loss of life through terrorist activity. Our response was to try to bring these criminals to justice, so we deployed FBI agents and evidentiary teams.

Not all Americans believed that we were at peace, and among those were the SEALs who regularly deployed to the Central Command. They saw the carnage at the Marine barracks in Beirut in 1983; they saw the body bags with American sailors being carried from the USS *Cole*. Many of them thought our nation was not doing enough to meet this growing threat, and more than a few thought that they were being unnecessarily restrained.

For example, in late July 1996, a naval task force was hastily assembled when it was thought that Imad Mugniyah, the Hezbollah security chief and the most wanted terrorist in the world, was aboard the freighter *Ibn Tufail* as it made its way around the Arabian Peninsula and into the Persian Gulf. He was the man responsible for the deaths of 241 Marines and sailors in Beirut, and he was believed to be the commander of kidnap squads who took nearly one hundred Westerners and foreign nationals hostage in Lebanon from 1982 to 1992. The task force, with a complement of Marines and two SEAL platoons, shadowed the *Ibn Tufail*. They were in position to seize the ship and had a plan to capture this infamous terrorist. The SEALs were to fast-rope onto the vessel and seize control. The Marines would then come aboard and do a thorough search.

"We were locked and loaded, sitting aboard the helos," one of the SEAL assault leaders recalled, "and the helos were turning on deck, ready for liftoff. We had the ship in international waters and we had the force in place. We even had the diagrams of the internal ship spaces. Then the word came down—'mission canceled.' We were told that there was insufficient intelligence; that he may not have been aboard. We were absolutely stunned. It really shook our Marines; this guy killed over two hundred of their brothers. I still think about it. It was my platoon's one chance to make a difference, and we were stood down. If it had been after 9/11, we would have taken that ship, or any other vessel in open waters, if there was a hint that there might be a terrorist leader aboard." The aborted 1996 mission to capture Mugniyah was a "spin-up and spin-down," when special operations forces are loaded aboard choppers and even moving toward the target when the order is given to cancel and turn back. For the special operators, it is a brutal feeling. There have been many spin-ups and spin-downs for the SEALs in recent years, and they have gotten used to the emotional roller coaster they create. There has been much subsequent debate as to whether Mugniyah was or was not aboard that ship in the Gulf in 1996. On February 12, 2008, Imad Mugniyah was killed by a car bomb in Damascus, Syria. The identity of his assailants remains unknown.

THE MOST SUSTAINED SEAL activity of the mid-to-late 1990s were operations to support the oil embargo imposed by the UN on Saddam Hussein and enforced largely by the U.S. Navy. In a campaign to block oil from being smuggled out and contraband in, SEALs boarded ships bound to and from Iraq. This activity was known as VBSS—"visit, board, search, and seizure." Saddam tried to get his oil to market by sneaking it out in tankers. SEALs, fast-roping from helicopters, boarded the tankers in international waters and detained them.

It was a cat-and-mouse game, with the SEALs swinging aboard at night, while the tankers raced for the safe-haven territorial waters of friendly Arab states. In the summer of 2001, just a few hours before dawn, two American helos caught up with the *Saddam Maru*. This was not the real name of the ship, but until the SEALs boarded and were able to make a closer inspection, it would do.

On a moonless night in the Persian Gulf two H-60 Black Hawks carrying a complement of SEALs approached the ship. Inside the lead helo, the rope master tossed out a length of fast rope, a thick, feltlike line that served as a fireman's pole for getting SEALs from a hovering helo to their target.

In the cockpit, the Navy pilots, wearing night vision goggles, deftly matched the speed of the tanker and kept the Black Hawk in a hover over the deck. These were fleet pilots, adept at hovering above moving vessels.

"Can you hold it there, sir?" the rope master said in his boom mike. "We'll do our best," the pilot's voice replied in his earpiece. "Roger that. First man is on the way."

The rope master tapped the thigh of the SEAL seated on the metal deck with his legs hanging out, and the SEAL popped from the door of the helo and dropped into space. Other SEALs took his place and vaulted into the void. Then another.

It was a rough boarding. A gust of wind pushed the helo above its hover point and two of the SEALs ran out of fast rope before their boots hit the deck. One tucked and rolled, but another was knocked unconscious. When the second helo came in with its load of SEALs, the fast rope became entangled in a boat davit and one of the SEALs came close to going over the side. He managed to grab the guardrail and scramble back onto the deck of the tanker.

With the platoon medical corpsman tending to the downed SEAL, the team gathered on the long foredeck and moved across the darkened, thousand-foot-long ship to the aft superstructure.

A load of oil like that carried by the *Saddam Maru* meant $10 million or more in Saddam's pocket. And this U.S. mission was a combined effort that largely put Saddam out of the illegal oil business. The two skills that combined to shape the SEALs' victory in this dangerous contest were VBSS and CQD, or Close Quarters Defense.

VBSS is a core SEAL maritime skill. During SEAL Qualification Training, the new men are introduced to this skill, usually with the pier-side boarding of a derelict ship, moored at a deserted dock for training purposes. During the SEAL squadron predeployment training, this evolution moves up a notch or two. VBSS drills are scheduled aboard naval vessels, in port and under way, and on offshore oil platforms. When possible, these exercises are conducted with noncompliant role players, usually at night.

Moving as a team through the target platform or ship in the dark requires the highest order of discipline and professionalism—and many hours of practice. Team commanding officers and squadron commanders are always looking for opportunities aboard naval vessels, merchantmen, and oil rigs where their SEALs can practice these skills. Naval task force commanders at sea off San Diego and Norfolk are constantly pestered by SEALs preparing for deployment; they especially want to train against ships under way at sea. Since the attack on the USS *Cole*, those afloat commanders have been a great deal more responsive to these requests. They have to train their crews in counterboarding measures, so it's been a win-win situation.

Surprise may be achieved during stormy weather or on a mild, cloudless day. Once aboard, they move like a football offense breaking from the line of scrimmage. The element of surprise, hopefully; violence of action, always.

As Saddam's financial situation worsened, he became more dependent on smuggled oil. With the approach of the coalition invasion of Iraq, the game took on a spy-versus-spy tone, with moves and countermoves on either side. The Iraqi tanker crews took a number of measures to oppose the boarding parties. One of the most successful was welding up entryway hatches and porthole windows to deny boarders access to the interior of the ship. Since the oil smugglers operated close to Iraqi-friendly shores, they only had to delay their attackers until they could make a run for a safe haven.

Stopping these tankers became a breaking-and-entering drill—could the SEALs get inside and take control of the ship before these armored tankers could turn and make a dash for friendly territorial waters? And, of course, there were restrictions on the SEALs trying to make these entries, among them a prohibition against using explosive breaching charges. (A breaching charge is a small explosive charge that blows open a locked door or hatch.) The SEALs who had to play the game thought the rules were silly; given a free hand, they would have put an end to Saddam's tanker-smuggling operation in short order. But explosive entries were out. As it was, thanks in part to the Yarrow Entry, they eventually won—and still played by the rules.

Close Quarters Defense, or CQD, became a favored technique for measured force projection in the early and mid-1990s, and was adopted for SEAL training by the Naval Special Warfare Center in 1996. Prior to CQD, there had been a number of hand-to-hand techniques and martial disciplines used by SEALs, but none were wholly satisfactory. The SEALs needed a skill set that was versatile and effective and could be mastered in a reasonably short period of time. Given all that SEALs must learn and do, they really don't have the time for extensive training in martial arts; they needed tools that are combat focused and efficient. This skill set also had to be adaptable to heavily armed men working as a team in a dynamic environment and in a range of operational environments—aboard ship, in buildings, in caves, and in open country. And, finally, it had to be suitable in a threat environment that could range from compliant noncombatants to armed opposition—individually or in a crowd. The answer became CQD.

Close Quarters Defense is a blend of martial artistry, commando-style fighting, and the spiritual demands of a warrior. The word *defense* in the name is misleading; in reality, it is more of an offensive skill. CQD skills are a system of team-based moves, strikes, bars, or holds, and the tactical communications necessary to manage different levels of violence and force projection. CQD is a "behind-the-gun" tactic, in that the practitioner maintains the ability to use his weapon.

"You have to understand how fast we move when we're clearing a house," another SEAL said. "Speed is everything, but we have to move safely. And we have to move as a team. We're always ready to shoot, but we very seldom need to. The objective during the takedown of a house or residence is usually an individual and, occasionally, the house itself—a bomb factory or a weapons cache. So when we encounter someone, we have to quickly judge if that person poses a threat and meet that threat with the proper amount of force. Every situation is different. I've been on operations that involved clearing a large home and a lot of different things are going on. On the first floor, two of the guys have just disarmed a bodyguard and taken him down hard—hard enough that he needs help from the platoon [medical] corpsman. On the second floor, another two guys are trying to soothe a grandmother who thinks the world is coming to an end. And up on the third floor, one of the guys is cuffing and searching the bad guy we came to get while his brother SEAL is trying to calm down the guy's wife. We've been known to crank that dial all the way to the left and all the way to the right on the same operation. Full right is a bullet, and full left is handing out a candy bar. Either way, we have to get it right."

In the SEALs' mission to board the *Saddam Maru,* Close Quarters Training came in very handy. The SEALs boarding the *Saddam Maru* in the summer of 2001 knew it was going to be a challenge, so they came aboard with a full platoon. The previous day, a Canadian special operations team had boarded this same tanker. They had worked on it for close to forty-five minutes, but they could not crack the armadillo-like deckhouse that had been welded tight and was further strengthened with double-reinforced steel at the normal entry points. This vessel had additional steel plating on various portions of the deck housing, so that no single cut into the bulkheads of the pilot house could provide an access. The tanker's crew, on later questioning, felt that they were invulnerable—that the counterboarding and entry-denial measures recently installed on the vessel had made them safe from the allied boarding parties. But the Iraqi crew was totally unprepared for the SEALs' "Yarrow Entry."

Lieutenant (jg) Sean Yarrow was on his first SEAL deployment. He was big for a Navy SEAL—six-two and two hundred pounds. Yarrow grew up in Pittsburgh and graduated from the Naval Academy in June 1998. He went through BUD/S with Class 222. In June 2001, he found himself deployed with a SEAL platoon in an ARG—an Amphibious Ready Group—on patrol in the Persian Gulf. The ARG was fully engaged in MIO and anti-oil-smuggling operations, and his platoon was doing its share of the boardings. Yarrow was a newly minted SEAL officer trying to contribute to the operations of his platoon. Yarrow, like the other members of his platoon, had training in CQD.

The oil-smuggling game was being played with intensity during the summer of 2001, and at that time the Iraqis had the upper hand. SEAL boarding parties would swoop down upon a tanker carrying contraband oil. The Iraqi master would turn his vessel for the safe haven of friendly territorial waters and the race was on. Could the SEALs crack the steel nut of the tanker pilothouse before the ship made it from international waters to a safe haven?

At that point in time, the SEALs' method of cracking the secure deckhouse of a tanker was to find a convenient weather-deck hatch, and begin cutting. Usually, they went for one of the pilothouse hatches, which were the closest to the ship control station. No sense in cracking a lower-deck hatch and finding an internal passageway hatch welded shut. After getting aboard and setting up external security, the SEAL breaching team fired up its Quick-Saw, a gas-driven rotary saw with an eighteen-inch diamond-tipped blade for cutting metal, and went to work. As the boarded tanker put its rudder over to run for freedom, the scream of a saw blade biting into metal echoed across the weather decks and into the night. That summer, the Iraqis began welding a secondary level of three-eighths-inch steel and I-beam spacers, which slowed the cutting-and-entering process considerably. This double-steel reinforcement took too long to breach, and the boarding SEALs simply couldn't get through in the allotted time. Things were leaning in the Iraqis' favor.

Sean Yarrow's role in the platoon at that time was that of the assigned third officer, or "third-G." He had limited tactical duties in the platoon and some administrative responsibilities, but his primary job as a new first-tour officer was to watch and learn. His leadership duties in the platoon were limited. He was a "new guy"—a rookie officer. When the platoon boarded a tanker and set up its security and entry teams, his job was to roam the decks of the ship with a hooligan, a crowbar-like lever arm, and look for an easier way.

While his SEAL platoon mates attacked a pilothouse door, Yarrow poked and pried at other hatches and portholes, trying to force one of them open. In the course of his duties, he noticed that the center forward-facing window to the pilothouse was not welded shut, as were the others. This single window had to be kept free so that the helmsman could see to steer the ship and was perhaps the only source of ventilation in the pilothouse. However, the window was all but inaccessible. All the forward-facing pilothouse windows were on a sheer metal face that composed the forward bulkhead of the ship's superstructure. In fact, due to tanker design, these windows were often set in a reverse slope to provide for easier viewing of the forward decking and to assist in conning the ship during docking operations.

But Sean Yarrow had an idea. After an earlier unsuccessful attempt to cut into a different tanker before it passed into Iranian territorial waters, he vowed to give his idea a try the next time out. "Yarrow had a good idea to come in through the front bridge windows," said Chief Don Latham, the platoon chief petty officer, "but getting over the pilothouse to the front window, often at night, when you don't have a lot of time, is tricky work. It's like being a window washer on a high-rise building in a combat situation. And those tankers, even when they're loaded, can pitch and roll." The Iraqis had begun welding rebar, then hinged plates, across the window in front of the helm; but in the absence of a periscope, they needed to see out from somewhere in the pilothouse. Basically, there was no way they could weld double plating to a window that they needed to have open at least part of the time. But Sean Yarrow was ready for them. Now when the platoon boarded a ship, both Yarrow and his chief were in rappelling harnesses with two men assigned to belay them. In a series of training exercises, the SEALs had worked out a system of ropes and belay points. While the breaching team began cutting at one of the hatches, Yarrow, armed with a Quick-Saw, would swing down to the vulnerable window and begin to cut at the rebar or the single sheet of steel plating.

"I would sling my weapon and fire up the saw," Yarrow said. "Chief Latham would be there with his weapon to give security while I did the cutting. We were like a couple of spiders swaying in the wind, but we got the system down so that we always beat the breaching team into the pilothouse. We'd found a way in, and unless the Iraqis came up with something new, we could now win the race. Usually, it took us no more than ten minutes to get inside and take control of a ship." Chief Don Latham said of Yarrow, "Like the rest of the platoon, I wasn't so sure about Yarrow's idea—it seemed a little harebrained when he proposed going in over the front of the pilothouse. But it worked, and it worked every time."

Now, aboard the *Saddam Maru,* Yarrow and Latham could see that the pilothouse windows of the ship had a decidedly reverse slope, so they had to work at a difficult angle. The vessel also had both rebar and a single hinged plate on the front pilothouse window. When the Iraqi crewmen on watch heard the SEALs clamoring on the roof of the pilothouse, they immediately bolted the window. The tanker turned and made for the nearest Gulf state's territorial waters; the clock was ticking. The two SEALs pressed themselves in, close to the face of the superstructure, and broke out their tools.

By this time, Yarrow could hear the whine of the gas engine from the Quick-Saw of the SEAL breaching team at the pilothouse door. Soon the sound of his own saw joined it. For those inside, it would have sounded like dueling chainsaws biting into steel. Clamped onto the front of the pilothouse like a couple of insects, the two SEALs were working against the clock, trying to force open the window before the tanker crossed out of international waters. Yarrow sliced through the rebar and then began on the movable plate. He cut an access hole, tossed the saw inside, and then wriggled through the opening. Depending on the situation, the first man through an entry would toss in a flash-bang—a small grenade designed to temporarily blind and stun those inside. Seeing no one, Yarrow made the entry without the fanfare. Chief Latham, still outside, struggled through the opening.

Yarrow moved across the deserted pilothouse to where the other SEALs were still trying to cut through the door. As Yarrow was considering how to force the door open from his side, an Iraqi crewman approached him from behind. The crewman was too close by the time Yarrow turned around, so he couldn't bring his primary weapon up to bear. It was now Close Quarters Defense time.

Reflexively, Yarrow gave the Iraqi a hand-strike to the sternum and the man went down, conscious but stunned. Chief Latham, who was even bigger than Yarrow, was still trying to get through the opening and could not assist him. Yarrow slung his MP5 submachine gun and, with his knife, began to cut at the ropes that secured the hatch. Enter a second Iraqi. Yarrow quickly drew his SIG Sauer 9 mm sidearm and ordered the man to lie on the deck. He appeared to be unarmed, but he kept coming. Yarrow gave him a barrel strike with the pistol and the second Iraqi went down. He had nearly cut through all the ropes at the pilothouse door and Chief Latham was almost through the window access when a third Iraqi came at him. Another barrel strike and he, too, joined his friends on the floor.

"The Iraqis do that sometimes," Yarrow said. "They have orders to fight to the death, but they really aren't going to do that. So they have to do something, show some physical resistance. If they have a gun or a knife, then they're in serious trouble. Usually, they just need to be hit and put down, and their honor is intact. Normally, we do everything in pairs or as a team, which is a lot safer. But this time I was alone. When I look back on it, it was just like a drill at CQD training."

"It was a scene out of the movies," Latham said, recalling the incident. "By the time I got into the pilothouse, Mr. Yarrow was standing there, pistol in one hand, knife in the other, and a pile of Iraqis on the deck. It took only a few more minutes to get the rest of the platoon in and we owned the ship." The sortie of the *Saddam Maru* was the beginning of the end of the Iraqi oil-smuggling operations. The route their tankers had to follow required that they be in international waters for at least part of the journey. With the "Yarrow Entry," the SEALs were now consistently boarding and stopping these tankers. The Yarrow Entry was passed down to new platoons coming into theater and became part of SEAL platoon predeployment training.

This challenging and largely successful SEAL mission came to an end on September 11, 2001. On that day, the history of the United States and the Navy SEALs entered an entirely new era.

CHAPTER 7

TERROR AND DESTINY: MIDEAST AND ANTITERROR OPERATIONS

SEPTEMBER 11, 2001 – TODAY

THE MISSIONS:
Support regional and global operations against the Taliban and al-Qaeda, the Iraqi military, terrorism, and piracy

On September 11, 2001, the U.S. Navy SEALs' phones started ringing off the hook, and they've been busy ever since.

"When we got word of the attack on America, we couldn't believe it," said SEAL Randy Lowery, officer in charge of the SEAL platoon in Bahrain. "We were shocked, angry, and we wanted to get our guns into the fight. But where and who? That took a while to sort out. The only thing we knew was that the training exercises were over; from now on it was going to be real world. Half the platoon was in Kuwait and the other half was in Bahrain. The first thing we did was get the guys back from Kuwait and get our gear together. That didn't take long, as we pretty much keep up to speed while on deployment, but there's always something to do. Now there was a clear reason to do it. For those first few days we sat at the unit in Bahrain, checked our gear, and watched those Twin Towers come down again and again on the TV replays."

On 9/11, Navy SEAL Bob Schoultz was working inside the Pentagon on assignment as senior military assistant to the assistant secretary of defense for special operations. "I was where every good team guy needs to be when the caca hits the fan, I was in the gym working out," he quipped. "I did not know an airplane had hit the Pentagon. I heard the fire alarm siren go off. I thought it was a drill, so I casually got dressed and I went outside. I stepped out and I saw twenty-five thousand of my closest friends leaving the building, going down to the river. What the hell happened? They said, 'we think an airplane hit the building.' I thought, 'I've got to find my boss, he needs me now.' So I fought my way back into the Pentagon, and I actually was sitting right there with the secretary of defense and my boss while they were trying to figure out what the heck was going on. There were still numerous airplanes that weren't responding to IFF [identification, friend or foe] and [we didn't know] how many more airplanes were going to come in and were going to hit what."

Chris Osman recalled his feelings when his SEAL platoon was selected to deploy overseas several days after the attacks. "We were one of two platoons in a high state of predeployment readiness. You're happy that you're going but you feel bad for the guys in the other platoon. And I remember leaving and I was like, 'Oh man. Sorry you didn't get picked.' And one guy looked at me and he's like, 'Screw you, dude.' We were allowed to go home for one night. We basically got about seven or eight hours off to go home and say goodbye to our families. And then we filled out last will and testaments. We filled out life insurance paperwork. We filled out power of attorneys for all of our families. So, it was the real deal."

Weeks later, Osman and his SEAL platoon were assigned a maritime mission in the Persian Gulf to intercept a top-tier target related to Osama bin Laden's earlier terrorist attacks. "The name of the ship was Alpha 117," Osman remembered. "That's the ship that Al-Qaeda used to smuggle the explosives into Africa for the two U.S. Embassy bombings that killed over 200 people. They wanted that ship taken down and our platoon was given the green light to do it. I remember our task unit commander saying over the radio, 'I don't care what you do, how you do it, but you're gonna get on that boat and you're gonna take it down.' All of the joking and the grab-assing goes away and it's game time; so it's unzip the bags, put all the gear on, check the weapons. Make sure there's a round in the chamber. We raced up to the stern at 40 miles an hour [in a rigid-hulled inflatable boat] in the middle of the night, hooked and climbed up the side of the ship—probably about 25–30 feet in the air— and jumped over the railing. We probably had about four or five people that had already made it over the railing, and we were setting a security perimeter when the doors opened and people started coming out. At that moment, we couldn't even wait for the rest of the platoon, so we started the assault on the ship with four or five people. There was a seriousness about what we were doing that I hadn't experienced before. The professionalism rose to the challenge and all of us just never really said anything. Never talked, nothing. We just operated and that's what all that training and that sacrifice is for. So when that phone call happens, you can do that job. That ship takedown took about three minutes."

On 9/11, there were twelve Navy SEAL platoons deployed

worldwide. Some of these platoons were aboard units of the fleet with Amphibious Ready Groups; others were assigned to Naval Special Warfare Units, overseas shore facilities that serve as home base for deployed SEAL platoons. There were SEALs in Europe, South America, and Korea, as well as throughout the Pacific. At that time there was an emphasis on placing NSW assets in the Middle East, but there was no concentration of those forces.

Since 2001, the main focus of SEAL operations has been Afghanistan and Iraq. SEALs were in the mountains, towns, and cities of those nations, because that's where the enemy was. They were deployed elsewhere as well, since the foes are global, but Iraq and Afghanistan were to be the SEAL focus of attention. After September 11, when the enemy fled to the mountains of Afghanistan, SEALs became mountain fighters; and when the enemy hid in the cities of Iraq, SEALs became urban warriors.

The attacks of 9/11, operations in Afghanistan, and the invasion of Iraq quickly drew the full attention and deployment commitments of the American military, including the SEALs. For the SEALs, all deployments became combat deployments, and that's the way it has been for close to a decade and a half. There were maritime operations associated with the initial combat operations in Iraq, but for the most part, SEALs have taken their work inland, to the mountains in Afghanistan, then to the cities and villages of Iraq, and then back to Afghanistan.

When new technologies or perishable intelligence presented opportunities with short lead times, SEALs became adept at compressing their reaction time to take advantage of this real-time intelligence capability. That's what SEALs are best at: changing tactics and adapting methods to meet new threats and changing environments. One thing has remained constant from Vietnam up through the intervening years to the current conflict: good intelligence makes for good operations. It was as true then for a platoon in the mangrove swamps of the Mekong as it is for today's SEALs, whether they were in the mountains of Afghanistan or the streets of Baghdad. And it's hard to find good intelligence without help from the locals.

Before 2000 and the war on terrorism, the SEALs were a built-in Navy force. They usually deployed with units of the fleet and to theater commanders such as the Pacific Command, European Command, Central Command (the Middle East), or Southern Command (Central/South America). While on those deployments, they were attached to a parent command—afloat or ashore—under a conventional-force command structure. SEAL platoons deployed with little command presence and limited logistic or operational support.

After Vietnam, the need arose for smaller, raiding-type coordinated special operations and interventions like those in Panama and Grenada, so Congress established the beginnings of a Joint Special Operations structure that included the SEALs. Many in the Army and Navy didn't like this, as they lost some control over their special operations components. But when 9/11 happened, it seemed like everything that happened between 1986 and 2001 was to prepare special operations and the SEALs to step into this new role in dealing with al-Qaeda, the rise of nonstate actors, terrorism, and smaller-scale interventions. The deployment of SEALs with beefed-up staffing and combat-support capability in self-contained squadrons was put in place just in time for the heavy combat rotations that followed 9/11.

Many of the most effective SEAL operations are the ones we'll never hear about because they're classified and may remain so for a very long time.

In the wake of September 11, 2001, the war in Afghanistan quickly turned into a ground campaign spearheaded by CIA operatives and led by special operations soldiers. The visible military targets of the Taliban and al-Qaeda were rapidly eliminated by air strikes, but the majority of the terrorists were hiding in caves and tunnels under the rocky mountains of Afghanistan. The U.S. special operations forces in Afghanistan included elements from the Army, Navy, and Air Force. Navy SEALs were on the ground in force—regardless of the fact that Afghanistan is a landlocked country and even drinkable water is sometimes hard to find.

In the war on terrorism that began in 2001, there have been many occasions for personnel recovery, where troops have had to go in harm's way for a fallen or captured brother or sister. In the Navy, the highest award for bravery is the Navy Cross, second only to the Medal of Honor, and two of these were awarded to Navy SEALs for personnel recovery.

One of these actions took place in November 2001, barely two months after the attacks of September 11. In the early days of the liberation of Afghanistan, the Taliban and their al-Qaeda allies were fighting the advance of the Northern Alliance fighters every step of the way. In the vast reaches of northern Afghanistan, there were pockets of fierce resistance. Americans on the ground at that time were of two persuasions: Army Special Forces and CIA personnel, with a sprinkling of British special operators and Navy SEALs, all working closely with the Afghan resistance under the banner of the Northern Alliance. CIA officers in the area had the best working knowledge of the Northern Alliance and some of the best Arabic language skills.

On November 25, a prisoner revolt broke out inside the Qala-i-Jangi fortress at Mazar-e-Sharif when al-Qaeda and Taliban prisoners seized the prison armory and two-thirds of the compound. The large prison courtyard became a battleground. Two CIA operatives were separated from their element, and the rescue team that was sent for them was blocked by heavy fire from the former captives.

As the battle raged, a single Navy SEAL, Stephen Bass, then working with a British commando unit, crawled forward under heavy fire to reach the two fallen men. His Navy Cross citation reads that Bass "was engaged continuously by direct small arms fire, indirect mortar fire, and rocket propelled grenade fire. He was forced to walk through an active anti-personnel minefield in order to gain entry to the fortress." They located one of the CIA men and he was alive, but the second American was still missing. After darkness settled onto the battlefield, the SEAL again moved forward "by himself under constant enemy fire in an attempt to locate the injured citizen. Running low on ammunition, he utilized the weapons from deceased Afghans to continue his rescue attempt." After dark he fought his way to the downed American, who had been killed in the fighting.

The SEAL didn't know the fallen American, but he risked his life to reach him and recover his remains, those of the first CIA officer to be killed in Afghanistan. His name was Johnny Spann.

WHILE THE AFGHAN NORTHERN Alliance and their American special forces allies completed their north-to-south sweep, the command of Captain Bob Harward set up shop in Kandahar. Called Task Force K-Bar, this component had become the authority for special operations forces (SOF) missions in central and southern Afghanistan. K-Bar, named for the military-issue knife carried by SEALs and Marines, was open for business by the first week of January 2002. It was a joint task force made up of both SOF and conventional elements from the Army, the Navy, and the Air Force, as well as a number of Marines and personnel from "other governmental agencies," or OGAs, including the CIA. It also included SOF troops from a number of allied nations. Task Force K-Bar had a SEAL-centric command-and-control structure and bore the imprint of its SEAL commander.

Navy SEAL Captain Bob Harward was the passionate leader of Task Force K-Bar, a job for which he was ideally suited. When the attacks came on September 11, Harward was Commander, Naval Special Warfare Group One in Coronado, and he was quickly ordered to Afghanistan. For the first time, a Navy SEAL commanded a task force five hundred miles from blue water.

Fortunately, this was not Bob Harward's first trip to Kandahar. Harward went to high school in Tehran while his father served as the American naval attaché to the shah of Iran's government. Tehran, like Beirut, was at one time a safe, cosmopolitan city with a substantial Western presence. In the mountains not far from the city center, the skiing was excellent. Harward learned Farsi and a working command of Pashto, and prior to attending the Naval Academy, he and two of his high school pals spent a summer hitchhiking in Afghanistan. Now Harward was back in Afghanistan.

In January 2002, Harward's planners began working on a twelve-hour "boots on the ground" mission to put special operations forces, led by a SEAL platoon, into the al-Qaeda strongpoint at the Zhawar Kili cave complex in Afghanistan's Khost province. The Zhawar Kili Valley and cave complex was some 150 miles northeast of Kandahar and had long been suspected of being the site of an al-Qaeda training camp. What made the Zhawar Kili Valley unique was its location—it opened up right onto the Afghan-Pakistani border. Fresh intelligence suggested that a number of fleeing al-Qaeda were using the valley to slip out of Afghanistan and into Pakistan. When it was determined there was a chance this might be a possible escape route for Osama bin Laden himself, the planning became urgent. That's when Harward sent for SEAL Lieutenant Chris Cassidy.

"What's up, sir?" Cassidy asked. Harward said with a grin, "Fresh intel says we may have a hot one for you. You ready to go back out?" Cassidy knew the answer, but glanced at his chief petty officer for confirmation. "The platoon's up, sir. We're always ready."

Harward looked at his watch; it was already late afternoon. "Put your platoon on alert and let's start working up the operation. We'll insert you just before daylight tomorrow morning. Todd has the details on the target along with the latest intel." Cassidy found Lieutenant Commander Todd Seniff, the watch officer, to find out where they were going. It was then that Cassidy learned about the Zhawar Kili caves.

The cave complex in the Zhawar Kili Valley and its use as a Taliban and al-Qaeda stronghold were well known, even before September 11. Oddly enough, much of this underground warren had been built with American support and American money during the decade-long Russian occupation. Millions of dollars in aid and arms had been given to the Afghan resistance. This rugged valley, within sight of the Pakistani border, was a major resupply point and haven for the mujahedeen in their struggle against the Russian-backed Kabul government. When the Taliban gained control of the country, they occupied the valley and made the extensive cave complex available to their al-Qaeda allies. In 1998, President Bill Clinton sent cruise missiles into the complex in response to the bombings of our embassies in East Africa.

Many of the allied SOF components had cumbersome planning and approval procedures and mission preparation windows, some taking as long as forty-eight hours. So did Navy SEALs, but they were quick to discard them. "In the early days at K-Bar," Chris Cassidy recalled, "nobody could get out the door quicker than SEALs. We were very good at this. All I had to do was turn my guys out of the rack and tell them to saddle up. We'd begin the mission briefing on the helo pad and finish it on the ride to the insertion point. Nobody else could move that quickly." Hour by hour, Zhawar Kili grew in importance and scope. The prospect of senior al-Qaeda cadres hemorrhaging from Afghanistan into Pakistan put a move into the valley on the fast track. Since it was to be a large operation with both SEALs and Marines involved, Harward installed Lieutenant Commander Todd Seniff as his ground force commander. Chris Cassidy and his SEAL platoon would be supported by a contingent of Marines.

On January 6 and January 7, 2002, the Zhawar Kili Valley was bombarded with TLAMs (Tomahawk Land Attack Missiles) and JDAMs (Joint Direct Attack Munitions). Precision-guided cruise missiles and smart bombs found their way to previously plotted GPS coordinates, slamming into cave entrances, fortifications, and dwellings as part of the pre-ground-attack package.

At about 3 A.M. on January 7, 2002, three large helicopters idled on the edge of the tarmac at Kandahar International. There were no lights showing, just the collective scream of jet engines. Lieutenant Commander Seniff led his seventy-five-man assault element from the task force compound to the giant whirring metal insects. They broke into three groups, twenty-five men to each bird, filing up the rear boarding ramps in good order. The planning, the preparation, and the briefings were behind them now. They were on their way downrange.

The assault element would be inserted by three Marine CH-53 Super Stallion helicopters. Normally, SEALs are transported by special operations MH-53 Pave Lows, an electronically sophisticated helo, but the Pave Lows have only two engines. The Marine CH-53s have three engines and are configured for heavy lift and troop movement. They were ideal for insertion work in the mountains of Afghanistan, where altitude degrades helicopter performance. Seniff, the SEAL platoon, and assorted mission specialists were aboard the lead helo. The Marine security element was on the other two birds.

Harward followed him aboard and yelled over the turbine whine, "Kick some ass!"

"Aye, aye, sir!" Seniff shouted back. Harward shook Seniff's gloved hand and gave him a thumbs-up, then hurried back to the exit ramp of the big helo. He quickly boarded each of the other two helos to wish the Marines good hunting as well.

The crew chief of Seniff's helo came over to him and yelled in his ear, "The other birds are loaded with a good head count, sir! Ready when you are!"

Seniff looked up at the crew chief. They were bathed in dull red light, enough to see by but not so much as to affect their night vision.

Outside, the air had been cool, even comfortable, but inside the body of the Super Stallion, sweat from heavily armed men mingled with the burned-kerosene odor of jet exhaust. Seniff gave the crew chief a single thumbs-up, then turned both thumbs out, palms up, in a jerky motion: pull chocks; let's go. The big CH-53s lifted in turn, ran out over the length of tarmac to gain what ground speed they could within the security of the airport perimeter, and soared quickly. No sense in taking chances with ground fire at this stage of the game.

High over the southernmost range of the Hindu Kush, the three big helos found their KC-130 tanker and topped off their fuel loads. The CH-53s couldn't complete the trip unrefueled, so it was decided they'd make the in-flight refueling on the way in. A midair refueling between a fixed-wing aircraft and a helicopter at night calls for a great deal of airmanship; the Marine pilots pulled it off smoothly and professionally. Now they were inbound for the Zhawar Kili Valley. With the refueling behind them, Seniff had just begun to relax a little when a voice crackled in his headset.

"Hey, Todd, we got a problem." It was Seniff's pilot in the lead helo. "The TOC [tactical operations center] just radioed that one of the Predators has some thermal activity at the primary insertion site; looks as if there may be a few locals moving about. They recommend the secondary. How about it?"

This was not good—the news that there were people moving on the ground meant that they might not be able to land where they wanted to. The plan called for them to insert at the head of the valley just before dawn and sweep down the valley northwest to southeast from the highest elevation to the lowest—7,500 feet down to perhaps 6,500. The first alternate was the middle of the valley, which meant they would have to move up the valley on foot, then back down. They say a battle plan doesn't survive the first shot being fired. *Hell,* Seniff thought, *we're not even on the ground yet.*

"What do you think, Chuck?" Seniff said to the pilot. Normally, SEALs flew with Air Force special operations pilots who trained extensively for this kind of operation. But Seniff and the other SEALs were coming to respect and trust the capabilities of their Marine flyers.

"We'll take you where you want to go, Todd, but if it's all the same, I'd just as soon not fly into ground fire."

And we don't want to insert into a hot LZ, thought Seniff. "Tell the TOC we're going for the first alternate. Let me know if there's any more intel."

"Roger that, Todd." The lead pilot gave instructions to the other helos, and Seniff settled back to wait out the ride. He told himself not to worry about what he could not control. Easier said than done.

The insertion into the secondary site went without incident. The Marine Super Stallions, their pilots flying with night-vision goggles, swooped in and dropped to the valley floor. The three helos were on the ground no more than fifteen seconds. As they lifted back into the air, the men on the ground scrambled to form a loose perimeter—seventy-five pairs of American boots at seven thousand feet.

A few minutes later, all was quiet. It would be another hour before they had good light on the valley floor, and there was a lot to do before that time. It was a clear night, with no moon and no breeze. A burned-sulfur smell still hung in the air from the JDAMs and TLAMs. Seniff and the others were curious as to what the air and missile strikes had accomplished.

The fifty-man Marine security detachment was headed up by Captain Lou Taladega. His gunnery sergeant had helped to liberate Kuwait City as a young lance corporal during the Gulf War. There were seventeen SEALs in the platoon, including Seniff. In addition to SEALs and Marines, there were two Air Force sergeants from the Combat Control Teams, two FBI agents, two Explosive Ordnance Disposal (EOD) technicians, an Army chem-bio specialist, and a Navy linguist who would serve as an interpreter. One of the Bureau agents was a former Navy SEAL with experience on the FBI Hostage Rescue Team. The other was a former Marine Corps infantry officer. Both were officially along for evidentiary purposes, not combat duty, but either one could be an experienced gun in the fight if it came to that.

The operation itself was to be a quick in-and-out sweep of the valley. They all carried a day's ration of water and a PowerBar or two. All wore body armor, and their weapons and ammunition loads were tailored for a fast-moving assault. This was a large, heavily armed, multidimensional SWAT team. The SEALs who were to check out the caves were prepared for close-quarter battle. The Marines would provide security. Their duties included setting out sniper positions for overwatch of the men working on the valley floor and to serve as a blocking force. They were also prepared for urban battle and light infantry work as needed. Close-quarters battle or close-quarters combat usually refers to fighting inside buildings or inside the compartments of a ship, while urban battle has to do with fighting outside in a city or town—street fighting.

The terrain was more than rugged. The floor of the valley was desert hardpan, very much like Camp Billy Machen, the SEAL training facility near the Chocolate Mountains in Southern California. The sides were steep, boulder strewn, and cut by deep wadis. The rim of the canyon sides averaged some fifteen hundred to a thousand feet above the valley floor, a nice perch for Taliban or al-Qaeda snipers. Seniff spoke into the boom mike of his radio.

"Lou, you there?"

"Right here, sir."

A SEAL of Taladega's rank would call a SEAL lieutenant commander by his first name, but Lou Taladega was not a SEAL; he was all Marine.

"Get moving. Get your guys to the high ground as soon as you can."

"Roger that, sir. We're on it." There was a quiet rustling as

Taladega's Marines left the insertion perimeter and began to pick their way up the rocky slopes that led from the valley floor.

Seniff soon heard a voice in his headset: "Bulldog One in place." The Marine element on his right was in position. A few minutes later, he heard, "Bulldog Two in place." Seniff breathed a sigh of relief; his overwatch Marines were in position. He found his SEAL platoon commander.

"Okay, Chris, take us out of here." With a hand signal from his platoon officer, the SEAL platoon chief put the platoon of SEALs into a loose diamond formation and they began to move in a northwesterly direction up the valley. The non-SEALs arrayed themselves with Seniff and Cassidy within the security of the moving diamond. Once on the move, they began to check out the cave entrances that lined the walls of the valley floor. The TLAM and JDAM strikes had done little or nothing to the infrastructure of the caves. There were craters at many of the cave mouths, but no significant damage to any of the entrances. They reached the head of the valley an hour after they had inserted and began the process of working their way back, carefully moving into the caves as they went. These were not just holes dug into the steep valley sides; they were sophisticated, interconnected tunnel complexes reinforced with steel I-beams and brickwork. The tunnels were several hundred yards deep, and there were more than seventy of them. The SEALs quickly searched caves while the Marines scrambled along the rough high ground to provide security. In many ways, their job was more difficult than that of the search elements moving on the valley floor.

Back on the valley floor, the search teams couldn't believe what they were finding. "It was incredible," Seniff reported. "There were thousands of tons of ammunition and explosives— thousands of tons! There were tanks, artillery, and antiaircraft guns. There was enough weaponry to outfit an army."

Each cave had to be checked carefully, for there was the ever-present threat of an ambush or booby traps. It was tedious, time-consuming, dangerous work.

"We were on a search-and-destroy mission," explained one of the SEALs, "but there was no way we were going to destroy that much munitions and equipment. We were scheduled to be on the ground for twelve hours and we barely had a hundred pounds of C-4 explosive with us."

The force moved methodically down the valley, trying to get a rough inventory of what they were finding. It was hard to catalog it all; there were thousands of crates of ammunition and explosives—literally millions of pounds of ordnance. Some of the caves held classrooms and training facilities. There were jail cells and safe-house accommodations that included passports and freshly laundered clothes. The caves were wired with electric lights, but there was no power. The search teams had only their flashlights.

"This was a classic terrorist-training and terror-export operation on a scale we couldn't imagine," said one of the FBI agents. "Al-Qaeda terrorists could be trained, equipped, given false documentation, and filtered across the Pakistani border. Who knows how many terrorist bombers were trained here and sent against targets in the West?"

As the teams moved from cave to cave down the valley, Taladega's Marines leapfrogged along the high ground on either side to provide security. Communications were marginal, but everyone now knew this was the biggest al-Qaeda base and terrorist training facility ever found. By late afternoon, they arrived at the extraction point near the end of the valley, just a few miles from the Pakistani border. Most of them had been up for more than thirty-six hours. They were tired and hungry, and it was getting colder.

"Camel Packer, this is K-Bar actual. You there, Todd?"

"Go ahead, sir." Even over the encrypted transmission, Seniff could recognize Harward's voice.

"New orders from higher command, Todd. They want you guys to stay in there for another day."

"Say again, K-Bar!" Seniff was shouting now. His radio batteries were low, and he wanted to make sure he had understood his commander. He knew the inbound extraction helos were only five minutes out.

"I say again, we want you to stay there. Can you safely go to ground and stay overnight, over?"

"Roger, wait one." Seniff quickly turned to Taladega. "Lou, can we dig in here for the night and hold?"

"There's a small abandoned village on the rim of the valley. We could take shelter there and set a good defensive perimeter. But we better get on it. It'll be dark soon, and it's going to get cold."

"How're your guys holding up?" Seniff was well aware that the Marines had been through a really tough scramble across the valley walls, some of them at altitudes over 8,500 feet.

"They're a pretty tired bunch, sir," Taladega reported, "but they're Marines. We'll make it happen."

Seniff glanced at the others. Everyone was excited with the day's find, but they were all weary. There were seventy-four American souls in that valley besides himself, and he was responsible for them.

"K-Bar, this is Camel Packer. Roger your last. We will move out from here to the security of the village on the east rim of the valley. Any chance of a resupply, over?"

"Negative, Camel Packer. We'll get you at first light tomorrow morning, so you'll have to make do with what you have, over."

Which is nothing, Seniff thought. "Understood, K-Bar.

We're moving to the village and will check in when we go to ground for the night."

"Good copy, Todd, and good luck. K-Bar out."

In the fading light, the American force made its way up to the little village on the rim of the valley. It was more a collection of huts than a village, one- and two-room dwellings made of stone and mud. The bombs and cruise missiles of the previous evening had done little to the cave infrastructure in the valley, but they had frightened all the locals away. They had fled, and the village was abandoned. The only inhabitants were chickens, a half dozen goats, and two cows. Weary after a hurried two-mile trek from the valley floor and an elevation gain of twelve hundred feet, the assault force filed into the village for the night.

Seniff huddled with his two element commanders. "We have a good perimeter here," Taladega reported. "We have a third of my Marines on guard duty and the others resting. They're pretty tired, so we'll rotate them every two hours. Either the sergeant or myself will be on the perimeter at all times."

"Thanks, Lou," Seniff replied. "Your guys did one helluva job today. Any activity out there?"

"Nothing close by, but we can see them signaling with lights in the hills to the west and north. They know we're here, and they're talking about it."

"I'm going to have a look around," Seniff said to Cassidy and Taladega. "Let me know if you see or hear anything. I don't want any of those gomers [the name SEALs often used for al-Qaeda and Taliban fighters] slipping back in here and surprising us."

Back in the tactical operations center at Kandahar, Bob Harward was reading Seniff's report. "Holy shit," he exclaimed when he got to Seniff's estimate of the enemy stores they had found. Harward turned to his watch officer. "Get Todd's report out to the SOC [Rear Admiral Bert Calland, special operations commander for General Tommy Franks's Central Command] right away."

Word was racing through CENTCOM that the Zhawar Kili complex was by far the largest al-Qaeda arms cache and training base found to date. Predator drones and P-3 Navy surveillance aircraft now had the valley under constant surveillance. The following morning, Lieutenant Chris Cassidy led a squad of SEALs along with a few Marines and an Air Force combat controller over a ridge to the west of Zhawar Kili. As they left the valley rim, they spotted a group of some thirty armed men moving below them. It appeared that al-Qaeda was starting to get organized and wanted their valley back.

"They were shuffling along in a loose formation," as a platoon SEAL described it. "Most of them had weapons that they carried draped over their shoulders and some had bandoliers of ammunition. They were turned out in mountain garb—robes, turbans, and sandals. We watched them with binoculars for a while before they saw us. A few of them fired at us, but we were well out of effective range. We had position on them and most of us were just itching to get a few rounds downrange. The lieutenant [Cassidy] just turns to the air controller and says, 'Take care of them.' By now they are only three or four hundred yards away."

"So our controller breaks out his map, gets on the radio, and raises a section of Air Force F-15E Strike Eagles. They talk for a moment, and then he turns to the rest of us. 'It's on the way,' he says. 'Look the other way and keep your mouth open; there'll be a pretty good shock wave.' A few seconds later, four five-hundred pounders land right in the middle of those guys. The concussions felt like someone was punching you in the kidneys. We went down to the strike area and there was nothing but sandals, body parts, and a few mangled weapons. They'd simply been erased."

There was some reluctance on the part of senior commanders to believe that the SEALs could have found that quantity of stores and munitions in such a remote mountain location. But once digital images of the stockpiles in the Zhawar Kili began arriving through the satellite communications (SATCOM) link, the upper-echelon commanders became believers. Seniff was then able to get all the JDAM smart bombs he wanted.

"It all came through Pakistan," Seniff explained of the huge quantity of stores and munitions. "We found heavy vehicle tire tracks leading from the Pakistani border into the valley. They brought it in by the semitrailer load. This stuff must have come in through the port of Karachi, then up through western Pakistan, each warlord taking his fee as it passed through his district. Borders don't mean too much here. Clan boundaries and smuggling routes do. We could see the border guards from the lower end of the valley. No one can tell me they didn't know what was going on there." While the search crews toiled in the caves, Cassidy and his reinforced SEAL squad continued to range out from the valley cave complex, looking for caches of al-Qaeda material and documents. By the seventh day and into the eighth, the Americans in the Zhawar Kili Valley were fully acclimatized and used to hard living—sleeping on the floor and cooking over an open fire. They couldn't get any dirtier, and all but the Marines were wearing local gear.

Throughout the operation the Air Force combat controllers rained JDAMs into the valley. On the seventh day, Harward informed the SEALs they would be pulled out the following day and told them to make all preparations for leaving the Zhawar Kili Valley and redeploying back to Task Force K-Bar at Kandahar. That afternoon, the SEALs and EOD technicians set out to blow the last cave the old-fashioned way—with C-4. They had found barrels of diesel oil and a small quantity of gasoline in this cave. They divided their C-4 into three charges and primed them with time fuse and blasting caps. The first two charges detonated with little or no effect, and seemed like firecrackers compared to the 2,000-pound JDAMs. When the third charge went, the ground began to move . . . and kept moving. It seems that there were fuel and ammunition stores buried well inside the cave, munitions they hadn't found—until now. All night long the rumbling continued as more cached stores and fuel fed the ongoing explosion. With this final demolition, all the caves in the Zhawar Kili Valley had been demolished or collapsed, and the weaponry hid in the wadis and ravines destroyed.

"We all left that valley ten or fifteen pounds lighter than we entered it," Todd Seniff reported. "I'd say we worked twenty hours a day and never slept for more than a two-hour stretch. We were dirty, hungry, cold, or hot most of our waking hours. It was wonderful. Had they taken us from the Zhawar Kili Valley and dropped us into another valley, we were good to go. There is absolutely nothing like being given an important and difficult mission and seeing your men accomplish that mission."

On the morning of January 14, two Marine MH-60s landed to collect a third of Seniff's force. That afternoon they returned to collect the last of the SEALs and the Marines, and one well-fed and totally rehabilitated Afghan dog. The SEALs' coming ashore for the first strategic-reconnaissance missions in the heart of Afghanistan was a large step for the maritime component of America's special operations forces. So were the many initial platoon-sized, direct-action missions conducted by Task Force K-Bar. But the mission into the Zhawar Kili Valley was as unique as it was propitious. Never in their history had SEALs conducted an airborne assault that far inland. Never before had they operated with a ground force that large, let alone provided the command and control on the ground for such a force. Zhawar Kili laid the groundwork for the larger multi-unit, multi-service operations that the SEALs would conduct in Iraq.

"We learned a lot at Zhawar Kili," SEAL Lieutenant Commander Todd Seniff recalled. "We directed some 404,000 pounds of ordnance into that valley. Not since Vietnam have that many bombs been dropped into that small of an area, and never that much so close to friendly troops. We did it routinely. As far as I know, it was the largest ground-controlled aerial bombardment in history. This was probably the largest and most important al-Qaeda training and resupply facility in Afghanistan, bigger than Tora Bora. We closed it down barely four months after the September 11 attacks. I'm proud of the role I was able to play in this operation. What made it happen was the way the ground force worked together: the Marines, the SEALs, the CCTs, the Bureau [FBI] agents—all of them. Every man contributed. We sweated it out during the day and froze our butts off at night, but we made it happen."

"Zhawar Kili was a turning point for us," recalled Captain Bob Harward. "It showed that even with a large, complex objective we could plan and execute the mission in a very narrow time window. And once on the ground, we could adapt to various contingencies as they arose. After Zhawar Kili, the joint command structure was much more willing to give us the job and tell us to simply do it, rather than having us reporting back up the chain every step of the way for direction and permission. It all seems routine now, but not back then. Think about it: SEALs in the mountains running direct-action and strategic-reconnaissance missions. No one thought we could do it, let alone do it better than anyone else."

Todd Seniff is now Commander of Naval Special Warfare

Group One at the Naval Amphibious Base at Coronado, California. SEAL Teams One, Three, Five, and Seven report direction to Seniff and Group One. Chris Cassidy was selected by NASA to be an astronaut in May 2004, two years after he took part in the SEALs' Zhawar Kili caves operation. From 2006 through 2008, he served as Capsule Commander (CAPCOM) in the Mission Control Center. During his NASA career, Cassidy completed six spacewalks, totaling 31 hours, 14 minutes, and accumulated 182 days in space. He is currently in charge of the extravehicular activity, or spacewalk, branch within the Astronaut Office.

ON MARCH 4, 2002, U.S. Navy SEAL Neil Roberts was all alone, fighting for his life near the top of a snow-covered mountain in Afghanistan.

Operation Anaconda was one of the biggest ground attacks of the initial Afghan campaign, and it was an attempt to clear entrenched al-Qaeda and Taliban fighters. Neil Roberts and his teammates made up a reconnaissance element that was trying to insert on a nearly ten-thousand-foot mountaintop in support of a joint special operations mission to oust al-Qaeda and Taliban forces from the Shah-i-Kot Valley. While trying to land near the summit, the MH-47E Chinook helicopter took enemy RPG and small-arms fire.

The helicopter, though badly damaged, managed to clear the insertion site and crash-land a few miles away. But as it veered away from the insertion, Neil Roberts fell from the craft and found himself on the ground, alone and surrounded by an entrenched enemy. His teammates at the crash site, as well as other SOF elements in the area, knew immediately that Roberts was still fighting but was in mortal danger. He was heavily outnumbered, and time was against him.

The SEAL senior chief petty officer in charge of the element immediately set up security at the helicopter crash site and directed the rescue of his team and the helicopter aircrew. But knowing that Roberts was on the ground, alone and fighting for his life, the senior chief asked to lead a team back to the original insertion site, in spite of the numerically superior force that held the ground. His Navy Cross citation reads: "After a treacherous helicopter insertion onto the mountain top, he led his team in a close-quarter firefight. He skillfully maneuvered his team and bravely engaged multiple enemy positions, personally clearing one bunker and killing several enemy within. His unit became caught in a withering crossfire from other bunkers and closing enemy forces. Despite mounting casualties, he maintained his composure and continued to engage the enemy until his position became untenable."

The valiant rescue attempt by Neil Roberts's teammates was met and defeated by overwhelming force and firepower. The episode turned into a complex fourteen-hour running firefight in rugged mountain terrain and waist-deep snow, an engagement that became known as the Battle of Takur Ghar. The SEAL senior chief did a magnificent job of caring for his wounded men and fighting off a determined enemy, but he had no choice but to withdraw. In the end, U.S. Navy SEAL Neil Roberts fought the enemy alone in a close-quarters firefight and was killed in that fight, possibly after being captured. "I will tell you very candidly," the task force commander, Major General Frank Hagenbeck, said of Roberts, "that individual had been captured by three al-Qaeda members and we knew exactly where they were. We saw him on the Predator being dragged off by three al-Qaeda men." Hagenbeck reported that Roberts had evidently been executed.

In the larger fight to save Roberts, and then to successfully recover his remains, six more Americans died on that mountain in Afghanistan. The loss of these men shocked many in the special operations community, and was a sobering look at the cost of going back for one of our own. Yet it remains an embedded tradition in SOF culture that the many, at substantial risk, will come back for the one.

Neil Roberts had left a letter with his wife with instructions that it should be opened if he failed to return. It read in part: "My time in the teams was special . . . I loved being a SEAL. I died doing what made me happy. Very few people have the luxury of that." The balance of the letter was devoted to thanking his family for their love and support. He was thirty-two when he died, and he left behind a wife and young son.

Quickly on the heels of Operation Anaconda, thirty Chechen al-Qaeda fighters were spotted leaving the valley on foot. SEALs and other special operators from Neil's unit managed to be inserted by helicopter in the path of the fleeing Chechens. Though this SEAL element was outnumbered two to one, they were the ones waiting in ambush. After a fierce firefight and with only minor SEAL casualties, they killed them to a man. No quarter was asked and none was given.

One of the men that the SEAL senior chief carried through the snow as they were driven off from the rescue of Neil Roberts had his lower leg severely mangled. He was rushed back to the States, but nothing could be done to save his leg. It was amputated just below the knee. A year later, this same SEAL warrior was back in Iraq and had his gun back in the fight—on a prosthetic leg. He was behind enemy lines conducting special operations as the 3rd Infantry Division and the 1st Marine Expeditionary Force pushed toward Baghdad. "Not a problem," he said. "The docs did a great job. I can do anything on the new leg I could do on my old one. I'm still good to go."

ON THE EVE OF the American invasion of Iraq, the SEALs were preparing to stage their biggest operation in their history so far, an attempt by more than 250 Naval Special Warfare personnel to capture two of Iraq's key offshore oil platforms and three land-based pumping facilities without their being blown up and triggering an environmental disaster. The capture operation was planned as a coordinated attack just before the Army and Marines pushed in from Kuwait.

"You have to go back to the invasion beaches at Normandy," recalled retired SEAL Vice Admiral Robert Harward, then the SEAL task force commander for operations in Iraq, "or some of the larger amphibious operations in the Pacific to find that many men on an operation. And even then, maybe not that many people moving at the exact same time. We've never seen the likes of this in our community, and we may never see it again." He added, "From the outset, we knew it would be the largest coordinated SEAL operation in the history of Naval Special Warfare. As it turned out, more SEALs went in harm's way that night than were deployed at any one time during the entire Vietnam War. We had a lot riding on this one."

The Iraqi oil platforms were rigged up to explode, U.S. intelligence reports suggested. One of the platforms could load 1.6 million barrels of oil onto tankers in a single day. If it was blown up, the disaster would be twelve times worse than the *Exxon Valdez* oil spill—to say nothing of the economic losses. There were political stakes, too: at the time it was thought that oil revenues could be one of the main sources of income for a new, democratic Iraq, and these funds would offset the need for the United States to sink taxpayer dollars into the country.

"I had visions of our SEALs being blown off the terminal at the last minute and into a sea of burning oil," recalled Admiral Harward. "We could do nothing but watch the gigantic oil slick that would blot the northern end of the Gulf from the Shatt al-Arab waterway to the Kuwaiti border. Eventually, it would work its way east and south and foul the Saudi desalinization plants."

For the critical off-shore attacks, the SEALs would be supported by the Special Boat Teams. There has always been a bond between the SEALs and the "boat guys," the Naval Special Warfare specialists who drove the eleven-meter, rigid-hull inflatable boats (RHIBs) and the sleek and fast sixty-five-foot Mark V patrol boats. This relationship goes back to when detachments from Boat Support Units One and Two, the forerunners of the current Special Boat Teams, deployed to Vietnam with SEAL Teams One and Two. They drove SEALs to work right after dark and came back for them just before sunrise. And sometimes, when the SEAL squads found themselves with more Viet Cong than they had bargained for, the boat guys "came in hot" and took them out of harm's way.

Two nights prior to the night of the operation, the SEALs' mission was to conduct reconnaissance and gather intelligence, to boost the odds that the SEALs and other allied forces could capture Iraq's key oil facilities at the beginning of the invasion a few days hence, and to capture them before they were blown up. Again, the two offshore platforms were the key facilities and would be the most difficult to secure. The recon SEALs were traveling about thirty feet underwater in two Mk VIII SEAL delivery vehicles or SDVs. They were "riding wet," wearing wet suits and fully exposed in the water in the free-flooding SDVs, breathing air from the mini-sub's on-board air supply. The SDVs' lighted displays flashed digital images of sonar and GPS coordinates.

After a two-hour underwater journey in their mini-subs, the SEALs briefly surfaced as they neared their targets. The platforms were lit up like Christmas trees, and the vast complexes were each strung out over nearly two miles of ocean. The SEALs already had lots of intelligence to plan their actual assault, from overhead imagery to construction and mechanical schematics, but they needed to inspect the platforms themselves. As any SEAL will tell you, there is no substitute for close-up "eyes on a target."

"We pulled up to the outboard loading platform pad and tied the boat off to one of the platform legs," recalled one of the SEALs on the mission. "After we tied up the boat we came up under the platform and went to work. We took a lot of pictures and made notes about the latticework and access wells. And we listened a lot. We wanted to get an overall impression of their activity and alert status, and to see if there were any obstacles in making the platform boarding from surface craft."

"This was a good operation for us," one SDV pilot reported. "We had a good GPS fix before we made our dive, and my navigator took me straight to our platform. The Gulf is a strange place. Three months later and the temperature there could have been in the low eighties. Cool water is better. It usually makes for better visibility. As it was that night, we could see about twenty feet."

Of the two offshore platforms, MABOT (Mina al-Bakr Oil Terminal) was clearly the most active. Right up until the invasion began, there was a constant parade of tankers at MABOT. In the weeks leading up to hostilities, a full complement of four tankers were often seen at MABOT, as if Saddam wanted to pump as much oil as possible before the invasion. This was the last gasp of the corrupt UN oil-for-food program, which Saddam Hussein had managed to use to his own advantage, politically and militarily. If this facility alone could not be taken intact and fell victim to intentional sabotage, the environmental disaster would be huge. On the positive side of the ledger, MABOT alone could create billions of dollars in oil revenue.

The Khawr al-Amaya Oil Terminal (KAAOT) was a smaller facility with less capacity. It then operated at a capacity of some two hundred thousand barrels per day. KAAOT was deliberately blown up by the Iraqis during the Iran-Iraq War, at a huge environmental cost to the area. Repairs had been ongoing to this offshore terminal, but many international oil shippers still questioned its safety. Yet its potential economic benefit to the postwar recovery of Iraq was substantial. And like MABOT, it remained capable of an environmental disaster.

"One of the problems was its sheer size," recalled one of the SEALs on the MABOT operation. "Picture if you can four platforms connected by a latticework highway some twelve miles out into the Persian Gulf. The first is an inboard platform used as a helo platform to offload personnel and supplies. The second one, some three hundred meters farther out, is the first loading platform. It's as long as a football field and can handle two tankers, one on either side, for loading. The third, another loading station, is another three hundred meters out from there. Both the loading platforms are crammed with plumbing and holding tanks for servicing the tankers. The forty-eight-inch pipelines come out of the seabed and up to these platforms. The last platform, again some three hundred meters from the second refueling station, is the berthing and living quarters. Sitting on this platform is a four-story building. It's a huge platform—the whole facility was huge. That's why we, the force who was to board the platforms, were going to be a large one—at least large for a SEAL special operation."

For two hours, the teams of SDV reconnaissance SEALs snuck around the bottom of the huge MABOT platform, inspected the below-the-water sections of the structure for mines, and discreetly took above-water pictures and video. Recalled one of the SEALs, "It was pretty quiet, but the platforms themselves were pretty well lit. We stayed in the shadows underneath; they never knew we were there."

The good news was the SEALs couldn't find any explosive charges positioned underwater on the platform. But there were many critical spots above water they couldn't see, and they could not rule out the possibility that they were rigged to blow.

Before they left the Iraqi MABOT oil platform that night, the SDV SEAL recon team leader took a chance. He expected to be a member of the assault team on the platform a few days later, and he noticed a perfect place to access the structure—a ladder leading out of the water straight up onto the structure. He swam over to the ladder and quietly climbed up a few steps to check if it was secure. It was.

The SEALs then vanished into the water.

AT 10 P.M. ON March 20, 2003, armed with the intelligence gathered on the reconnaissance mission, Lieutenant Chuck Forbes and three groups of SEALs were drifting peacefully under a starlit sky in three eleven-meter RHIBs, holding their positions just three hundred yards away from the MABOT oil-tanker-loading platform, waiting for the order to strike. The Iraq War was about to begin.

Lieutenant Chuck Forbes was an experienced SEAL platoon commander. He had been around the teams for a while, and then some. He was a mustang officer, which meant he had prior enlisted experience. In the planning for this coordinated operation—a mission to secure the Iraqi oil export infrastructure intact—it became apparent that the MABOT terminal would be the most important and perhaps the most dangerous of the five targets, consisting of two offshore oil complexes and three land-based pumping stations. The smaller KAAOT oil platform would be attacked by another SEAL element and the SEALs' close allies, the Polish GROM. The task group commander had wanted one of his best men on the MABOT platform. Forbes was selected to lead the SEAL force against this key installation. He was chosen for his leadership skills as well as his operational experience.

Forbes had grown up in Naples, Florida, and enlisted in the Navy shortly after high school. After boot camp, he received orders to BUD/S, where he graduated with Class 130 in 1984. He had two deployments as an enlisted man before being accepted into a Navy educational program that sends outstanding sailors back to college on their way to becoming commissioned officers. It took Forbes a little over two and a half years to complete his four-year degree—in nursing. He was commissioned as an ensign in the Navy Nurse Corps, a former Navy SEAL in a largely female community, perhaps the only one ever. For the next three years, he attended to his nursing duties at Balboa Naval Hospital. In the early 1990s, an oversupply of Navy nurses and an exodus of officers from the Teams allowed Forbes the opportunity he had been looking for. In 1994, he returned to the Teams and began operational training for duty as a platoon officer. This was his third deployment since his return to the Teams.

While the MABOT oil platform complex was a difficult and dangerous target, it was still the kind of leadership challenge that a SEAL officer waits his whole career for. As a former enlisted man and Navy nurse, Chuck Forbes had simply waited longer than most. And he would have to wait a while longer as yet another team of SEALs were to perform a final underwater recon of the two offshore platforms.

Some 250 Navy SEALs and allied support personnel were poised to strike this platform, the nearby KAAOT platform, and three onshore oil pumping stations. They included allied Polish GROM Special Forces, British Royal Marines, U.S. Marines, and a host of allied support aircraft overhead. But they were being ordered to hold their positions, so all the pieces of the complex assault could be moved into place for the simultaneous attacks on five targets. All had to be taken by surprise at the same time.

While their brother SEALs closed for their simultaneous raids on oil pumping facilities ashore, two SEAL assault elements moved into position to attack the offshore terminals. The moon was not yet up, but the terminal was brightly lit up, and the three rigid-hulled craft were trying to stay just outside the bubble of illumination thrown out from the series of platforms that constituted the terminal. The boats were heavily laden with SEALs and their support personnel.

"We can't stay here much longer, sir," Chief Jim Collins said to Lieutenant Chuck Forbes. Collins was in charge of the SEALs' three-RHIB flotilla. "And if we get any closer, they're sure to see us. Hell, they may have already seen us."

This was the exact situation that Forbes had feared and tried to avoid. He glanced at his watch; he could feel the element of surprise slipping away. Aboard his little fleet of three boats were forty-nine souls—thirty-one SEALs, twelve Special Warfare Combatant Craft crewmen, two Navy EOD techs, two interpreters, an Air Force combat controller, and himself. Forbes was responsible for all of them.

"Screw them!" muttered Lieutenant Forbes. He wasn't cursing the Iraqis. He was furious at his commanders several layers up the chain of command, who still wouldn't let the SEALs move forward.

"We're compromised!" radioed Forbes to his commanding officer. "We need to hit this platform now!"

The SEALs were ducking down trying not to be seen, but they were starting to drift into the illumination bubble of the structure's floodlights. The SEALs wore green jumpsuits and body armor stuffed with ammunition, and black balaclavas over their faces. By now, Forbes was sure they'd been spotted. SEALs usually like to attack very fast, but tonight they were like ducks floating dead in the water. They'd wanted to approach the plat-form by sneaking up to the target underwater, but against their advice, the mission planners put them in open, exposed surface craft so the SEALs' movement and timing could be coordinated by radio with the other pieces of the assault.

"We gotta wait ten minutes," said the mission commander over the radio. In the sky above, spotters in U.S. aircraft were relaying real-time intelligence into the SEALs' earpieces on the radio network, counting off the fortified positions, machine-gun nests, and sandbags on different points of the complex. The SEALs' boats were drifting so close to the platform, Lieutenant Forbes recalled, he could see Iraqi figures running around on it. "I could see one guy who looked like he was surrendering waving a white handkerchief or something, but we couldn't be sure."

Planning and rehearsals for MABOT and KAAOT were built around intelligence that the oil terminals were staffed by civilian oil workers with a token security force, just like the onshore pumping facilities. The SEALs were supposed to first secure the valving that controlled the flow of oil to the terminals to prevent the oil workers from venting crude into the Gulf. Once the pipelines, valving, and storage tanks were secured, the assaulters would then move to clear the terminal of any Iraqi personnel. Plumbing first, then people. That was the plan right up until they approached the attack launch window. But in the last forty-eight hours, U.S. intelligence had detected an ominous development—the Iraqi oil workers manning the platform, it seemed, were replaced by heavily armed elite Republican Guard troops, the most feared unit in Saddam's military. It was assumed that they would fight to the death. The intelligence reports had them aboard the offshore platforms with heavy weapons, RPGs, and crates of explosives.

"This really shook us up," Chuck Forbes said. "I had visions of us moving to the valves and some Republican Guard dude sitting on the platform with a detonator in his hand, waiting for us to get close to the explosive charges on the pipelines. I talked it over with some of my senior enlisted men, and they concurred. So I took it up to Captain Harward, who then commanded the SEALs on the eve of the Iraqi invasion. He readily agreed. At the eleventh hour, we decided to take out the opposition first, then secure the infrastructure."

The SEALs were operating under liberal "rules of engagement." They were free to shoot anybody doing anything other than surrendering. By now, the SEALs were sure they'd been spotted by someone on the MABOT platform. It was time to move. Forbes took a deep breath and turned to his special boat team chief. "Let's do it, Chief. Take us in hard."

"Stand by to run in on step," Chief Collins said quietly into his lip microphone. In the other two craft, the coxswains acknowledged the order and passed a warning to those embarked in their boats. "Hang on, everybody," Collins said in a conversational tone. "Stand by . . . and hit it!"

There was a growl as six turbocharged engines quickly revved to full power and bellowed in unison. All three boats flew across the top of the water toward the MABOT platform. The roar of the engines canceled all conversation, yet Forbes whispered aloud to himself, "Oh please God, let us get on that terminal before they have time to react." The "pucker factor" was through the roof. The SEALs assumed that at any moment their fragile boats could be ripped apart by heavy machine-gun fire or rocket-propelled grenades. Or the oil terminal could erupt in a fireball and take them with it.

The SEALs' plan was simple: gain footholds on the platform, take control of the Republican Guard troops as fast as possible, race to at least a dozen critical nodes and chokepoints on the structure where explosives were probably rigged up, and stop them from being blown. If the SEALs couldn't move fast enough, it was possible that the last thing in their lives they'd ever hear would be a small primary detonation, followed by a gigantic fireball.

In the lead boat, Lieutenant Forbes aimed his assault rifle's laser pointer at the platform's access ladder so the boat pilot could guide them in. The boats reached the edge of the platform. The SEALs quickly scaled the ladders, fanning out toward preassigned spots on the platform. In the distance, Forbes could see groups of Republican Guard troops clad in oil-worker uniforms freeze in their tracks, shouting something the SEAL couldn't understand. Other Iraqis were waving, and others were diving to the floor.

Relieved, Forbes thought they were surrendering. But then he heard it. It was the last sound on earth he wanted to hear, and it erupted from somewhere deep in the bowels of the MABOT oil platform. It was the distinct sound of a muffled explosion. Forbes braced himself for what he assumed would be the last moment of his life. But nothing happened, and he never found out what the noise was.

Forbes recalled, "We swarmed over that housing complex as fast as we could get from the RHIBs up to the platform level and to the main structure. With the Republican Guard now in place, our ROEs were very liberal and for good reason. If there was any sign of noncompliance by an Iraqi or one of them made a sudden move, like he was reaching for a detonator or even a cell phone, we had authorization to shoot to kill. Any sudden movement was all it took for them to earn themselves a bullet. Really, we didn't know what to expect; we were ready for anything.

"When I say things could have gone a lot worse, I mean a whole lot worse. They were very well armed. We found AK-47s, RPGs, antiaircraft guns, even SA-7s—the Russian-made heat-seeking antiaircraft missiles. And a ton of explosives. While most of us dealt with the Republican Guard, the search teams found charges made up to sections of the pipeline and the valving. They were not primed or wired up, but the charges were in place. It took a while to find all of it. From the time we went aboard until we had the terminal secure was about an hour and a quarter."

"We treated those Iraqis really well while the search teams moved about the facility," recalled one of the SEALs on the operation. "They were bound and gagged, but we drug out a stack of mattresses for them so they wouldn't have to lie on the steel decking. We were so relieved that they didn't put up a fight, we were downright nice to them." Chuck Forbes praised his task force planners and his platoon SEALs. "They deserve a lot of credit, for getting that many people aboard the terminal that quickly. The Iraqis seemed to know we would come sooner or later, but were clearly surprised at how quickly we were on them."

"It was as if they just didn't want to die for Saddam," mused one SEAL. "That, or destroying their nation's oil export capability was just not in them. It was as if they were just going through the motions—doing just enough to make it look like they were going to fight or blow the terminal, but their hearts weren't in it."

By the time Forbes's SEALs had cleared the berthing and living platform, they managed to round up twenty-three Iraqi Republican Guardsmen. To their relief, all of the priming charges and detonators were still in their packing crates. After declaring the facility secure, Forbes called in the U.S. Marine security force that would hold the terminal while the coalition forces occupied Basra and pushed northward for Baghdad.

At the KAAOT oil platform, the Polish GROM commandos enjoyed much the same success as the SEALs on MABOT, although there was not the same presence of the Republican Guard, nor were there the caches of weapons and explosives. With the taking and securing of the offshore terminals, along with coastal and inland infrastructure, the vital oil export capability had been made safe for the Iraqi people.

The SEALs, the GROM, and their support elements suffered no loss of life, and only a few combat wounds, that night of March 20–21, 2003. All five objectives, including the onshore oil pumping stations, were secured with minimal damage to the installations and no environmental consequence.

Shortly after American armored columns set off from Kuwait to Baghdad, another group of SEALs and GROM commandos seized another important piece of Iraqi infrastructure, the Mukarayin hydroelectric dam, located some sixty miles northeast of Baghdad on a tributary of the Tigris River.

The success of the SEALs' lightning raids on the Iraqi oil and hydroelectric facilities prevented an environmental disaster, furthered U.S. political, military, and economic ends, and helped achieve the objective of quickly toppling Saddam Hussein.

IN 2006 AND 2007, a detachment of U.S. Navy SEALs played a critical role in a pivotal campaign in the Iraq War: the Battle of Ramadi, the capital of strategic Anbar Province. The SEALs' experience in Ramadi serves as a vivid microcosm of their experience throughout many battles and engagements of the long conflict. At the start of the battle, al-Qaeda terrorists and their insurgent allies had conquered much of the province, established a parallel government in many areas, and were in the process of forging a radical Islamic caliphate in the region, terrorizing local sheiks and inflicting atrocities and fear upon the population. When the battle was over, U.S. forces allied with Iraqi army, police, and tribal sheiks had recaptured most of the province and ushered in an era of fragile relative stability that largely endured until 2013.

The Battle of Ramadi was one of the fiercest extended campaigns of the Iraq War. For insurgents and foreign jihadis yearning to make a name for themselves, Ramadi was the Terrorist Super Bowl. For the SEALs it was a bloody, epic experience of land combat, urban warfare, and full-spectrum special operations. In the spring and early summer of 2006, the American and allied Iraqi forces were dug in at three main bases around the strategic Sunni-dominated provincial capital of Ramadi: Camp Ramadi; Camp Blue Diamond, at Hurricane Point on the banks of the Euphrates on the northwest side of Ramadi; and Camp Corregidor, a besieged outpost on the eastern side of the city. These bases supported a number of smaller strongpoints scattered across Ramadi, including a very brave and embattled company of Marines at the Government Center outpost in central Ramadi. Next to Camp Ramadi was an installation referred to as "Shark Base," where many of the SEALs were stationed. All were under the threat of continual attack, and most took fire on a daily basis. The Marines at the Government Center fought off continuous attacks.

The insurgents had all but confined the Army and the Marines to their bases. Most patrols were made in force and usually resulted in contact. The insurgent grip on the city and the province also threatened the traditional authority of the Anbari tribal leaders. At this point there were really few options left for the Americans and their Iraqi army allies in Ramadi. It was becoming increasingly evident that they either had to drive the insurgents from the city or be forced to hunker down on their bases and in their bunkers, and watch the insurgent presence continue to escalate. It was unclear just exactly how they would rid the provincial capital of these insurgents, but they now realized that it would take a major effort to drive them out.

In the Battle of Ramadi, the SEALs had three interconnected missions: to train Iraqi military and police personnel, to conduct sniper missions, and to execute direct-action operations targeting terrorist and insurgent leadership. Throughout the battle, the SEALs reported to their own chain of command, but they also worked closely with an Army brigade commander responsible for the Ramadi "battlespace," and with the Army, Marine, and Air Force troops assigned to the brigade task force he commanded.

In May 2006, there were some twenty-one major tribes in the greater Ramadi area. Only six of these were friendly to the Americans; the rest were hostile or, at best, sitting on the fence. The people of Ramadi were caught in the middle. The tribes and the people knew there was a fight coming, and they were waiting to see who was going to be the winner. That month, there was a change in the American military leadership in Ramadi and a new leader stepped into the role of the commander of the Ramadi area of operations, U.S. Army Colonel Sean MacFarland. He was most experienced with armored units and held a master's degree in aerospace engineering from Georgia Tech.

MacFarland had an offhand, self-deprecating manner like that of a Jimmy Stewart or Gary Cooper, something the SEALs in Ramadi picked up on immediately. Along with an easygoing and approachable demeanor, he brought solid experience to Ramadi. He was a counterinsurgency veteran, having worked in the footsteps of highly regarded Colonel H. R. McMaster in the northern Iraqi city of Tal Afar. He also brought with him a number of seasoned veterans, what one Army officer called the Tal Afar mafia.

There were two battle plans on the table. The "Fallujah model" called for a full-on assault—a single operation. As one Army officer put it, "We would just line up shoulder-to-shoulder and push the bastards west into the water." The "Tal Afar model" was more subtle. It was a modified inkblot strategy that called for a rolling assault—taking the city one neighborhood at a time. No one, it seems, wanted a solution that would demolish a major Iraqi city and draw the negative media attention that attended the battle for Fallujah in late 2004, and a large number of refugees.

"To some extent," explained the new brigade commander, "the final plan for Ramadi was one born of necessity. Ramadi is significantly larger than either of the other two Anbari cities. We simply lacked the overwhelming force to achieve a Fallujah-style offensive operation." The SEAL task unit commander in Ramadi, a Lieutenant Commander named Jack Williams, became a critical, value-added force for Colonel MacFarland in the Battle for Ramadi. The SEALs and the Ramadi task unit, their role in the brigade battle plan and their participation in the Battle of Ramadi evolved as the battle unfolded. In the overall scheme of things, they were a small element and their operational portfolio did not require that they go out into the streets and fight in the way the Army and Marine, infantry and armor, were going to be asked to fight. Jack Williams saw this as an opportunity to do what he had come to Ramadi to do—to make a difference.

Williams recalled, "We were to train the Iraqi army scouts and make them better soldiers. We were also to conduct tribal engagement and to make ourselves useful to the brigade commander. But I had a great deal of latitude in the disposition of my task unit and in executing those orders. When Colonel MacFarland arrived, he was tasked with the job of taking Ramadi. I think he saw his job as twofold. First, he had to execute his battle plan, which became one of pushing out into the city and establishing outposts—to reclaim Ramadi, step by step. Second, he had to engage the local tribes and encourage them to work with us against al-Qaeda. When I learned the Army and the Marines were going into the streets to take back Ramadi, I told Colonel MacFarland, 'Sir, what can we do to help?' He basically wanted one thing from me; he wanted me to kill insurgents. So he incorporated the SEALs in his battle plan in that role. We joined the battle by helping to establish the combat outposts."

Establishing a combat outpost in insurgent-held Iraqi territory was a dangerous, complex, and dynamic venture with a lot of moving parts. From the Army and Marine point of view, it was a difficult but proven counterinsurgency tactic. For the insurgents, it was an in-your-face push that moved the line of battle farther into their territory. For the SEALs, it was an offensive operation that allowed them to use their direct-action skills to best advantage.

In early June 2006, the SEALs in Ramadi were poised to strike the enemy in a way they had not done in their forty-five-year history: as a sustained direct-action force dedicated to supporting conventional troops in retaking a major urban area over a battle lasting many months. The focus of SEAL operations would be to support the 1st Brigade Combat Team, 1st Armored Division of the United States Army in the battle to retake Ramadi. The order of battle on the eve of this struggle pitted four American Army battalions, one Marine battalion, and two Iraqi army brigades against an unknown and fluid number of entrenched insurgents. All told, there were some 5,500 Americans and 2,300 allied Iraqis going into the Battle of Ramadi and a Navy SEAL task unit with some thirty combat-ready SEALs.

The battle began on June 17 with two combat outposts (or "COPs") being stood up simultaneously in the southwest and southeast sides of the city. A third outpost was established on June 18 in the southeast sector near Camp Corregidor. These respectively were COP Iron, COP Spear, and COP Eagle. These initial COPs were designed to block insurgent infiltration activity from the south. It took several days of fighting and building to seize and harden each of these three outposts and turn back the inevitable insurgent counterattacks. Over the course of the next seven months, thirteen COPs and many Iraqi police stations were established, then defended on a daily basis.

SEALs were involved from the beginning in nearly all of these operations. "The build-out was a seventy-eight-hour mission with the first forty-eight hours the most critical," said Army Captain Mike Bajema. "I had to plan for rest breaks for all the engineers, builders, and drivers. The actual mission began with getting the security package in place and that started with the Navy SEALs."

"We had gone in a few nights earlier to do our own recon of this COP site," SEAL Lars Beamon said of the COP Falcon operation. "It was one of our few maritime operations we conducted in Ramadi." COP Falcon was the first joint combat operation conducted by Captain Bajema and the SEALs. There would be more. Their relationship from the beginning was typical of the Army-SEAL bonding.

"We inserted by Marine rigid-hull inflatable boats (or 'RHIBs') off the Habbaniyah Canal and patrolled in on foot," Beamon said of the SEAL recon. "Once ashore, we conducted a careful reconnaissance. We made a point to move about an extended area so we wouldn't tip off the exact location of the new COP. Yet we were able to get some good IR [infrared] pictures of the COP buildings. This was a pretty dangerous area, down on the edge of the al-Mualemeen District. When we got to the neighborhood where the COP was to be sighted, we found two guys in the street planting an IED. We shot them both. Then we completed our recon and got back to the boats."

After dark on the evening of June 24, an expanded SEAL element was again inserted by Marine RHIBs. The SEALs, their EOD techs, a Marine ANGLICO (Army/Navy Gunfire Liaison Company—a Marine air controller), interpreters, and their contingent of scouts quietly made their way to the objective. "We didn't have to wait long to make contact," Beamon said, "as we killed an armed insurgent on the way in. It let the Army know we were on the job. We went into the target house, a tall three-story residence. The scouts and the terps [interpreters] explained to the residents what was coming, and they took it stoically. These are people used to war. We set up shooting perches in the upper stories, and called Mike to tell him we were in place. Our job now was to provide a sniper overwatch along the routes that the lead Army elements were going to use to get to the COP location."

As Army Captain Mike Bajema and his people were moving in, Lars Beamon and his SEAL snipers were moving out. Sometimes the SEALs will leave an overwatch element at the COP, but not this time. They patrolled out from the new COP, past the infantry and armor, to set up sniper overwatch positions along the routes they determined the insurgents were most likely to use to mount a counterattack. "Once the SEALs got in place on the outer perimeter," Mike Bajema said of the Falcon operation, "we were as prepared as we could be to defend the battlespace around the COP. Now the Army engineers, the Navy Seabees, and the support elements rolled into Falcon and started a forty-eight-hour, nonstop build-out of the site. Trucks began to ferry equipment and building materials in from Camp Ramadi, often taking sniper fire as they came and went. They dropped more than two hundred twelve-foot concrete-wall T-barriers, set up two thousand meters of concertina, and strung God knows how many feet of electrical wire."

Inside the perimeter of the new COP, engineers and soldiers alike worked at a fever pitch, laying concertina wire, moving supplies, and carrying sandbags amid the drone of generators. Outside the outpost grounds, between the new concrete-barrier walls and the tanks and Bradley fighting vehicles on the outer security perimeter, soldiers patrolled the streets, carefully searching the upper stories of buildings for insurgent activity. Skirmishes happened often. Overhead, F/A-18 fighters and drone aircraft circled the new COP while keeping human and electronic eyes on the surrounding area. At night, there were AC-130 gunships overhead as well. And well outside the foot patrols and the armor, Lars Beamon and his snipers kept watch on the streets of Ramadi, specifically along the routes the insurgents might take to get to those building COP Falcon. This was a relatively new game for the SEALs and the insurgents, and a learning experience for both.

SEALs train for this and know how to conduct sniper over-watches, but usually in the context of covering a single special mission like a raid or an assault, or to protect a conventional force patrolling in the street. They also train for these over-watch operations with the idea that they would be shooting from positions unknown to or hidden from the enemy. And for the most part, their training is for short-duration missions. Now they were going out sitting in shooting positions from two to four days at a time.

The insurgents knew the city and the neighborhoods far better than the Americans. If they didn't intuitively know the location of the best and most likely shooting perches the SEALs might use, they quickly learned. They also learned how to move in the dead spaces where they were screened from their enemy's fields-of-fire, both from the COPs and from the sniper overwatch positions. For the insurgents moving on the street, these were life-and-death lessons in trigonometry; those who didn't master this skill, or were careless or less nimble, were quickly killed. They learned from bitter experience just how ac-complished these sailors with sniper rifles could be. The SEALs took a grim harvest of insurgents in Ramadi, especially early on during the building of the initial COPs. In many cases, each of these insurgent deaths was a mistake on their part—and a les-son learned. They soon began to understand the methods and tactics of these skilled urban shooters and to develop counter-measures.

"Shooting these guys was very easy at the beginning," a SEAL sniper said. "They were careless. One time two insur-gents were heading for a new COP on a motor scooter. One had an AK-47 and the other an RPG launcher. One of our snipers got them both with a single round—one shot, two kills. But it gradually got harder. It was a Darwinian thing. We shot most of the stupid ones, and that left the smarter ones to evolve and survive. But we evolved as well. And even for some of the hard-core fighters out there, all they had to do was make one wrong move at the wrong time or take one too many chances. When they crossed an open area, we might not get the first one, but we'd get the second—and the third if they were dumb enough to try it. We're SEALs and we were very good when we got to Ramadi. For the insurgents in Ramadi or who came to Ramadi, they became good or died in the process."

This was the first time in their history that SEALs had operated in direct and continuous support of conventional forces in combat, and the SEALs had nothing but admiration for the soldiers and Marines. SEAL Lars Beamon said, "The bravest and noblest men in uniform are those Army specialists and Marine lance corporals. They're our most courageous and patriotic fighting men, and they're out there day in and day out. For many of them, it's becoming year in and year out. We SEALs are honored to call them brother warriors."

The respect went both ways. Army Captain Mike Bajema said, "When those SEALs first came back into COP Falcon, some of them had been out there seventy-two hours on sniper overwatch. They were hot, hungry, and dead tired. Still, they would join a line of Army soldiers to carry endless supplies of sandbags to the rooftop fighting positions before eating and resting. Now that's what really makes them special—they don't act special. We worked with the SEALs of Charlie Platoon of SEAL Team Three in Ramadi for those first three terrible months, and they were always there for us. And we'd go anywhere in Ramadi to help them out if they got in trouble. They were our brothers.

"I think what made us a big fan of the SEALs," Bajema continued, "was the respect they showed us. Here we were a company of dogface Army soldiers, and here they were these BTFs—big tough frogmen. I think they secretly liked it when we called them that. Right from the start, they treated us as equals, and they'd been in the battlespace longer than we had. They had tremendous intelligence assets and resources, and they went out of their way to share information with us."

Colonel MacFarland, the Army brigade commander during the Battle of Ramadi, recalled, "I didn't know what to expect—I had never worked with SEALs before. The SEALs were exactly what I had hoped for and in some ways, even more. They were very interested in working as a part of a team, as well as being incredibly good at what they do. I won't say that their competence surprised me, but I wasn't sure just how adept sailors with guns would be in a counterinsurgency fight. It quickly became evident to me that they were tremendously effective and versatile warriors who were highly motivated and thoroughly professional. I can honestly say that with the exception of our Army SOF components, I had never worked with warriors of such high caliber. My soldiers and junior leaders came to respect the Big Tough Frogmen and would do anything for them. The losses that the SEALs suffered in Ramadi cemented that relationship in my mind. Anyone who shed blood, sweat, and tears in Ramadi with us will always be a part of our band of brothers. The names of those SEALs lost in action were inscribed on our [division] memorial plaque in Germany when we got home. We like to think that this respect was mutual."

Colonel MacFarland explained of the SEALs, "I gave them a wide range of missions, all of which they accepted without complaint and executed superbly. They helped us establish our COPs by sending in small kill teams to help seize the buildings we wanted, then they moved out to positions outside the perimeter in order to disrupt any enemy counterattack. At COP Falcon alone, they killed some two dozen enemy fighters in those first twenty-four hours as they attempted to disrupt our COP construction. We also employed SEALs as part of our counter-fire fight—inserting them near historic enemy mortar points of origin. The enemy feared snipers above all else and for good reason. Our sniper teams were incredibly lethal. I tried to put them in the seams of the battlespace—places where they could go because of the small size of their patrol elements and the places where we couldn't go. They also helped us to train new Iraqi army and Iraqi police recruits at Camp Ramadi after they returned from their basic training, raising the competence level of the soldiers and policemen in Ramadi to well above their peers elsewhere. Finally, the SEALs conducted targeted raids on individuals on which they had developed target folders. They shared their intel with us at intel-fusion and targeting meetings, and were happy to pass over targets best suited to conventional forces."

A driving force in the emerging Army/SEAL partnership in Ramadi was the need for precision shooters in the battlespace and the ability of the SEALs to shoot. It requires talent and a great deal of time and training to create a combat sniper. And it's not just a matter of pure precision shooting. There are the issues of patrolling through hostile territory to get into position, and adjusting to the difficult and imperfect conditions found in a combat environment. This is not match shooting; it's combat sniper work—precision, long-range killing. Competition shooters often make poor snipers, and a good sniper is sometimes an average marksman in long-range match competition. A military sniper must be able to shoot, but he has to be a functioning member of the patrol and the combat team. As a group, the SEAL snipers are among the best combat snipers in the world. In short, the SEAL Teams have talent and the weapons, and their shooters are given a lot of time on the gun.

The most successful SEAL sniper in Ramadi was also one of the greatest snipers in U.S. military history. He was a burly, affable, soft-spoken Texan, a former professional cowboy named Chris Kyle.

Petty Officer First Class Chris Kyle was the lead sniper in Charlie Platoon and in Ramadi. He was also a shooting legend in the SEAL Teams. This was his third combat tour and second tour as a platoon sniper. On his first tour he was among the first SEALs in Iraq, serving as an M60 gunner on a SEAL desert patrol vehicle during the pre-invasion operations to take and hold the Iraqi oil terminal junctions and petroleum pumping infrastructure. On his previous rotation, he was one of the SEAL snipers in the Battle of Fallujah in 2004. He was wounded there and was still being treated for that injury, but that didn't keep him from taking part in the Battle of Ramadi. It was in Ramadi that his shooting took him into the ranks of the military sniper elite.

Chris Kyle grew up on a working ranch in Texas. He was used to hard work, dealing with cattle, and shooting on the open range. A solid work ethic is a key ingredient for a sniper. It's a difficult and hard-won skill. Eyesight, nerve, judgment, and patience all have their place in the making of a sniper, but to be *really* good, you have to work at it. SEAL sniper training is a popular and sought-after school for the platoon SEALs, yet few SEALs who enter this training realize just how hard they must work. It's a mentally and physically demanding calling.

Kyle spent a year on the professional rodeo circuit as a saddle bronc rider before joining the Navy at twenty-four for SEAL training. He graduated with BUD/S Class 233. Kyle was a big man, perhaps six-two and 230 pounds. Big shooters have an advantage with a higher human-mass to weapon-mass ratio. He had a soft manner, almost shy in explaining his duties. Early in this tour in Ramadi he worked with the Marines at Hurricane Point and trained Iraqi army scouts at Camp Ramadi. But when the battle started, he became a pure sniper in a very target-rich environment.

"We did a lot of shooting," Kyle said of those initial months of the battle. "And there were a lot of bad guys to shoot at. I have to credit my teammates with a lot of my success. They spotted for me and provided the security, so I could focus my time and attention on the gun." When asked which gun, he answered immediately. "Three hundred WinMag [.300 Winchester Magnum]. The best sniper rifle in the world—a Remington 700 rifle set up for the .300 WinMag cartridge. It's a great round with a lot of punch—very heavy and a very flat trajectory. Its only downside is the noise and the flash. Even with a suppressor it has a loud bark, and it's hard to mask the muzzle flash. It lets everyone know exactly where you are."

In addition to the favored .300 WinMag, the SEALs also use two other sniper weapons. One is the SR-25, a semiautomatic rifle designed by Eugene Stoner and manufactured by the Knights Armament Company. The Navy calls it the Mk 11 Mod 0 Sniper Weapons System. This rifle uses the NATO 7.62 match-grade ammunition, combining this superb round with an accurate, semiautomatic capability. It's a true sniper weapon that enjoys a great deal of utility in a standard firefight. The other is the Mk 12 Mod X Special Purpose Rifle, a "sniperized" version of the M4 rifle. It's a highly accurate version of the standard SOF rifle with a sound suppresser and scope. The Mk 12 also has the option of frangible .556 ammunition that has applications for reducing collateral damage in long-range shooting situations. All of these weapons have their place in mission-specific environments. Some of the SEAL snipers favored the SR-25 in Ramadi since they seldom made a shot longer than four hundred yards, well within the capability of the weapon, but with the ability to quickly engage multiple targets. But most preferred the absolute precision and stopping power of the .300 WinMag. It's a punishing weapon, for shooters as well as those on the business end. It has a brutal recoil, and SEAL snipers, perhaps more than other military snipers, put a lot of rounds through their weapons. The SEALs also have a .50-caliber sniper rifle in the inventory, but it had limited use in Ramadi. The SEALs have recently been looking at the next generation of special-purpose sniper weapons in the .338- and .408-caliber range.

"You can always tell one of our snipers," a SEAL platoon chief said. "They walk around with one shoulder lower than the other. That's why it sometimes helps to be a bigger guy; you can take the recoil from all those training rounds without developing an unconscious flinch-type reaction in anticipation of the kick."

Chris Kyle estimated the number of enemy kills he made in Ramadi at well over a hundred, plus the nearly twenty he accounted for in Fallujah. "These were the confirmed kills," he said in his quiet, precise way, "the ones who were shot dead on the street. We don't count the ones who managed to crawl off and probably bled out. But I didn't have too many of those." His longest shot was "a little over 1,400 yards," Kyle estimated.

In Ramadi, the insurgents came to know and fear Chris Kyle. They called him *al-Shaitan Ramadi*—the Devil of Ramadi. There was a reward out for Kyle and his fellow snipers. Al-Qaeda in Iraq (AQI) would pay twenty thousand dollars to any insurgent who could kill a sniper and bring in his weapon. It has been estimated that something close to eleven hundred insurgents were killed during the Battle of Ramadi. A third of those have been credited to the SEAL snipers.

The insurgents also had snipers, and some of them were highly skilled shooters. Most of them use the Dragunov sniper rifle, a dated, semiautomatic 7.62 mm weapon of Soviet design.

Neither the weapon nor the insurgents who had them were in the same league with the SEAL shooters and their guns, but they were still a threat for the Americans patrolling the streets of Ramadi. Ninety-six Americans died in the nine months during the Battle of Ramadi. All but two of those were soldiers and Marines. One wonders how many more would have been killed in the battle without the grim harvest of snipers like Chris Kyle. After Kyle left the SEALs in 2009 to devote more time to his family life, he wrote a bestselling book and was in the process of writing another when, tragically, he died at a Texas shooting range while trying to help a fellow American veteran of the Iraq War.

The rules of engagement, or ROEs, are the restrictions and guidelines that govern military activity and combat engagements, and they apply to the snipers as well. These rules can vary from region to region and situation to situation. In Ramadi, the ROEs allowed for an enemy combatant to be taken under fire if he was armed and moving with tactical intent, or clearly presented a threat to soldiers or civilians. There were finer points to these ROEs, but their purpose was to allow for the killing of bad guys while safeguarding innocents. An insurgency is a battle for the people, and killing an innocent civilian may do far more harm than the good that comes from killing an insurgent who deserves a bullet. This becomes a complex issue with the insurgents hiding among the people. In the early days of the battle, when the first combat outposts were being established, there were more than enough targets in the form of armed insurgents moving tactically in the streets.

In Iraq, it was SOF policy regarding snipers that for every enemy KIA or WIA there had to be a statement from the shooter and a statement from a witness, usually the sniper's shooting partner or spotter. Accompanying these statements there had to be an operations summary that outlined the tactical and operational conditions that accompanied the shoot. Given the heavy toll of human life taken by the SEAL snipers in Iraq and Ramadi, these measures were put in place to protect the shooters should there be a question of impropriety.

It really all comes down to the decision of the man on the gun. He must decide whether a shooting is justified—as to whether the man in the reticle of his scope qualifies for and deserves a bullet. It also goes much deeper; it goes to the heart of the shooter—his instincts and his judgment, even his compassion. Few warriors have the opportunity and burden, on an ongoing basis, to end a human life. To a man, the SEAL snipers in Ramadi were serious and professional about their duties, and proud of the fact that they had not exceeded their moral or statutory boundaries.

THE FIRST SEAL TO die in battle in Iraq was Marc Lee, who made the ultimate sacrifice on August 2, 2006, in Ramadi.

By the first week in July 2006, Ramadi was blazing hot. The temperature often reached 120 degrees, even as the battle raged for control of the streets. Five new combat outposts had been established as the Americans and the Iraqi army edged into the city, the last of these being COP Grant on July 5. The insurgents now knew the strategy of the Americans and were determined to stop them. But another player was beginning to show itself on the battlefield of Ramadi—the Iraqi police. The Americans and the new Iraqi army continued their push into the city, reclaiming neighborhoods and doing what they could to keep them insurgent-free and safe. The tribal sheiks began to see that the Americans were serious—that they were successfully executing their battle plan and beginning to bring parts of

Ramadi under control. So the tribal leaders began to encourage their young tribesmen to join the fledgling police force in Ramadi. On July 17, the Jazeera Police Station was established. This was one of the few functioning police stations in Ramadi since the insurgency began, but others would follow.

The COP strategy, as SEAL Commander Collin Green put it, was to "isolate, seize, clear, hold, and build." In Ramadi, in July, "hold" was the operative term. Once the new COPs were put in place, they had to be held and defended. To do this, the area around each COP had to be purged of insurgent elements and the streets had to be patrolled—to keep them clear of insurgents and to let the people know that those streets now belonged to the Americans and the Iraqi army. The plan called for the police to be the most visible force in the streets, but that would come later. Most of July was taken up with patrolling the streets around the COPs and beating back insurgent counterattacks. In addition to keeping patrols on the streets, there were cordon-and-search operations to flush out the last of the insurgent presence in the cleared areas. It was on one of these operations that the first SEAL was killed in action in Iraq.

During the early morning hours of August 2, an element of Navy SEALs and their Iraqi scouts were engaged in a cordon-and-search operation. They had launched from COP Falcon. The SEALs were working with the Army, who had roads blocked with tanks and Bradleys. The drill was to set up security around a dwelling, knock on the door, and ask to search the premises. This permission was granted in most cases, with the scouts conducting a thorough search. They were looking for insurgents and evidence of insurgent presence. The first block of their assigned area was cleared without incident. On the second block, the SEALs in security positions were taken under fire by small arms, including sniper fire. The insurgents had chosen this day to come out in force against the American and Iraqi patrols.

A sniper round narrowly missed Ryan Job (pronounced Jobe), a first-tour SEAL from Seattle, Washington, but the bullet glanced off a wall and into the top of his weapon, sending shrapnel into his eyes and face. One eye was destroyed by the impact and the other severely damaged. Job's brother SEALs—including Chris Kyle—quickly gathered around him to provide cover while the platoon corpsman gave him aid. Among those who moved to cover Job and lay down a base of protective fire was Petty Officer Marc Lee. The operation quickly shifted from a cordon-and-search operation to getting Ryan Job safely off the battlefield.

The element commander, Lieutenant Lars Beamon, called for a casualty evacuation. A Bradley fighting vehicle came from COP Falcon for Job while the SEALs and scouts set up a security perimeter. Job was evacuated to the hospital on Camp Ramadi without further incident. The rest of the patrol returned to COP Falcon to rearm, as most of their ammunition was expended in the exchange. Everyone in the patrol was shaken by this serious wounding of Ryan Job. Out on the streets, the insurgents pressed their attack and several Army patrols were in heavy contact. ISR (image surveillance reconnaissance) from orbiting F/A-18s reported several bands of armed insurgents moving in the area where Job was hit.

With the other Army patrols in contact and the enemy mounting counterattacks, Beamon made a difficult decision. He ordered his SEALs to gear up and get ready to return to the fight. They were tired and battle-weary, but that's why SEALs train to such a rigorous standard. The F/A-18s orbiting over the city kept them advised of the insurgent locations. The Bradley fighting vehicles carried the SEALs back to the vicinity where

Job was wounded, and they continued their patrol. This time they were without their Iraqi scouts. Their operating procedures called for them not to go into the battlespace without Iraqis in their patrol element, but this time the scouts did not want to return to the fight. The streets of Ramadi had turned extremely dangerous, and it was the first time many of them had seen a SEAL go down. With Army patrols in close contact, the SEALs returned to the battle without their scouts. Their mission now was to support the soldiers engaged in this street battle.

The SEALs cleared one house from which they had received insurgent fire, and moved to the next. As this structure was being cleared, an enemy sniper from across the street found himself with a clear shot at an American in a second-story window. His target was U.S. Navy SEAL Marc Lee, from Hood River, Oregon. Petty Officer Marc Lee, twenty-eight, was struck in the head and died instantly.

Lieutenant Lars Beamon called in the Quick Reaction Force and made his second under-fire extraction. This time there was no rush to get a teammate to the hospital; the platoon medic told his officer that their teammate was dead. In the blink of an eye, the first Navy SEAL died in Iraq, on the battlefield in Ramadi.

The death of Marc Lee just hours after the wounding and blinding of Ryan Job shook the entire task unit. Indeed, Army Captain Mike Bajema and his Bulldogs felt the loss of a brother as well; Charlie Platoon had conducted many of their operations from COP Falcon. These casualties came thirteen months after eleven SEALs were killed in Afghanistan during Operation Red Wings. There had been no deaths in that intervening period.

"The loss of wounded Ryan Job and the death of Marc Lee was hard on everyone," SEAL Jack Williams said. "It was hard on me. But those soldiers and Marines went out there every day, and we'd have felt terrible sitting back cleaning our guns or reviewing target folders while they were fighting for their lives on the street. It wasn't an option for us. We were in Ramadi and we wanted our guns in the fight; we wanted to make a difference. Beamon did his duty—what was expected of him as a combat leader. Anything short of that would have been dereliction of duty." Reflecting on his decision to go back out, Beamon said: "I think about it a lot—every day in fact. I'd give anything to have Marc back. I'd give anything for Ryan to see again. It was my decision, and I'll live with it. I'm not sure I could live with myself if we'd stayed in the COP while our Army brothers were out there in close contact. That's just not who we are."

A short time later the Ramadi SEAL compound known as Shark Base was renamed Camp Marc Lee.

The decision to take to the streets in support of the Army and Marines in the Battle of Ramadi had largely been that of Jack Williams. As a SEAL task unit commander he did not have to support Sean MacFarland and his brigade battle plan in this way. He might well have directed his SEALs to continue in their roles as trainers and continue to only provide the Army and Marine battalions with intelligence and targeting information—not shooters. Or he could have restricted his operations to those traditionally considered "special," keeping his SEAL operators poised for high-value targets, such as key foreign fighters and known al-Qaeda operatives. Instead, he said to Colonel Sean MacFarland, "Sir, what can we do to help?" and he meant just that.

In late September, Squadron Three and the task unit at Ramadi were looking at their last few weeks in Ramadi before their scheduled rotation back home. A SEAL task unit from SEAL Team Five was to relieve them and take up the battle.

But those at Camp Marc Lee were beginning to notice some changes. Days went by without taking fire on the base. Over at Camp Corregidor, the SEALs were still taking fire daily; they still couldn't go to the toilet or to chow without a helmet and flak jacket, but there was a feeling that things were getting better. The COP strategy was beginning to pay dividends; those neighborhoods around the COPs were gradually being purged of insurgents and insurgent violence. Tribal policemen were seen more frequently on the streets near the COPs. In these areas, there were the beginnings of normal life and commercial activity. There were still districts within the city fully under insurgent control, but their influence was shrinking.

On their final operation, the Corregidor SEALs from Squadron Three were scheduled for a thirty-six-hour overwatch operation. The SEAL squad on the operation was already packed and ready to leave for Camp Marc Lee on the first leg of their journey home. The other platoon squad was back at Camp Corregidor staging their equipment for redeployment. A contingent of scouts from the 1st Iraqi Brigade at Corregidor were with the SEALs. The mission was to set in two mutually supportive overwatch positions to protect a platoon of soldiers stringing razor wire along the rail line that ran across the southern outskirts of the city. By this stage of the game, it was a familiar drill—familiar, but they were taking nothing for granted this close to the end of the tour.

This was not the first time they had operated in this sector of the Mala'ab District, and the SEALs knew it to be dangerous turf. The insurgents were still active, both offensively and in planting IEDs. Only two weeks earlier two soldiers with an improvised explosive device clearance team had been killed in action nearby. It was from this sector that insurgents gathered to launch attacks on COP Eagle. The last SEAL operation into this area had led to a forty-five-minute firefight and six enemies KIA, with the SEAL element maneuvering in a running gun battle for half a mile to get back to COP Eagle.

On this operation, the SEAL elements patrolled out from COP Eagle on foot and seized two buildings that were about a block from each other. Lieutenant Sean Smith was in command of the easternmost overwatch while Lieutenant (jg) John Seville had the other. Seville was the Delta Platoon assistant officer in charge or AOIC. There were twelve to fourteen men in each element. A third of them were SEALs, the rest were Iraqi army scouts. They settled into their positions at about 3 P.M. on September 29. Both had excellent fields of fire to protect the soldiers who would be working along the rail line after sunup. The scouts dealt with the building residents and held security on the lower floors while the SEALs set in shooting positions on the roof of the third floor. They were exposed on the roof but protected by a short, stucco-and-concrete wall that bordered the open, flat roofs. In order to make their shooting positions more secure, they cut holes in the wall with loop charges. Their positions were tactically solid, and both overwatches were in communication with the tactical operations centers at Camp Corregidor and COP Eagle.

"As soon as it became light, we knew it was going to be a day of fighting," John Seville recalled. Seville was a former enlisted Marine who took his degree and commission at Texas A&M. Instead of returning to the Corps, he opted for a commission in the Navy and for SEAL training, graduating with BUD/S Class 247. This was his second combat rotation in Iraq as a SEAL. He had spent time in Ramadi in the summer of 2005. Seville had begun this tour with his SEAL squad working out of Shark Base, before it became Camp Lee. With the persistent insurgent presence in south and eastern Ramadi, he had been detailed to

Corregidor to help Sean Smith and the 1-509th—the storied Army Band of Brothers.

"The insurgents were out moving early, scouting our position," Seville said of the mission. "We shot two of them and the other overwatch to our east, shot one. Then civilians began blocking off the streets with rocks and trash to warn people away. By midmorning, vehicles began pulling into view. Someone inside would send a few rounds at us, and then they'd drive off. These were long-range, drive-by shootings. At noon, we got hit by an RPG that dusted up everyone inside our building."

From his command position in the other overwatch some 150 meters to the east, Sean Smith could see the RPG strike and knew Seville's overwatch was under siege. So was his position, for that matter. He also trusted John Seville as a capable combat leader; he and his SEALs, all seasoned veterans, could hold their own in a fight.

While their position on the roof at Seville's overwatch was reasonably secure from direct fire, they were vulnerable to indirect fire and rockets—grenades and RPGs. Into the early afternoon, both positions were under steady insurgent fire. It seemed that on this day the insurgents in the Mala'ab were focusing on the SEALs rather than the soldiers stringing wire along the railroad. The SEALs watched as individual insurgents tried to maneuver close to the overwatch buildings. They were able to drive most of them off, but not all. At Seville's overwatch, one of them managed to get in close, under the guns of the SEALs on the roof. It was from there that the insurgent managed to hurl a grenade up to the roof. It was a well-placed toss.

U.S. Navy SEAL Petty Officer Mike Monsoor was on one knee behind the covering wall. The grenade hit Monsoor in the chest and dropped in front of him. He leaped to his feet, then dropped to the ground to smother it with his body. John Seville was a few steps to Monsoor's right and another SEAL was less than five feet to his left. Both Seville and the other SEAL were in prone shooting positions; they had no room or time to maneuver away from the grenade to avoid the blast.

Mike Monsoor was the only one of the three who could have dived away from the grenade that had landed in their midst. In the split second it took for Monsoor to assess his position relative to the vulnerable position of his brother SEALs, he made a fateful decision. He dropped on the grenade and absorbed the blast with his body armor and his body.

"He never took his eye off that grenade," John Seville said of Monsoor's last courageous act. "His only movement was down toward it. He undoubtedly saved my life and probably saved Danny's [the SEAL to Monsoor's left] as well. We owe him."

Mike Monsoor was twenty-five and on his first combat rotation as a SEAL. He was handsome, just over six feet, easygoing, and a devout Catholic. On his first try at SEAL training, he failed, only to return more determined than ever. The second time he succeeded. At SEAL Team Three, his quiet presence and cheerful willingness to carry "the pig" (the M48—the current version of the 7.62 squad medium machine gun) made him a well-liked and respected member of his platoon and his team.

This was not Mike Monsoor's first courageous act on the battlefield. On May 9, not quite a month after the task unit had arrived in Ramadi, Monsoor and his element were engaged in a firefight with insurgents. Moving through the streets, one of his teammates was taken down by enemy fire. Shot through the legs, he was exposed and immobile in the street. Monsoor raced to his side, shooting on the move. Enemy rounds kicked up the dirt around him. He helped to drag the fallen SEAL to safety while continuing to lay down suppressing fire with his M48. For his courage under fire, he was awarded the Silver Star.

After the grenade exploded, there was a great deal of confusion. Seville and Danny, on either side of Monsoor and the smothered grenade, both absorbed shrapnel, mostly in their legs. Neither was able to walk. Three of the scouts on the roof, shaken at the sight of three SEALs down, ran from the rooftop down into the safety of the building. The fourth scout went fetal, unable to move from fear and shock. They needed help, but the blast had also knocked out the SEAL radios. John Seville crawled to the immobilized scout and took his radio, calling to the other overwatch position to say he had men down. Bobby, the fourth SEAL on the roof, was only slightly wounded. He managed to drag Monsoor away from the building wall edge to assess his wounds, but there was little to be done; Monsoor was still alive but his breathing was labored. Calling the other scouts back onto the roof, Seville managed, with some difficulty, to get them to take up positions and return fire.

At the other overwatch, Sean Smith and his SEALs were already on the move. Knowing that Seville and his team were hit and needed help, they broke from their position. The second they stepped into the street, they were in a running gunfight as they battled their way to Seville's location. The fire was so intense that Smith's Iraqi scouts refused to leave the protection of their overwatch building. Smith and his four SEALs didn't have that luxury. There were brother SEALs in trouble, and they had to get to them.

"It seemed like it took them forever to get to us," Seville said of the wait, "but time was distorted for me. It was probably inside of ten minutes. That was pretty quick considering they were moving under fire. I was experiencing a lot of pain and a lot of frustration. And I remember how badly Mikey was hurt. I knew we had two priorities until the medevac arrived—win the fight and keep Mikey alive. Bobby, a professional warrior to the core, had taken Mike's M48 back to the wall and was firing down on the enemy."

Lieutenant Sean Smith called for a casualty evacuation and two Bradley fighting vehicles were dispatched from COP Eagle. The three wounded SEALs were rushed back to the COP and on to the hospital at Camp Ramadi, but it was too late for Mike Monsoor.

"I met Mikey at communications school during our predeployment training," Seville said, recalling his friend. "He was from Garden Grove—your typical Southern California boy. He drove a Corvette and always had a laid-back, I'm-cool, no-sweat attitude. But that was just on the surface. He took important things seriously. When we were working, he was always there, one hundred ten percent and all business, yet in a nice way. When Mike was around, things seemed to go better—easier. Mike came from a very loving family, and when you met his folks, you could understand how he came to be such a likable guy and such a great team player. Y'know, he never made a big deal about it, but somehow he always managed to go to Mass on Sunday. He was our best and now he's gone. We all miss him."

At the division headquarters of the U.S. Army 1st Armored Division in Stuttgart, Germany, there's a dedicated field of honor with a planting of evenly spaced trees. By each tree is a small monument with a plaque to honor a fallen member of the 1st AD. Among these soldiers are two sailors—two SEAL petty officers: Marc Lee and Mike Monsoor. Mike Monsoor became the fifth Navy SEAL to receive the Medal of Honor, and the second since 9/11. He alone among these SEAL heroes chose to give his life in a willful and deliberate act to save his teammates. Monsoor had options. He could have turned away from that grenade and saved himself. His teammates might not have died from the blast. Mike Monsoor chose instead to protect his teammates. *Greater love hath no man than this, that a man lay down his life for his friends:* John 15:13. This was Mike Monsoor.

The Navy SEALs and their colleagues in the American military and intelligence services and in the Iraqi police and military helped the tribes and people of Anbar Province overthrow al-Qaeda and establish a period of fragile relative stability in the area that endured for more than five years. Tragically, in the wake of the American military pullout in 2011 and the continued political paralysis of the Iraqi government, large sections of Iraq fell back into insurgent and terrorist control in 2013 and 2014.

Whatever the future holds, nothing can detract from the valor of the SEALs and the many other Americans and their allies who fought and died to try to bring stability to Iraq and Afghanistan.

IN 2009 TO 2012, three near-flawless SEAL operations—two rescues of a total of three Western civilians from Somali kidnappers, and the killing of Osama bin Laden, a man directly tied to the murder of more than three thousand civilians—made news headlines in such a spectacular fashion that they pushed the traditionally secretive SEALs into the stratosphere of global media attention. In particular, these high-profile operations thrust into fame a Naval Special Warfare (NSW) component known as "Development Group," whose existence is almost never acknowledged by the Department of Defense (DoD). One of the very few exceptions is a public Navy document dated May 9, 2014, titled "NSW Command Brochure," which identifies the location of the Naval Special Warfare Development Group as Dam Neck, Virginia, and tersely describes the duties in this way: "Manages RTD&E [research, testing, development, and evaluation]; develops maritime, ground and airborne tactics for NSW and DoD-wide application." *

With each of the three operations, a common element was how routine they were for the SEALs, in large part because of their training. As one former SEAL observed, "In the SEAL teams, you train and train, you go over things over and over, you do a ton of dry runs. When the door gets blown and you go in, you don't even think. It's just second nature and you resort to muscle memory and your training. You know that the guy right next to you is doing the same thing, so there's not much thinking involved, just acting and reacting."

The first operation was the rescue of Richard Phillips, captain of the merchant ship MV *Maersk Alabama*, on Easter Sunday, April 12, 2009. Phillips was tied up, with an AK-47 pointed at him from inches away by one of three Somali pirates who were holding him hostage inside a small enclosed fiberglass lifeboat being towed to calmer waters in the Indian Ocean by the American guided missile destroyer USS *Bainbridge*. Ransom negotiations had stalled. At the White House, newly elected President Barack Obama monitored the operation closely.

Three SEAL snipers positioned on the warship's fantail peered through the night scopes of their sniper rifles. The SEALs waited until a moment appeared when all three pirates were simultaneously visible, and they squeezed their triggers. Three shots hit their targets less than one hundred feet away, and three pirates were killed. The hostage was freed. Many details of the flawless operation were made public, creating a global media sensation. Tom Hanks starred in a movie about the incident that grossed over $200 million in worldwide ticket sales.

---

* Publisher's note: The DoD's Office of Security Review requested the redaction of further references in this book to NSW's Development Group, to which the authors have complied.

THE SECOND MISSION, DUBBED Operation Neptune Spear, occurred two years after the rescue of Captain Phillips, on May 2, 2011, and was by far the most famous special operations raid in history. The climax of a ten-year manhunt led by the CIA, the operation resulted in the killing of Osama bin Laden at his compound in Abbottabad, Pakistan. The raid was run from a U.S. base at Jalalabad, Afghanistan, and was personally monitored by video feeds by President Obama and his officials from the White House Situation Room and by CIA Director Leon Panetta from CIA headquarters at Langley, Virginia.

The raid included twenty-three SEALs (or twenty-four, according to some accounts), a Pashto translator, and a dog—a Belgian Malinois combat dog named Cairo. "We think we found Osama bin Laden," the SEALs were reportedly told a few weeks before the mission, "and your job is to kill him," prompting cheers from the SEALs. The SEALs had the rare luxury of weeks of sustained planning and as many as one hundred assault rehearsals for the takedown on specially built mockups of bin Laden's lair. In many ways it was a fairly straightforward compound raid, the kind that SEALs have a lot of experience with and train for routinely, stressing speed, surprise, planning, and flexibility.

The whole operation took less than forty minutes. When one of the helicopter pilots began losing control of his craft while descending toward bin Laden's compound, he expertly conducted a soft crash-landing that safely deposited the SEALs to the site. The emergency landing required the SEALs to improvise and reshuffle their plan of attack, but managing this kind of last-minute crisis was also routine for the SEALs, who smoothly and methodically cleared the guesthouse and the first and second floors of the compound, advancing toward the third floor, where they found bin Laden. "What SEALs are good at is what I consider pickup basketball," explained one SEAL. "We all know how to play the game. You hear the saying in the teams, can you shoot, move, and communicate? We all know how to shoot, we all know how to move efficiently and tactically, and we can communicate clearly. So when something goes sideways we're able to play that pickup basketball and kind of read off each other."

Al-Qaeda founder Osama bin Laden and several other adults were killed in the raid, including bin Laden's twenty-three-year-old son and the courier who inadvertently led CIA analysts to pinpoint the location of bin Laden's hideaway. A dozen children were unharmed. Bin Laden was reportedly killed just eighteen minutes after the helicopters landed, dispatched by a shot to his right forehead and one or two rounds to his chest.

Bin Laden may have had at least fifteen minutes to contemplate his fate in the darkness of his bedroom after the early noises of the SEALs' arrival at the compound, which was soon punctuated by gunfire (the SEALs weapons were silenced but at least one man in the compound fired a burst from an AK-47), people wailing, and the noise of doors being blown off. Bin Laden might have initially thought a Pakistani force was entering the compound, but this impression probably shifted abruptly to total uncertainty. Because of the position of his window and the layout of the compound, if bin Laden looked outside, he wouldn't have seen the SEALs or their aircraft on the ground. Bin Laden could have reached for his nearby AK-47, but he didn't. The SEALs had the authority to capture bin Laden if he made conspicuous moves to surrender, but he didn't. The world's most notorious terrorist had neither the courage to fight nor the brains to surrender, or he may have simply figured his time had come. His fate was sealed. The SEALs collected

SEALs emerge from the water during tactical warfare training, 1986. The SEAL in the foreground is armed with an M-16A1 rifle, the standard of the day, equipped with an M203 grenade launcher. *(National Archives)*

Final resting place of one of four SEALs who died in Grenada operations, 1983. *(U.S. Navy)*

Panama, 1989: four Navy SEALs died in the operation to disable dictator Manuel Noriega's getaway Learjet. The damage is from rocket and small-arms fire by the SEALs. *(SEAL Museum)*

Members of SEAL Team Four aboard ship prior to the Panama operation. *(U.S. Navy)*

Everybody inside, outside! A squad of SEALs on a HALO—high altitude, low opening—training jump leave the rear of a C-130. *(U.S. Navy)*

From the sea. A squad of SEALs emerge from the water, still breathing on their Underwater Breathing Apparatus. *(U.S. Navy)*

SEALs leapfrog ashore. A SEAL fire team crosses the shoreline, two moving, two covering. *(U.S. Navy)*

A Special Boat Team RHIB, having delivered its SEALs to the side of a target, breaks away. *(U.S. Navy)*

A Special Boat Team gunner engages a training target with a twin .50 caliber mount. *(U.S. Navy)*

Two Special Boat Team 82-foot MK V Special Operation Craft. *(U.S. Navy)*

A Navy MK V Special Operation Craft, a 50-ton, high-speed boat, is squeezed into a C-5 Galaxy aircraft from the 349th Air Mobility Wing, California, 1999. *(National Archives/U.S. Air Force)*

GOPLAT entry. A SEAL fast ropes onto an gas/oil platform as part of a VBSS exercise. *(U.S. Navy)*

An MH-53J Pave Low delivers SEALs to a target. *(U.S. Navy)*

VBSS—vertical boarding search and seizure. A SEAL squad fast ropes from an H-60 onto a target ship. *(U.S. Navy)*

(Right and below) In January 2002, an American special operations element led by Navy SEALs entered a key al-Qaeda strongpoint at the Zhawar Kili cave complex in Afghanistan. They discovered thousands of crates of ammunition and explosives, and millions of pounds of ordnance, along with training facilities, jail cells, and safe-house accommodations. (*U.S. Navy*)

A SEAL platoon operating in Iraq pauses for a photo amid a collection of captured weapons and photos of Saddam Hussein and his son Uday. *(Courtesy of Michael Branch)*

SEALs inspecting a shipping container at Iraq's Mina Al Bakr Oil Terminal (MABOT) at the outset of the invasion of Iraq. Their quick action helped to prevent an environmental disaster. *(U.S. Navy)*

Navy SEALs Matthew G. Axelson, Daniel R. Healy, James Suh, Marcus Luttrell, Eric S. Patton, and Michael P. Murphy in Afghanistan. With the exception of Luttrell, all were killed on June 28, 2005, while supporting Operation Red Wings. *(U.S. Navy)*

SEAL Team Three, Charlie Platoon, in Ramadi, Iraq. The unobscured faces are, from left, Marc Lee, Ryan Job, and Chris Kyle: all fallen SEALs. Marc Lee was the first Navy SEAL to be killed in Iraq. *(U.S. Navy)*

(Right and below)
The very affable and
very brave petty officer
Michael Monsoor, on
patrol and at work in
Iraq, 2006. *(U.S. Navy)*

Adm. William H. McRaven takes command of U.S. Special Operations Command, Aug. 8, 2011. McRaven assumed command from Adm. Eric T. Olson and was the ninth commander of USSOCOM. *(Photo by Mike Bottoms, USSOCOM Public Affairs)*

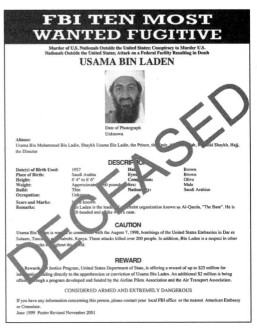

The aftermath of OPERATION NEPTUNE SPEAR, 2011. *(U.S. Department of Defense)*

In a now all-too-familiar ritual, a SEAL senior chief petty officer pounds his SEAL Trident into the coffin lid of a fallen brother—in this case that of Special Warfare Operator 3rd Class Denis Miranda, killed in action in Afghanistan, September 2010. *(U.S. Navy)*

A new cycle starts as the next generation of Navy SEALs begin their journey. Here BUD/S trainees crawl through the cold surge and surf toward to their SEAL instructor. They will become Navy SEALs, but first they must become Navy frogmen. *(U.S. Navy)*

as much evidence from the house as they could carry, put bin Laden in a body bag after taking photos and DNA samples, and safely withdrew toward the base in Afghanistan before local Pakistani security forces had a chance to respond to the site. Ever since the SEALs began their antiterrorism mission in 1980, they had rehearsed and conducted thousands of compound raids and night raids on high-value targets, and that experience paid off in the bin Laden raid. For the SEALs, it was pure muscle memory.

When President Obama announced the death of Osama bin Laden, America rejoiced. Within days, after Vice President Joe Biden inadvertently revealed the involvement of the SEALs, they became the subject of intense worldwide fascination.

For the SEALs, it was a day at the office, a very successful one, but they then turned their focus on their next missions. Two of the SEALs involved in the raid later told their stories publicly, causing a whirlwind of controversy in the SEAL community and the media.

ON THE NIGHT OF January 25, 2012, Jessica Buchanan lay on a mat in an open field in Somalia, enduring her ninety-third day of captivity by a gang of local kidnappers. Nine armed gunmen slept just feet away from her.

The thirty-two-year-old American aid worker was suffering from an acute urinary tract infection that was triggering complications to her kidneys, and she had only sporadic access to medicine. She had spent three months outdoors, sometimes trying to sleep in torrents of cold rain and immobilized by pain. "They treated us like animals," she recalled. She thought she would soon be dead. Negotiations for her release and the release of her fellow captive, Danish relief worker Poul Thisted, were stalled.

"Please tell God that I need some help," Buchanan prayed as she gazed at a star she chose to represent her late mother. "We need to get out of here." She heard rustling noises on the edge of the camp. Suddenly, her captors were jumping to their feet and cocking their weapons. "Then everything exploded," she remembered. "Instant Armageddon. Gunfire broke out in every direction, and even the shock waves were terrible." Her mind was overpowered with a single sensation: "Oh God, oh God, oh God . . . I cannot survive this." Fearing that a rival gang was attacking the camp, Buchanan pulled a blanket over her head and thought, "Okay, well, this is it. This really is truly the end." Then she felt a hand grabbing her blanket and calling her name. She was shocked to recognize that it was an American-accented voice.

The SEALs appeared from the darkness, penetrated the camp perimeter, and achieved total surprise. In moments all nine kidnappers were dead and both hostages were safe. Buchanan later explained, "It was unbelievably hard and fast. I gained instant insight into why the SEAL teams are said to train with such intensity. The depth of violence in the attack hits you all the way down to the bones."

"Jessica!" a voice called. "This is the American military. We've come to take you home. You're safe." Those words, according to Buchanan, "were more beautiful than any piece of music I'd ever heard." A SEAL picked her up in a fireman's carry, trotted her away from the campsite, gave her medication, and placed her flat on the ground. The SEALs formed a protective bubble around her and lay on top of her as a human shield until the rescue helicopters landed. She felt as if "I was surrounded by magical heroes. They brought this terrible explosion of violence that popped the locks on our invisible prison. They reached in there and snatched us out alive—I couldn't see how, but I was impossibly alive—and there we were, getting the hell out of there."

Buchanan later explained what happened next: "I can't believe I did this, but I had a small, little powder bag that they had let me keep. And inside, I had a ring that my mom had made, and I thought, I can't leave it out here in the desert. And so, I asked him [a SEAL] to go back and get the bag for me. And, I mean, these men are just—they're incredible. I mean, he goes back out into a war zone, basically, to go get my ring." She added, "I don't start breathing until we actually lift up off the ground. And they hand me an American flag that's folded. I just started to cry. At that point in time I have never in my life been so proud and so very happy to be an American."

Soon, her father got a call from the president of the United States. "I have great news for you," he said. "Your daughter has been rescued by our military."

The SEALs "were heartbreakingly polite," Buchanan wrote. "They made special efforts to be kind, these athletic hunter-killers who had just taken out a camp full of armed men." The hostages were evacuated to an American base in Djibouti, and soon, before Buchanan had a chance to fully express her feelings or thanks to the SEALs, they were gone.

"They just vanished," Buchanan remembered. "They came out of darkness and disappeared back into it. I mean, it's incredible."

IN THE TURBULENT AGE since September 11, 2001, the U.S. Navy SEALs were used as never before. They succeeded in a wide spectrum of combat operations around the world and played a role in some of the most significant military operations of the era.

EPILOGUE

Today, on the day before they complete SEAL qualification training and become U.S. Navy SEALs, dozens of young SEAL trainees climb up a hill at Fort Rosecrans National Cemetery, overlooking the Pacific Ocean.

They pause to assemble amid the graves of fallen SEALs. Each of the SEALs-to-be carries a Ka-Bar knife specially engraved with the name of a different Naval Special Warfare member who was killed in action, and the date and name of the battle in which they fell. It is the student's responsibility to learn all they can about that person, to find their gravestone, and read aloud the teammate's name.

A guest speaker, often a former SEAL, addresses the students in a private talk that focuses on the heritage of Naval Special Warfare, and the personalities and character of individual SEALs the speaker might have known. The ethos of valor and sacrifice that is instilled throughout SEAL training suddenly becomes real when the students put names and faces to those values.

A sailor named Paul Coover wrote of the ceremony, "On clear days, visitors to Rosecrans can often see the Navy's boats, ships and aircraft operating near the horizon. On cloudy days, those missions—both training and live—are shrouded in a thick fog that envelops the peninsula. The carriers and rigid-hull inflatable boats, the planes and helicopters and people all working toward the same purpose then become invisible, but that doesn't mean they cease to exist."

The U.S. Navy SEALs have traveled far since their ancestor units were forged in the maelstrom of World War II. From the rich heritage and heroic sacrifice of the Naval Combat Demolition Unit sailors, UDT sailors, Scouts and Raiders, and OSS Maritime Swimmers who operated in the waters off Europe, the Pacific and Korea; to the SEALs who operated in the jungles of Vietnam, the battle zones of Grenada, Panama, the Persian Gulf, Iraq, Afghanistan and Africa, the mission of Naval Special Warfare has evolved from a narrow portfolio of demolition work and beach reconnaissance into a broad spectrum of maritime and "over the beach," land-based special operations, including the specialties of antiterrorism and hostage rescue.

The SEALs and other American special operation forces (SOF) have often faced an extremely dynamic landscape, both operationally and politically. As the Cold War peaked in 1961 and 1962, President John F. Kennedy ordered the Army, the Navy, and the Air Force to develop capabilities in unconventional warfare. This hastened the birth of the Navy SEALs, but it was not until 1986, when Congress directed the formation of the U.S. Special Operations Command, that SOF had a legitimate chair at the Defense Department table.

The new organization would be headed by a four-star commander in chief, or CINC, and would have parity, at least on the organizational chart, with warfighting commands like Pacific Command, European Command, or Central Command. The creation of SOCOM was an unpopular decision among the service components who have traditionally resisted elite units, and especially those elite units who seriously compete for talent and treasury. There was even resistance within the SOF components that were made to leave their parent service for duty under the fledgling SOCOM. Some senior SEAL commanders said they would regret the day that the SEALs left the protective skirts of the Navy; they said they would be awash in Army green as the smallest service component of the new joint command. But in recent years, there has been grumbling among some in the Army and elsewhere that SOF has become too SEAL-centric, in the wake of some highly publicized successful missions and SEAL officers taking top leadership roles within the Special Operations Command structure.

The SEALs and their forefathers have experienced many hard-fought victories. They have also endured tragedies, failures, and long stretches of combat inaction and periods of major drawdowns, like the years after World War II and the Vietnam War. Recently, the SEALs have also endured a spate of publicity about current operations that many SEALs and former SEALs find extremely uncomfortable.

Modern warriors must grapple with the threats of combat, battlefield wounds, adjusting to life back home, and illnesses like post-traumatic stress disorder, to name a few. The SEALs are no exception. Then there is the horror of witnessing comrades or civilians die in the course of battle, experiences that can enter the realm of the spiritual. One day in 2010, the year before he oversaw the raid that eliminated bin Laden, Admiral William McRaven, a career Navy SEAL, appeared at the door of an Afghan farmer whose sons were among five civilians accidentally killed during a raid by his men. "Sir, you and I are very different," McRaven said to the farmer. "You are a family man with many children and many friends. I am a soldier. I have spent most of my career overseas away from my family. But I have children as well, and my heart grieves for you. But we have one thing in common. We have the same God. He is a God who shows great love and compassion . . . I pray today that He will show mercy on me and my men for this awful tragedy."

Looking to the future of the SEALs, Vice Admiral Albert Calland III, former commander of Naval Special Warfare Command, argued in 2003 for an approach that stressed fundamentals in an age of complexity: "There are a lot of mission areas out there, and so what I'm doing is bringing us back to really focus on our core competencies: direct action and special reconnaissance. Those are the hallmarks of Naval Special Warfare and have always been our strengths from the time of the frogmen and Scouts and Raiders and the Underwater Demolition Teams. And with that, small unit tactics, flexibility and being able to operate in all environments, things that have really been the focus of what we've done well." He added, "What's in front of us now in my view is a very dispersed enemy that's spread across the globe and continuing to disperse even more. You've got to go in with a small force. You've got to be able to maintain the element of surprise and that really aligns well with Naval Special Warfare and everything that we do."

Why do men become SEALs? For some, the strongest impulses are the patriotic ones, to serve and protect their nation, and by extension their community and family. For others, these values apply, plus the ambition to perform at the most elite level of military special operations, and to prove themselves in the most challenging conditions. Some SEALs were inspired to join by a father or friend's experience as a SEAL, or even by a SEAL book or movie. Others are attracted by the camaraderie, the thrill of danger and the unknown, and the adrenaline rush of new operations, traveling the world, shooting weapons, blowing things up, and jumping out of airplanes. And getting paid for it.

For a sailor named Norman Olson, the inspiration was a vision he had one day in 1955 on a California beach. "I was aboard a ship and we'd been off the Korean peninsula and came back," he told us. "The ship was going out of commission and I was being transferred to another ship and I went over to Coronado because they had a class I had to take. And on the weekend, I was down on the beach, and I looked out and I saw a volleyball net. I saw a handful of studly guys in tan shorts. And, the other thing that perked me up, they all had very attractive women around, and they had a lot of beer. I didn't know who they were and I started asking, 'Who the hell are they?' And they said they're Frogmen. And I said, 'Hmm, sounds pretty interesting.' " He jumped ship to become a UDT member, and later a SEAL, and spent thirty years on active duty.

The story of how Navy SEALs died in the mountains of Afghanistan during Operation Red Wings in 2005 has been widely told in books and movies and by Marcus Luttrell, survivor of the incident. In 2011, the father of one of the fallen SEALs, U.S. Army Vietnam Veteran Daniel Murphy, had this to say about his son and the brotherhood he belonged to:

"I am the father of Navy SEAL Lieutenant Michael P. Murphy. He was a Navy SEAL who was killed in Afghanistan on June 28th, 2005, and as a result of those actions was subsequently awarded the Medal of Honor. Michael was like all of the other Navy SEALs that you've ever met. They're extremely unassuming. They're quiet, humble, incredibly brave men who do some of the most dangerous missions in the world. There's only 2,000 of them. They are an extremely tight, extremely closed-mouthed, extremely small community that watches over each other. When I had heard about the capture and killing of Osama bin Laden by a special operations team, they had not reported yet who was involved. I knew myself that it was the Navy SEALs just by the operation that took place, how it went down. It was no doubt in my mind that those were Navy SEALs, those were Michael's teammates." Murphy has also said of the SEALs, "These are brave souls, brave people. It's what's happening every day. Forget politics, forget policy, forget what you're doing, there are men and women out there that are willing to stand up and say, 'I will protect your right to say what you think, to practice your religion.' That's a great thing. And that's what makes this nation great."

There are traditions in the Teams that only members of their unique brotherhood share. Since 1970, every SEAL has worn the Trident. Poseidon, the god of the seas, wielded a trident that gave him the power to both create storms and calm the waters. At SEAL funerals, there is a tradition of teammates removing their Tridents and embedding them in the coffin of their fallen comrade. Retired Vice Admiral Joseph Maguire told us, "Being a SEAL and wearing the Trident, you come from a long line of people who've sacrificed greatly to get you to where you are. Nobody who wears the Trident today earned that reputation. They inherited that reputation from the men who came before them. And while you have the opportunity to be a SEAL, what you have to do is keep that reputation intact, and make it just a little bit better than when they pinned a Trident on your chest. At a SEAL funeral, you're not just burying a warrior. You're not just burying a teammate. You're burying somebody that you love, somebody that you know, somebody that you trained with. You know his family. You know his children. For those of us who wear the Trident, everybody refers to each other as brother. And that is not just an expression. That's how everybody feels about each other. Because my teammate is more important than I am."

The SEALs are entering a period of uncertainty now, as

America enters the post–Iraq War and post–Afghanistan War era. The scale and pace of combat may drop off or change substantially and the nature of the future missions of the SEALs and other American special operations forces is unclear. The missions of foreign internal defense and partner nation training, or helping other nations fight terrorism, especially in the Middle East, Asia, and Africa, may increasingly dominate the SEALs' work in the immediate future.

But as long as there is instability and war, there will be the need for special warriors like the SEALs to conduct direct-action, special reconnaissance, personnel recovery, hostage rescues, and antiterrorism missions. "We live in an extremely dangerous and difficult world," observed Admiral Maguire. "And we have people who are willing to sacrifice everything for their country. I have no doubt in my mind that no matter where we as a nation go next, the first people in will be the SEALs."

For decades to come, there will be the need for individuals with the physical ability, durability, intelligence, mental toughness, moral maturity, personal ethics, humility, and patriotic devotion necessary to become U.S. Navy SEALs.

AFTERWORD

by Rear Admiral Garry J. Bonelli (USN., Ret.)
Chairman, Navy SEAL Foundation
Ninth Force Commander, Naval Special Warfare Command
Deputy Commander, Naval Special Warfare Command
Commanding Officer, SEAL Team Five
Frogman, UDT-12

*We asked Rear Admiral Garry Bonelli to contribute
the Afterword to this book because he exemplifies the
character and achievements of the U.S. Navy SEALs.
He has served the Naval Special Warfare community
for more than four decades.*

*Enlisting in the U.S. Navy in 1968, Rear Admi-
ral Garry Bonelli graduated from Basic Underwater Demolition/SEAL (BUD/S) training Class 51 in
Coronado, California. He made two ground combat
deployments in Vietnam as a Navy "frogman" with
Underwater Demolition Team 12. In 1974, Bonelli
became a member of the first reserve unit of Naval
Special Warfare.*

In 1976, while completing his master of science degree in mass communications, he received a direct commission in the Navy Reserve. Bonelli has served as the commanding officer of eight Navy SEAL reserve units. He was mobilized in 1990 in support of Operations Desert Shield and Desert Storm, and served as the commanding officer of SEAL Team Five. Bonelli is the only Reservist to ever command an active-duty SEAL Team.

In 2001, Bonelli was selected to serve as the deputy commander of Navy Reserve Readiness Command Southwest. In 2006, Bonelli was recalled to active duty again, and when selected to flag rank, served as the deputy commander, and then the ninth Force Commander of Naval Special Warfare Command.

Looking back on the late 1960s in America, a time many historians viewed as a period of social upheaval and change, I was an aimless urchin roaming the streets of the Bronx, New York City.

I knew nothing about U.S. Navy SEALs. Growing up in the big city, I looked at the accountants who lived in huge homes in nice neighborhoods in Connecticut and commuted to work in Manhattan. I thought accounting looked like a pretty good profession, so I played basketball at Pace University, and sometimes attended accounting classes. After two semesters, I flunked out.

It was 1968. I knew I was getting drafted. Vietnam came right in my face real fast. I talked with my dad and he said, "You know, if you go into the Air Force or the Navy you probably won't be in ground combat in Vietnam." I said, "That makes sense, but that's four years versus two years in the Army as a draftee." Two extra years was a lifetime for an eighteen-year-old. To make a long story short, I enlisted in the Navy, and went to the Great Lakes Recruit Training Command outside Chicago.

In Navy boot camp, I realized within twenty-four hours that there's the Almighty, and there's a Navy chief petty officer, and they're pretty close. This chief showed us an old grainy 16 mm film of guys scuba diving. It never dawned on me that the Navy would teach you how to scuba dive, so I raised my hand. The chief said, "Okay, kid, we're shipping you to Coronado." I said, "Coronado? What part of Vietnam is Coronado?" I took the car/pedestrian ferry across San Diego Bay before the bridge was built. It was paradise on the Pacific. I went to the beach and planted my feet firmly into the sands of the Coronado Silver Strand. When I looked up and down the mostly deserted beach, I thought, *Kill me, this is where I'm staying.*

However, my plan to stay out of ground combat in Vietnam failed. In fact, it failed twice. I was deployed in 1969, and then again in 1971. My first combat came sort of in a twisted way. We got to our command compound located on Da Nang Harbor, which was called "Frogville." You are issued your basic equipment load—your guns and your bullets and all that, and you put it all at the end of your rack (bed). That way, in the middle of the night, if you get called out, you can get all your gear immediately.

Suddenly there were flares going off and all types of noises. Somebody woke me up and my first reaction was to go to the foot of my rack to get my harness and my rifle. My seasoned frogman teammate told me, "Don't worry about that, leave your gear there."

"What do I need?" I said.

"Your bathing suit," he said.

"What are we doing?"

"We're going around the harbor to go surfing. We're looking for some Army guys that drowned, but we're then going surfing." So my first day in Vietnam I was on a surfboard. That's the truth.

I was fortunate to be part of the special operations community, both active and reserve, for forty-five years. The low point I can recall was post-Vietnam, during the mid-1970s drawdown. It was a morale buster because SEALs and frogmen were less valued. The powers that be thought that our country didn't need much in the way of special operations. It was a mistake, and we paid for it at Desert One during the aborted Iranian hostage rescue.

After Grenada and Panama, we've learned from our mistakes. That's why we have a joint unified special operations command in Tampa, Florida, led by a four-star admiral or general to standardize and professionalize all special operators and synchronize the missions they execute. It's a terrible fact of life; we learn more from our mistakes than we do from our successes. The SEALs today are better educated, better equipped, better resourced, and better led than at any time in our history.

In 1990, I answered a phone call on a Thursday night saying, "Bonelli, we need you and twenty-four guys here by tomorrow if possible." Desert Shield/Storm was kicking off. I said, "Yes sir!" We got called up, and ever since, the reserve component of Naval Special Warfare has been an important part of taking the fight to the enemy.

My proudest and most humbling moments were when I became commanding officer of SEAL Team Five in 1990, and eighteen years later, when Admiral Olson, then commander of the Special Operations Command, fleeted me up to be the ninth Force Commander of Naval Special Warfare Command.

People always ask me, "What does it take to become a SEAL?"

Today's training takes two and a half years. You get a kid who comes in the front door—and when I say the front door, only one in five young men gets to even start basic SEAL training known as BUD/S. Then you take all those ones that made it in the front door, and only one in four is going to graduate and become a U.S. Navy SEAL. Only the federal government could afford to make that type of national investment.

The average SEAL trainee today is usually a bit more mature, and more educated. They have the brains, the brawn, and what I call the "Rudy factor" (from the Notre Dame football movie). The heart! They'll never quit. The innate thread that runs through the teams since their inception back to World War II is that SEALs have hearts and minds that will never quit. They will never quit no matter what. SEALs are the type of professional warriors who get knocked down, get back up, get knocked down, get back up. That's the common thread. After multiple combat deployments, a SEAL is a warrior's warrior. But he's also learned to be a diplomat and a problem solver.

When people think of SEALs, they think of them kicking in doors during combat operations. That's true, but where our nation gets the most bang for their buck is with the diplomatic-problem-solving-type guy—the SEAL who can work with partners to expand their capabilities and their capacity to prevent wars and regional unrest. SEALs do a great job of building and sustaining relationships.

There's another innate trait SEALs have. It's a word that's not found in the English language: *teamability*. It's the ability not only to lead in a situation, but the ability to follow and contribute to the team and its mission.

Most military members wear some type of identifying patch or pin. With the Navy SEALs, it's called the Trident. The Trident depicts an American bald eagle perched on a Navy anchor, grasping Neptune's spear and a flintlock pistol. Wearing the Trident means everything to the guys. It's the most distinguishing emblem on their uniform or most any military uniform. You see a lot of American eagle images in our country, often with the bird's head held high, going full steam ahead. But on the SEAL Trident, it's one of the few times you'll see the American eagle with the head bowed. Why is the head bowed? It stands for humility. The best SEALs are humble warriors.

Since 9/11, I have a new group of heroes: the SEAL wives. They go through a lot and many of them have only known their husbands at war. These courageous women will never truly be appreciated for the sacrifices they make daily on behalf of our nation. The SEAL wives are the bulwark that keep our operators resilient and in the fight, time and time again. They bear the children who will raise their hands to defend our freedoms in the future.

My wife was the "first lady" of Naval Special Warfare for a number of years. Just prior to SEAL graduation ceremonies, my wife would make a point to meet the new spouses and the steady ladies of the guys graduating from SEAL training. She would tell them, "Believe it or not, ladies, during your time with these guys, they'll want to be with their fellow SEALs more than they'll want to be with you." You could see their faces registering disbelief. "You can either be a camper or a worrier," she'd say. "Campers take care of themselves, but worriers need a lot of attention. Your marriage will work better if you're a camper."

Any family will have their challenges. What's particularly challenging about our SEAL community is that our guys on average are gone 255 days of the year out of 365. They're in the fight, they're training for the fight, or doing some special training.

To help, SEALs and their families now enjoy and cherish the

benevolence of civilian, nonprofit support organizations such as the Navy SEAL Foundation, the SOF Care Coalition, and the NSW Family Foundation. Made up of mostly volunteers, these organizations help our teammates and their families during casualties, with educational support, transitions to civilian life, and the promotion of our rich Navy SEAL history and heritage.

In 2014, the Navy SEAL Foundation board of directors selected me as their chairman. If a SEAL is killed or wounded, the Navy is good about taking care of the family's immediate needs. Our SEAL Foundation ensures that the spouse is taken care of on an enduring basis, and the children of our fallen have their educational needs met all the way through college.

We advertise that for every dollar donated to the Navy SEAL Foundation, we give back 94 cents to our teammates and their families through a variety of meaningful and measured programs. That's a good return on investment.

If you're interested in helping support our SEALs and their families, I can't think of a better organization than the Navy SEAL Foundation.

For more information, please go to:

www.navysealfoundation.org

ACKNOWLEDGMENTS

We thank Carol L. Fleisher, Peter Hubbard, Steve Bass, Mel Berger, John Silbersack, Captain William Fenick, Senior Chief Joseph Kane, Nick Amphlett, Sharyn Rosenblum, Liate Stehlik, Andrea Molitor, Brian Barbata, Dave Davis, John McManus, Erasmo Riojas, Chip Maury, Tom Pitoniak, Jay Barksdale, Rick Kaiser, Garry Bonelli, Ruth McSween, and Mark Corcoran; the teams at HarperCollins, PBS, Oregon Public Broadcasting, and everyone who contributed to this book and the PBS special, especially the Naval Special Warfare veterans who helped us.

A very special thanks to Tom Hawkins, who reviewed our manuscript and made many valuable contributions and comments.

APPENDIX A

U.S. SPECIAL OPERATIONS COMMAND STRUCTURE

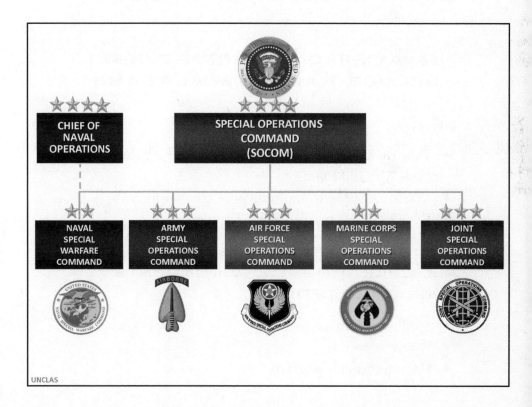

APPENDIX B*

NAVAL SPECIAL WARFARE COMMAND— MISSIONS AND STRUCTURE

NAVAL SPECIAL WARFARE (NSW) GROUPS 1 AND 2: SEAL TEAMS

SEALs

- Take their name from the elements in which they operate (Sea, Air, and Land)
- Maritime-focused, multipurpose combat forces
- Experts in the maritime environment

PLAN AND EXECUTE MISSIONS IN ALL OPERATIONAL ENVIRONMENTS, THREAT CONDITIONS

- Special reconnaissance
- Direct action
- Unconventional warfare

---

* Adapted from the NSW Command brochure: *http://www.public.navy.mil/nsw/news /Documents/ETHOS/Brochure.pdf.*

- Foreign internal defense
- Information warfare
- Security assistance
- Counter-drug operations, personnel recovery

INFILTRATE OBJECTIVE AREAS FROM

- Fixed and rotary-winged aircraft
- Tactical mobility vehicles
- Navy surface ships
- Combatant surface craft
- Submarines, undersea platforms

MAINTAIN A FORWARD PRESENCE
- Regional orientation
- Language skills
- Cultural awareness

Team patches of NSW Groups 1 and 2.

NSW GROUP 3 SEAL DELIVERY VEHICLE TEAMS

SEAL DELIVERY VEHICLE TEAMS

- Operate and maintain SDVs, DDS
- Sustained by underwater breathing apparatus
- Support clandestine reconnaissance, direct action and passenger delivery
- Replacing MK 8 MOD 1 SDVs with MK 11
  - Newer technology, greater payload
- Long-standing requirement for "dry" submersible
  - Evaluating dry combat submersible prototypes

NSW GROUP 4 SPECIAL BOAT TEAMS

SPECIAL WARFARE COMBATANT-CRAFT CREWMEN MAINTAIN AND OPERATE MARITIME SURFACE CRAFT

- Train extensively in craft and weapons tactics
- Conduct special reconnaissance, combat gunfire support, SEAL insertion and extraction
- Provide dedicated, rapid mobility in shallow water areas

UNIQUE SOF CAPABILITY—MARITIME COMBATANT—CRAFT AERIAL DELIVERY

CURRENT INVENTORY

- 11-meter Rigid-hull Inflatable Boat
- Special Operations Craft Riverine
- SEALION
- Security Force Assistance craft

NSW GROUP 10

ORGANIZES, TRAINS, EQUIPS, DEPLOYS, AND SUSTAINS SPECIAL-IZED INTELLIGENCE, SURVEILLANCE, RECONNAISSANCE, AND PREPARATION OF THE ENVIRONMENT CAPABILITIES

MISSION SUPPORT CENTER

- Reach-back capability state-side tailored to mission commanders' needs
- Supplies mission-planning support to deployed forces

CULTURAL ENGAGEMENT UNIT

- Embeds language/regional experts and female support technicians to support translation, tactical interrogation, and intelligence collection

NSW GROUP 11

ORGANIZES, MANS, TRAINS, EDUCATES, EQUIPS AND DEPLOYS RESERVIST SEALS, SWCC, COMBAT SUPPORT, AND COMBAT SERVICE SUPPORT CAPABILITIES

- Provides additional operational capacity to the active duty force including expeditionary support, joint military training exercises, counter-narcotics operations

NSW DEVELOPMENT GROUP

MANAGES RTD&E [RESEARCH, TESTING, DEVELOPMENT, AND EVALUATION]; DEVELOPS MARITIME, GROUND AND AIRBORNE TACTICS FOR NSW AND DOD-WIDE APPLICATION

MISSION SPECIALISTS AND SUPPORT PERSONNEL

CRITICAL TO NAVAL SPECIAL WARFARE OPERATIONS SUCCESS

- Explosive ordnance disposal, intelligence, communications, hospital corpsmen

COMPREHENSIVE PRE-DEPLOYMENT TRAINING

FULL-SPECTRUM LOGISTICS SUPPORT, RANGE PERSONNEL, AEROGRAPHERS, ELECTRONICS TECHNICIANS

- Information systems technicians, divers, mass communication specialists

APPENDIX C

OVERVIEW OF NAVAL SPECIAL WARFARE LEGACY UNITS

By Tom Hawkins

SEAL historian Tom Hawkins provided us with this overview of the history of the formation of the World War II predecessor Naval Special Warfare units of the U.S. Navy SEALs:

Amphibious Training Base, Little Creek, Virginia
During preparation for amphibious warfare operations in the Chesapeake Bay, two special-mission units were formed almost simultaneously at the Amphibious Training Base (ATB), Little Creek, Norfolk, Virginia, in late August 1942. Each was to perform specific missions in Operation Torch—the allied invasion of North Africa the following November; however, there is no evidence that either knew about the other or their assigned tasks during this period.

Amphibious Scouts and Raiders (S&R)
Amphibious Scouts and Raiders (Joint) were created specifically to reconnoiter prospective landing beaches and to lead assault forces to the correct beaches under cover of darkness. The unit was led by U.S. Army First Lieutenant Lloyd Peddicord as commanding officer, and Navy Ensign John Bell as executive officer. Navy chief petty officers and sailors came from the boat pool at ATB, Solomons, Maryland, and Army Raider personnel came from the 3rd and 9th Infantry Divisions. They trained at Little Creek until embarking for the North Africa campaign the following November. Operation TORCH was launched in November 1942 off the Atlantic coast of French Morocco in North Africa. One mission, under Army 1st Lieutenant Willard G. Duckworth, involved the launching of kayaks from the submarine USS *Barb* (SS-220). This was the first U.S. submarine-hosted operation of World War II involving specially trained reconnaissance personnel. Their mission was to infiltrate to a location off the Jette Principal at Safi,

Morocco, under cover of darkness to safely guide the destroyers USS *Cole* (DD-155) and USS *Bernadou* (DD-153) to near-shore gunnery positions.

S&R men also conducted pre-assault operations at Normandy several weeks before D-Day, June 6, 1944, and at the invasion of southern France later that August. After that the need for Scout and Raider capabilities in Europe ended; no other amphibious operations were envisioned in that theater. Many of the men returned to Fort Pierce to serve as instructors at the Scouts and Raiders School. Army personnel were returned to their parent units, and many Navy men were reassigned to sea duty or given the opportunity to join the Pacific units.

S&R teams performed a variety of actions and activities to guide ships and small craft throughout Operation TORCH, often under withering fire. They performed so admirably that all Scout boat officers were awarded the Navy Cross Medal. The Scout and Raider school was relocated to ATB, Fort Pierce, Florida, in February 1943, where, in the following July, it became an all Navy school.

S&R operations in the Mediterranean and Pacific Theaters also provided the framework for legacy capabilities now accomplished by today's NSW Special Warfare Combat-Craft Crewmen (SWCC) operators.

After Normandy, the Scouts and Raiders became all Navy personnel. Special Services Unit #1 was an earlier S&R-like unit formed in the South Pacific in 1942. The Scouts and Raiders returning from Europe were retrained in a school called Amphibious Roger for operations with SACO in China. Other S&R personnel were made part of ship's company in the Intelligence sections.

Special Mission Naval Demolition Unit

Also in August 1942 at ATB, Little Creek, a specialized naval demolition team was formed with two officers and seventeen enlisted men. They were led by Lieutenant Mark Starkweather (senior in command) and Lieutenant James Darroch. All were trained Navy salvage divers brought in from Hawaii. Their crash course included demolitions, commando tactics, cable cutting, and rubber boat training. Their singular mission during Operation TORCH was to remove the cabled boom blocking the Wadi Sebou River, which spilled into the Atlantic Ocean along the west coast of French Morocco. Removal of this boom would allow USS *Dallas* (DD-199) to proceed up the river and train her guns on the Port Lyautey airdrome in preparation for attack by Army Rangers that were previously embarked aboard *Dallas*.

The operation was launched just before H-Hour on November 8, 1942. The men operated at night from an open Higgins boat in very heavy seas and under direct enemy machine-gun fire. Several of the men were badly injured in the rough seas, and the first attempt was aborted. During a second attempt on the night of November 9, they accomplished their task. Their mission was so demanding and critical to the success of the invasion that every demolition man in the operation was awarded the Navy Cross Medal. This special-mission naval demolition unit was disbanded once the men returned from Africa.

The Naval Demolition Project

On May 6, 1943, the "Naval Demolition Project" was directed by the Chief of Naval Operations "to meet a present and urgent requirement." The CNO's directive outlined a two-phase project.

The first phase began with a letter to the Chief of the Bureau of Yards and Docks directing dispatch of eight officers and thirty enlisted men for duty with the Operational Naval Demolition Unit and Naval Demolition Unit Number No. 1, which was to be established at the ATB, Solomons, Maryland. Commander John C. Daniel was selected as Officer in Charge. Six officers and eighteen enlisted men reported for training at Solomons on May 14, and all came from the Seabee training camp at Camp Peary, Williamsburg, Virginia.

Led by Navy Lieutenant Fred Wise, these men were given a four-week course of instruction and sent immediately to participate in Operation Husky, the Allied invasion of Sicily, which occurred during the following July and August.

CDR Daniel submitted a letter report about this new capability on May 27, 1943. His report, which proposed an outline for the second phase, recommended an organization, outlined a detailed core training syllabus, and recommended a list of equipment needed to supply an operational combat demolition unit. He further recommended that the training program be detached from Maryland and relocated to ATB, Fort Pierce, Florida, to take advantage of good weather for year-round training.

Naval Combat Demolition Units (NCDUs)

On June 6, 1943, the Naval Combat Demolition Unit (NCDU) training school was established at Fort Pierce, Florida, and organized by Lieutenant Commander Draper Kauffman. He assembled volunteers from the Bomb and Mine Disposal School, Washington, D.C. (which he organized), and the Civil Engineering Corps and Naval Construction Corps (Seabees) School at Camp Peary near Williamsburg, Virginia, to fill the first training classes.

Kauffman is given credit for instituting the infamous "Hell Week," a period of intense instruction that remains a fundamental component in the modern-day Basic Underwater Demolition/SEAL (BUD/S) training program. By the end of Fort Pierce training there was an overall attrition rate of 65–75 percent, much like it remains today in BUD/S.

In some accountings, Kauffman has also been given credit for the establishment of the Underwater Demolition Teams (UDTs) in the Pacific during World War II, but this is not factual. The UDTs were formed in December 1943, while Kauffman was still at Fort Pierce. He left his training position at Fort Pierce in April 1944 to become commanding officer of UDT-5 in Maui, Territory of Hawaii.

Each NCDU was composed of one officer and five enlisted sailors to make up a single boat crew. The first NCDU class graduated in September 1943, after several months of arduous training with primary emphasis on demolition of submerged beach obstacles (submerged in a surf zone). Seven units were dispersed to the Third and Fifth Fleets in the Pacific, three units went to the Eighth Fleet in the Mediterranean, and only one unit went to England. By April 1944, however, a total of thirty-four NCDUs had collected in England in preparation for Operation Overlord, the amphibious landing at Normandy.

D-Day—The Bloody Sands of Normandy

For the assault at Normandy, each six-man NDCU was augmented with three U.S. Navy seamen brought in from Scotland to assist in handling demolitions. The resulting nine-man NCDUs were later integrated with U.S. Army combat engineers to form thirteen-man gap assault teams.

During the assault on June 6, 1944, NCDU men suffered 37 killed and 71
wounded, a casualty rate of 52 percent, making D-Day the bloodiest single
day in the history of Naval Special Warfare, although not one NCDU man
was lost to improper handling of explosives.

The NCDUs at Omaha Beach were awarded the Presidential Unit Citation, one
of only three presented for military actions at Normandy. The men at Utah
Beach were recipients of the only Navy Unit Commendation awarded for
actions on that awful day.

The Invasion of Southern France

NCDU men were engaged in combat only once more in Europe, and this was
during the invasion of southern France in August 1944. First code-named
Anvil and later Dragoon, several of the NCDUs from Utah Beach were
augmented with new units from Fort Pierce to participate in the last amphibious assault of the war in Europe. Once operations ceased in Europe,
all Fort Pierce trained men were sent to the Pacific and assigned to Underwater Demolition Teams.

NCDU men contributed greatly to the war in Europe, and their efforts are often
overshadowed by the Pacific UDTs. Indeed, in some historical accountings,
it has been written that UDTs performed work at Normandy and southern France; however, during World War II the UDTs operated only in the
Pacific.

Moreover, NCDU men have often been referred to as "frogmen" by some authors and historians; however, in those early days swimming was only a
test and a method of physical training. The men wore full combat dress,
and were taught to operate stealthily at night and during predawn hours
by wading in surf and carrying explosives to obstacles from rubber boats.

MacArthur's Frogmen

Many of the early Fort Pierce–trained NCDUs were deployed to the Pacific
Theater of Operations. NCDU-1 went to Alaska in August 1943 to participate in the Aleutian Islands Campaign—before actually finishing their
formal training class. These operations were a struggle over the Aleutian
Islands, which were then a part of the Alaska Territory. The NCDU men
were never engaged, since the Japanese had already departed the islands.
They were subsequently transferred to Waimanalo, Territory of Hawaii, to
be embedded with the provisional UDT-1.

NCDU-2, NCDU-3, NCDU-19, NCDU-20, NCDU-21, and NCDU-24 went
to the Southwest Pacific, and remained together for the war's duration
(the only NCDUs never to be subsumed into a UDT). Lieutenant (jg)
Frank Kaine was the leader of this group, which later became known as
"MacArthur's Frogmen."

NCDU-4 and NCDU-5 also went to the Southwest Pacific. They were the first
Fort Pierce men to actually be committed to battle in the Pacific, when they
operated with the 4th U.S. Marines at Green Island and Emirau Island in
the Bismarck Archipelago of the South Pacific at New Guinea. These men
were eventually returned to Hawaii and assigned duty with the UDTs.

Special Services Unit One (SSU-1)

A second and lesser-known group of Scouts and Raiders, code-named Special
Services Unit One (SSU-1), was established in the Pacific on July 13, 1943.

SSU-1 was a joint and combined international force, with personnel from Australia and the U.S. Army, Navy, and Marine Corps. They were trained in martial arts, hand-to-hand combat, mapmaking, rubber-craft operations, jungle survival, Pidgin English, underwater coral formations, and sea-creatures recognition.

Their operations, actions, and activities began in September 1943 at Finschafen, New Guinea, where they conducted near-shore and inland reconnaissance operations, often with indigenous personnel. Similar operations were carried out at Gasmata, Arawe, Cape Gloucester, and the eastern and southern coasts of New Britain, all without loss of personnel.

The focus of this organization was much different than their Atlantic counterparts, who conducted pre-assault reconnaissance and guided assault waves ashore. SSU-1 collected intelligence and trained and operated with indigenous personnel in the conduct of guerrilla warfare missions. They were later designated the 7th Amphibious Scouts and organized under staff intelligence sections, somewhat along the lines of their Atlantic counterparts.

Sino-American Cooperative Organization (SACO)

Many Scout and Raider personnel returning from Europe were given special assignment with the U.S. Naval Group in China, headed by Captain (later Admiral) Milton "Mary" Miles. He and his Chinese counterpart set up the Sino-American Cooperative Organization (SACO) to train, equip, and direct guerrilla forces against the Japanese occupation of China. To help bolster the work of SACO, Chief of Naval Operations Admiral Ernest J. King ordered 120 officers and 900 men trained for "Amphibious Roger" at the Scout and Raider School at Fort Pierce.

Amphibious Roger was a cover name for Navy personnel being groomed to support SACO and conduct raids on the Yangtze River. Many of these men never made it to China because the war ended. Those who did were used to train Chinese guerrilla forces and conduct reconnaissance operations with them until the end of the war. They were also tasked to locate and survey prospective landing beaches for a potential invasion of the Chinese mainland, report on Japanese ship movement, and provide weather reports to the fleet. They were later glamorized as the "Rice Paddy Navy."

Underwater Demolition Teams (UDTs)

On November 22, 1943, during the Tarawa landing at the Gilbert Islands, a chain of sixteen atolls and coral islands in the South Pacific Ocean, a submerged reef caused amphibious landing craft to founder far offshore, resulting in the loss of hundreds of U.S. Marines from enemy fire and drowning. After that experience, Admiral Kelley Turner, Commander of the 5th Amphibious Force, directed that 30 officers and 150 enlisted men be moved to Waimanalo ATB (on the "big island" of Hawaii) to form the nucleus of a reconnaissance and demolition training program. It is here that the UDTs of the Pacific were born.

The first UDT group became UDT-1 and UDT-2, "provisional" UDTs with strengths of about fourteen officers and seventy enlisted men each. They saw their first action on January 31, 1944, in the attacks on Kwajalein and Roy-Namur during Operation Flintlock in the Marshall Islands. Following Flintlock, the UDT men returned to establish a naval combat demolition training and experimental base on a beach near ATB, Kamaol, on the island of Maui.

Between December 1944 and August 1945, UDT men saw action across the Pacific in every major amphibious landing, including Eniwetok, Saipan, Guam, Tinian, Angaur, Ulithi, Peleliu, Leyte, Lingayen Gulf, Zambales, Iwo Jima, Okinawa, Labuan, Brunei Bay, and Borneo. On July 4, 1945, at Balikpapan on Borneo, UDT-11 and UDT-18 spearheaded one of the last and least-recorded offensive actions of the war, where they performed their now classic pre-assault reconnaissance and demolition operations.

A memorial to the founding of the UDT is being built at Bellows Air Force Station near the original Amphibious Training Base (ATB) Waimanalo.

Postwar UDTs

Thirty UDTs were organized during World War II. UDT-1 and UDT-2 were disbanded almost as quickly as they were formed, there were at most twenty-eight teams at any one time. All teams were trained at Fort Pierce except UDT-1 and UDT-2 (the provisional teams), and UDT-14, UDT-16, and UDT-17, which were made up largely of fleet volunteers, all trained in Hawaii.

Four fifty-man teams were established during the postwar period. UDT-1 and UDT-3 were home ported at ATB, Coronado, California; and UDT-2 and UDT-4 were sent to ATB, Little Creek, Norfolk, Virginia. All were organized under Amphibious Forces Pacific and Atlantic respectively. These were the only World War II maritime commando units to survive doctrinally after the war, and thus provided a direct lineage to the modern-day SEAL Teams.

Office of Strategic Services Maritime Unit

Undoubtedly the most influential World War II legacy unit that would eventually affect the capabilities of the Underwater Demolition Teams, and subsequently the U.S. Navy SEAL Teams, was a joint-service maritime component of the Office of Strategic Services (OSS). Many of its capabilities were later adopted by the postwar UDTs, and many of the same capabilities can be found in today's SEAL Teams.

On January 20, 1943, a Maritime Section was established within the Special Operations Branch of OSS, with responsibility for planning covert infiltration operations from the sea. On June 10, 1943, the Special Operations Branch was reorganized and the Maritime Unit (MU) was established with branch status. Its responsibilities included planning and coordinating the clandestine infiltration of agents, supplying resistance groups, engaging in maritime sabotage, and developing special equipment for operations from the sea.

OSS MU pioneered U.S. capabilities in maritime sabotage through use of special-boat infiltration techniques and tactical combat diving using flexible swim fins and face masks, closed-circuit diving equipment, submersible vehicles, and limpet mines. These capabilities were adopted by the UDTs in 1947 and became the hallmark of SEALs lasting through the modern day. OSS MU operations in the Mediterranean and China-Burma-India Theater also provided the framework for legacy capabilities now accomplished by NSW SWCC operators and resident in the NSW Special Boat Teams.

SEAL ETHOS/CREED

In times of war or uncertainty there is a special breed of warrior ready to answer our Nation's call. A common man with uncommon desire to succeed. Forged by adversity, he stands alongside America's finest special operations forces to serve his country, the American people, and protect their way of life. I am that man.

My Trident is a symbol of honor and heritage. Bestowed upon me by the heroes that have gone before, it embodies the trust of those I have sworn to protect. By wearing the Trident I accept the responsibility of my chosen profession and way of life. It is a privilege that I must earn every day.

My loyalty to Country and Team is beyond reproach. I humbly serve as a guardian to my fellow Americans always ready to defend those who are unable to defend themselves. I do not advertise the nature of my work, nor seek recognition for my actions. I voluntarily accept the inherent hazards of my profession, placing the welfare and security of others before my own.

I serve with honor on and off the battlefield. The ability to control my emotions and my actions, regardless of circumstance, sets me apart from other men. Uncompromising integrity is my standard. My character and honor are steadfast. My word is my bond.

We expect to lead and be led. In the absence of orders I will take charge, lead my teammates and accomplish the mission. I lead by example in all situations.

I will never quit. I persevere and thrive on adversity. My Nation expects me to be physically harder and mentally stronger than my enemies. If knocked down, I will get back up, every time. I will draw on every remaining ounce of strength to protect my teammates and to accomplish our mission. I am never out of the fight.

We demand discipline. We expect innovation. The lives of my teammates and the success of our mission depend on me—my technical skill, tactical proficiency, and attention to detail. My training is never complete.

We train for war and fight to win. I stand ready to bring the full spectrum of combat power to bear in order to achieve my mission and the goals established by my country. The execution of my duties will be swift and violent when required yet guided by the very principles that I serve to defend.

Brave men have fought and died building the proud tradition and feared reputation that I am bound to uphold. In the worst of conditions, the legacy of my teammates steadies my resolve and silently guides my every deed. I will not fail.

APPENDIX E

THOSE WHO MADE THE ULTIMATE SACRIFICE

The Navy SEAL Museum in Fort Pierce, Florida, is home to a memorial dedicated to honoring the Scouts and Raiders, NCDUs, UDTs, and Navy SEALs who have been killed in the line of duty. Here are the names of the men so honored as they are listed by the museum, as of the writing of this book.

WORLD WAR II & KOREA (1941–1953)

96 PERSONNEL

1. Howe, Kenneth E. "Rip"; Lt
2. Pirro, Carmon F. "Cuz"; Ens
3. Donnell, John Gerald "Jerry"; Lt
4. Olson, Richard Roderick; S1c
5. Tascillo, Matteo; Cox
6. Guess, Teddy O'Brian "Teddy"; MM1c
7. Vetter, Alvin Edward; Lt(jg)
8. Abbott, George L.; BM2c
9. Alexander, Henry Richard; SF2c
10. Bussell, John Edward; Ens
11. Cook, John William; S2c
12. DeGregorio, Carmine; S2c
13. Demmer, Peter Mathew; S2c
14. Dillon, Thomas Justin; S2c
15. Dombek, Walter Joseph; S1c
16. Doran, William Robert; S2c
17. Drew, Elmer Malcolm; S2c
18. Duncan, Harold E.; GM2c
19. Fabich, Henry Samuel; GM1c
20. Fleming, Andrew Jackson; CEM
21. Fuller Sr., John Anthony "Johnny"; GM2c
22. Gouinlock, George Linzy; Ens
23. Goulder, Preston Hardaway; GM2c
24. Greenfield, Edward Joseph; S2c
25. Harang, Richard David; MM1c
26. Herring, Clifford Palmer; GM2c
27. Hickey, Arthur Burton; QM3c
28. Holtman, Orvid J.; Lt(jg)
29. Hudson, Alton E.; BM1c
30. Jacobson, John A.; CBM
31. Jarosz, Edward Anthony; SF1c
32. McDermott, John Daniel; MM1c
33. McGeary, Donald C.; SF2c
34. Millis, Conrad Clarence; CCM
35. Mingledorff Jr., Ozie Claud; GM2c
36. Olive, Jesse D.; GM2c

37. Perkins, Frank James; BM2c
38. Pienack, Raymond Rudolph; GM2c
39. Sullivan Jr., Maurice Francis; S2c
40. Weatherford, Milton Parker; GM1c
41. Weckman, Lawrence I.; GM1c
42. Christensen, Robert V. "Bob"; SF1c
43. Weidner, Albert Garhardt "Gary";
    SF2c
44. Blowers, Ralph A.; W.O. (Carp.)
45. Nixon, Thomas Dervus; Ens
46. Black, Robert Armstrong "Bob"; QM1c
47. MacMahon, John Churchill; SP1c
48. Roeder, Howard Livingston "Red";
    CGM
49. Audibert, Benoit Bernard "Frenchy";
    CM1c
50. Kasman, Brennan W.; MM2c
51. Tilton, Edward; MM2c
52. Lauderdale, Kenneth Broughton; SF1c
53. Wannamaker, Richard C.; Ens
54. Prall, Carroll Bert; GM1c
55. Blettel, David; MM1c
56. Castillo, Guadalupe; S1c
57. Gamache, Wilfred Dolar; CCM
58. Hopkins, Robert Lee; CM3c
59. Lewis, William Robert; SM3c
60. Malfeo, Marvin Antonio; Ens
61. McKnight, Thomas Rex; GM
62. Rodriquez; James Lawrence
    "Wahoo"; MoMM2c
63. Rossart, Joseph William; MM2c
64. Scoggins, F.P.; SK1c
65. Sugden, William Lloyd; GM3c
66. LeBlanc, Lawrence Raymond "Ray";
    SF2c
67. Anderson, Edward Wilson "Andy";
    CM1c
68. Yates, Lee Carlton; Lt(jg)
69. Allen, Kermit; BM2c
70. Beason, Edwin Albert; CCM
71. Blackwood, Buress Lee; MM2c
72. Blanot, Harry Thomas; CM1c
73. Davis, Paul Harrison; RM3c
74. Dolan, Patrick Raymond;
    MoMM2c
75. Flemming, Joseph Leo; CM2c
76. Gordon, Paul Eugene; SF1c
77. Hilke, Earl Everett; MM2c
78. Kalman, Louis Emery "Shorty";
    GM2c
79. Maki, Eugene Elmer; CM3c
80. Mecale, John; BM2c
81. Rodman, James Emerson; MM2c
82. Runnels, Adrian; S1c
83. Sumpter, Frank Warren; MoMM3c
84. Szych, Chester; MM2c
85. Watkins, Thomas Jackson;
    EM1c
86. Willbanks, Herman Delmar; F1c
87. Eckert, Edmund P.; GM2c
88. Netz, Louis Gustave; GM1c
89. Lynch, Francis Joseph; Cox
90. Bock Jr., Leonard Joseph; S1c
91. Masden, Charles F.; S1c
92. Irish, Edgar William; GM1c
93. Esau, John Jacob; Cox
94. Frey Jr., Edward Ivan; Lt(jg)
95. Satterfield, Paul Veston "Satch";
    ENFN
96. Berry, Ronald Albert; SA

VIETNAM & COLD WAR (1954–1989)

103 PERSONNEL

1. Phipps, George Thomas; BM1
2. Cunningham, John Randolph "Jack";
   ATN2
3. McAllister, Thomas Anthony; GMG1
4. Dowd, Timothy Clement; SA
5. Painter, William Gissal; LTJG
6. Eskotter, Anthony Willis "Tony"; SA
7. Coates, Richard J.; SA
8. Samuelson, Leroy Oscar
   "Sam"/"Sammy"; SA
9. Walsh, Clifford Leroy; SA
10. Allard, Robert L. "Bob"; RM3
11. Salas, Joseph O.; CE2
12. Fox, James Earl; PH3
13. Marshall, Walter Alan "Horse"; SA
14. Geiger, Leroy Calvin "Gedunk";
    MMFN
15. Fauls Jr., Raymond A.; SN
16. Fleming, Robert R.; CM2
17. Melochick, Melvin F.; MM3
18. Chester, David A.; ENS
19. Fay, Robert Joseph; CDR

20. Gough, Marcell Rene; ET1
21. Machen, Billy Wayne; RD2
22. Dubak, Douglas R.; FN
23. Boston, Donald Earl; IC3
24. Mann, Daniel McCarthy; LT
25. Neal, Ronald Keith; RM3
26. Funk Jr., Leslie Harold; SM3
27. Antone, Frank George; SN
28. Keith, Roy Benjamin; SN
29. Williams Jr., Arthur C. "One Lump"; GMG1
30. Condon, Robert Eugene; LCDR
31. Fraley, Eugene Thomas "Gene"; ADR2
32. Risher III, Clarence T.; AMH2
33. Turner, Dennis R.; IC2
34. Frederickson, Delmar D.; SN
35. Pope, Walter Glen; BM1
36. Devine, David Eugene "Skinner"; SFP2
37. Zillgitt, Donald Henry; SK2
38. Patrick, Donnie Lee "Pat"; CS1
39. Brown, Gordon Curtiss; EMC
40. Albrecht, Joseph Alfred; MM1
41. Wagner, Robert Kay "Bob"; SK1
42. Tinnin, Eugene Sanford "Gene"; CWO1
43. Trani Jr., Frederick Eugene "Rick"; LT
44. Ramos, Roberto; ABH2
45. Wilson, David Allen "Willy Lump"; LSMC
46. Mattingly Jr., Harry Albert; GMG1
47. Worthington, Robert Leroy; HMC
48. Meyer, Lowell Wayne "Wayne"; MM2
49. Pace, Ronald Earl; QM2
50. Van Hoy, Kenneth Edward "Ken"; ATN1
51. Mahner, Lin Albert; HM1
52. Nicholas, David Lamprey; LTJG
53. Wolfe, Richard Ogden; HM1
54. Ashton, Curtis Morris "Butch"; AE1
55. Brewton, John Cooke "Bubba"; LTJG
56. Sadlik, John E.; ATR2
57. Donnelly III, John Joseph; RMSN
58. Durlin, John Stewart; SM3
59. Gore, James Raymond; BM3
60. Solano, Richard John; MM2
61. Thomas, Toby Arthur; FN
62. Williams Jr., Lawrence C.; HM3
63. Palma, Luco William; SN
64. Bomar, Frank Willis; ENC
65. Riter, James L. "Gasman"; EM3
66. Thames, James Franklin; LT
67. Birky, Harold Edwin; FN
68. Tolison, James Paul; ENS
69. Collins, Michael Raymond; LT
70. Moe, Lester James "Les"; TM1
71. Waters, Franklin Gerald "Jerry"; BM1
72. Dry, Melvin Spence "Spence"; LT
73. Goodson, Richard Calvin; GMT2
74. Watkins, James Lorenzo "Cookie"; EM3
75. Casco, Joseph M.; RM2
76. Squires, John J. "Jack"; EM1
77. James, John Mike; SA
78. Doheny, Richard William "Harpo"; HT2
79. Greer, Richard Allen; HT3
80. Kelly, Paul P.; FN
81. Harris, Mark Ewen; HTFN
82. McCarthy, Joseph Frank; GMG2
83. Choi, Rodney Gilbert; EN1
84. Bond, Richard David; QM3
85. Robinson, William Clinton; ENS
86. Hersey, Gary Francis; MR2
87. Schaufelberger III, Albert Arthur; LCDR
88. Langelier, David Philip; STG2 KIT
89. Butcher, Kenneth John "John"; MM1
90. Morris, Stephen Leroy "Steve"; HT1
91. Lundberg, Kevin Erin "Kodiak"; QM1
92. Schamberger, Robert Rudolf; ENCS
93. Blackiston III, Slator Clay; LT
94. Fusco, Arthur Albert; QM3
95. Sadilek, William Louis "Bill"; LTJG
96. Horn, Richard Michael "Rich"; EN2
97. Hall, John Francis; BTC
98. Station, Paul Christopher; LT
99. Lancaster, John Michael; MM2
100. Connors, John Patrick; LTJG
101. McFaul, Donald Lewis; ENC
102. Rodriguez III, Isaac Georgetti "Ike"; TM2
103. Tilghman, Christopher "Chris"; BM1

DESERT STORM & GLOBAL WAR ON TERROR (1990-PRESENT)

81 PERSONNEL

1. Greppin III, Ernest Haquette "Ernie"; LTJG
2. Dean, Carter Myers "Dino"; GMG2
3. Wilson Sr., Mark Russell; LT
4. Pruitt, Jason Early; BM2
5. Voight, Steven Mark; AW1
6. Moreland, Theodore Michael; QMC
7. Kimura, Keith Masao "Kiko"; HM2
8. Clearwater, Carl Jerome; STG1
9. Stone, Larry Allen "Allen"; YN2
10. Tucker, Brad Keith "Brad"; HM1
11. Bearden Jr., Michael Delane "Tatanka"; PR3
12. Burkhart, Chad Michael; GMG2
13. Danielson, Scott Michael "Scotty"; HT2
14. Blais, Rock Edward; LCDR
15. Roberts, Neil Christopher; ABH1
16. Bourgeois, Matthew Joseph "Meat"; HMC
17. Oswald, Peter George "Pete"; CDR
18. Pope II, Jerry Oreall "Buck"; ENS
19. Retzer, Thomas Eugene; IC1
20. Maestas, Mario Gabriel; IT2
21. Tapper, David Martin "Dave"; PH1
22. Ouellette, Brian Joseph; BM1
23. Fitzhenry, Theodore Dilworth "Fitz"; HMCS
24. Murphy, Michael Patrick; LT
25. Axelson, Matthew Gene "Axe"; STG2
26. Dietz Jr., Danny Phillip "DJ"; GM2
27. Fontan, Jacques Jules; FCC
28. Healy, Daniel Richard; ITCS
29. Kristensen; Erik Samsel "Erik"; LCDR
30. Lucas, Jeffrey Alan "Jeff"; ET1
31. McGreevy Jr., Michael Martin; LT
32. Patton, Shane Eric "Eric"; MM1
33. Suh, James Erik; QM2
34. Taylor, Jeffrey Scott "Jeff"; HM1
35. Lee, Marc Alan; AO2
36. Monsoor, Michael Anthony "Mike"; MA2
37. Schwedler, Joseph Clark; SO2
38. Lewis, Jason Dale; SO1
39. Carter, Mark Thomas "Badger"; SOC
40. Ghane Jr., Shapoor Alexander "Alex"; SO2
41. Hardy, Nathan Hall; SOC
42. Koch, Michael Eugene; SOC
43. Valentine, Thomas John "Tommy"; SOCS
44. Vaccaro, Lance Michael; SOC
45. Harris, Joshua Thomas "Josh"; SO1
46. Freiwald, Jason Richard; SOC
47. Marcum, John Wayne "Dusty"; SOCS
48. Shellenberger, Erik F.; SOC
49. Job, Ryan Curtis; SO2
50. Woodle, Ronald Tyler; SO2
51. Brown, Adam Lee; SOC
52. Thomas, Collin Trent; SOC
53. Smith, Adam Olin; SO2
54. Looney, Brendan John; LT
55. Miranda, Denis; SO3
56. Benson, Darrik Carlyle; SO1
57. Bill, Brian Robert; SOC
58. Campbell, Christopher George; SOC
59. Faas, John Weston; SOC
60. Houston, Kevin Arthur; SOC
61. Kelsall, Jonas Benton; LCDR
62. Langlais, Louis James; SOCM
63. Mason, Matthew David; SOC
64. Mills, Stephen Matthew; SOC
65. Pittman, Jesse Daryl; SO1
66. Ratzlaff, Thomas Arthur; SOCS
67. Reeves, Robert James; SOC
68. Robinson, Heath Michael; SOCS
69. Spehar, Nicholas Patrick; SO2
70. Tumilson, Jon Thomas; SO1
71. Vaughn, Aaron Carson; SOC
72. Workman, Jason Ray; SOC
73. Nelson, Caleb Andrew; SO1
74. Feeks, Patrick Delaney; SO1
75. Warsen, David John; SO2
76. Kantor, Matthew Geoffrey; SO2
77. Ebbert, Kevin Richard; SO1
78. Checque, Nicholas David; SO1
79. Leathers, Matthew John; SO1
80. Shadle, Brett David; SOCS
81. Kaloust, Jonathan H.; SO3

Source: The Navy SEAL Museum

NOTES ON KEY SOURCES

This book is based on interviews with more than one hundred men who have served in the U.S. Navy Naval Combat Demolition Units, Scouts and Raiders, Underwater Demolition Units, SEALs, and other Naval Special Warfare and U.S. military units. The interviews were conducted by the authors and by Carol L. Fleisher for the PBS special that accompanies this book. It is also based on declassified government documents and historical and journalistic accounts.

The book is also informed by Dick Couch's experiences as a UDT member and Navy SEAL, and by his research, reporting, and writing on SEAL operations and training for his books *The Warrior Elite: The Forging of SEAL Class 228* (Three Rivers Press, 2003), *The Finishing School: Earning the Navy SEAL Trident* (Crown, 2004), *Down Range: Navy SEALs in the War on Terrorism* (Three Rivers Press, 2005), and *The Sheriff of Ramadi: Navy SEALs and the Winning of al-Anbar* (U.S. Naval Institute Press, 2008).

The SEALs have been the subject of a tidal wave of books and articles in recent years. Those that were most helpful to our research are listed below, along with key source notes for each chapter.

ARCHIVES

Naval Special Warfare Command Historical Files, Coronado, California: a key source for our research was this remarkable collection of thousands of pages of declassified files dating back to 1942, covering a wide spectrum of Naval Special Warfare history. They include unit histories, after-action reports, cable and radio traffic, mission logs, intelligence reports and debriefings, interrogation reports, ships logs, letters, oral histories, personal diaries, lessons-learned studies, press clippings and photographs.

U.S. Navy Heritage and History Command Archive, Washington, D.C.
National Archives, Washington D.C.
John F. Kennedy Presidential Library, Columbia Point, Massachusetts
The Navy SEALs Museum, Fort Pierce, Florida
Materials donated to the authors from private collections

BOOKS

Herbert Best, *The Webfoot Warriors: The Story of UDT, the U.S. Navy's Underwater Demolition Team* (John Day, 1962).

T. L. Bosiljevac, *SEALs: UDT/SEAL Operations in Vietnam* (Ballantine Books, 1990).

Elizabeth K. Bush, *America's First Frogman: The Draper Kauffman Story* (Naval Institute Press, 2004).

Dennis J. Cummings, *The Men Behind the Trident: SEAL Team One in Vietnam* (Naval Institute Press, 1997).

Kevin Dockery, from interviews by Bud Brutsman, *Navy SEALs: A Complete History* (Berkley Books, 2004).

John B. Dwyer, *Scouts and Raiders: The Navy's First Special Warfare Commandos* (Praeger, 1993).

Francis D. Fane and Don Moore, *The Naked Warriors* (Appleton-Century-Crofts, 1956).

Bill Fawcett, *Hunters and Shooters: An Oral History of the U.S. Navy SEALs in Vietnam* (William Morrow, 1995).

Michael E. Haas, *In the Devil's Shadow: UN Special Operations During the Korean War* (Naval Institute Press, 2000).

Orr Kelly, *Brave Men, Dark Waters* (Presidio, 1992).

Don Mann and Ralph Pezzullo, *Inside SEAL Team Six: My Life and Missions with America's Elite Warriors* (Little, Brown, 2011).

Susan L. Marquis, *Unconventional Warfare: Rebuilding U.S. Special Operations Forces* (Brookings Institution Press, 1997).

James Douglas O'Dell, *The Water Is Never Cold: The Origins of the U.S. Navy's Combat Demolition Units, UDTs, and SEALs* (Brassey's, 2001).

Patrick K. O'Donnell, *Operatives, Spies, and Saboteurs: The Unknown Story of World War II's OSS* (Citadel Press, 2006).

United States Special Operations Command History, 6th Edition, 2008; and *United States Special Operations Command Fact Book 2014*; USSOCOM, MacDill AFB, Tampa, Florida.

PUBLICATIONS AND WEBSITES

The Blast, Journal of Naval Special Warfare, currently published by UDT-SEAL Association, 1969–2013 archive courtesy of Tom Hawkins

Ethos Magazine, published by Naval Special Warfare Command

http://www.history.navy.mil Naval History and Heritage Command

http://www.sealtwo.org SEAL history and reunion site maintained by Erasmo Riojas

http://www.navyfrogmen.com Naval Special Warfare archive, non-governmental

https://www.navysealmuseum.org National Navy UDT-SEAL Museum

KEY SOURCE NOTES

EPIGRAPHS

"You are not alive unless you are living on the edge": Patrick K. O'Donnell, *Operatives, Spies, and Saboteurs: The Unknown Story of World War II's OSS* (Citadel Press, 2006), p. 141.

"It's just the way we were, the teams and the men": Brian Biller, "Training, Teamwork Key to 45 Years of Navy SEALs," U.S. Navy Press Release, January 11, 2007.

"They just vanished. They came out of darkness": *Charlie Rose*, May 15, 2013.

"We must remember that one man is much the same": Robert Debs Heinl, *Dictionary of Military and Naval Quotations* (Naval Institute Press, 1966), p. 328.

Naval Special Warfare Command Organizations Chart: "NSW Command Brochure," May 9, 2014: http://www.public.navy.mil/nsw/news/Documents/ETHOS/Brochure.pdf.

CHAPTER I

Ken Reynolds on Omaha Beach, his biography and quotes in this chapter: interviews with Ken Reynolds and Carol Fleisher interview with Ken Reynolds. Additional D-Day detail: Combined Operations Headquarters, "Bulletin Y/35, Underwater Obstacles in Operation Overlord, November 1944," Naval Special Warfare Command historical file; "Combat Demolition Units of the Atlantic Theatre of Operations," (no date), World War II Command File, Shore Establishments, Operational Archives Branch, Naval Historical Center; Lt. (jg) H. L. Blackwell, Jr., "Report on Naval Combat Demolition Units (NCDUs) in Operation 'Neptune' as part of Task Force 122, July 5, 1944," U.S. Navy World War II Action Reports, Modern Military Branch, National Archives and Records Administration; "OMAHA BEACHHEAD (6 June–13 June 1944)," American Forces in Action Series, Historical Division, War Department, Facsimile Reprint, 1984, Center of Military History, United States Army, Washington, D.C.

"an epic human tragedy": S.L.A. Marshall, "First Wave at Omaha Beach," *Atlantic,* November 1, 1960.

"There were bodies, body parts, and blood": Seaman 1st Cl Robert Watson, 5th Engineer Special Brigade—6th Naval Beach Battalion, in Laurent Lefebvre, *American D-Day,* http://www.americandday.org/Veterans/Watson_Robert.html.

"a guy beside me had his arm blown off": Lou Mumford, "They were dying all around me," *South Bend Tribune,* June 5, 2012.

"The artillery and machine guns were generally sited": United States Fleet, Headquarters of the Commander in Chief, *Amphibious Operations: Invasion of Northern France, Western Task Force, June 1944,* http://www.eisenhower.archives.gov/research/online_documents/d_day/Report_of_the_Amphibious_Operations.pdf.

Bucklew on D-Day: Thomas B. Allen, "Untold Stories of D-Day," *National Geographic* website, http://ngm.nationalgeographic.com/ngm/0206/feature1/.

Starkweather and volunteers at Wadi Sebou: Francis D. Fane and Don Moore, *The Naked Warriors* (Appleton-Century-Crofts, 1956), p. 10.

"Slit trenches were dug for defending riflemen": Headquarters of the Commander in Chief, Navy Department, United States Fleet, *Amphibious Operations, Invasion of Northern France, Western Task Force, June 1944,* October 21, 1944, http://www.ibiblio.org/hyperwar/USN/rep/Normandy/Cominch/index.html#index.

"To accomplish this, men shinnied up the stakes," "was standing by to pull the fuses," "enemy rifle fire set off the charges": "Recollections of Lieutenant Commander Joseph H. Gibbons, USNR, Commanding Officer of U.S. Navy Combat Demolitions Units in Force 'O' during combat operations on Omaha Beach during and after the D-day landings"; adapted from Joseph H. Gibbons interview in box 11 of World War II Interviews, Operational Archives Branch, Naval Historical Center, http://www.history.navy.mil/faqs/faq87-3p.htm.

"Our craft hit a mine": Seaman 1st Cl Robert Watson, 5th Engineer Special Brigade—6th Naval Beach Battalion, quoted in Laurent Lefebvre, *American D-Day,* http://www.americandday.org/Veterans/Watson_Robert.html.

An exuberant *"F—k!"*: referred to as "the word that won the war," in Michael Accordino, *299th Combat Engineer Battalion—First On Omaha/D-Day,* http://www.299thcombatengineers.com/HistoryAccordino.htm.

"I ordered all hands to inflate their life belts": Fane, *Naked Warriors,* p. 63.

SEAL historian Tom Hawkins told us his theory of why the NCDUs are relatively unknown: "There are a lot of reasons why I think the NCDU men are not known for what they did. It's largely because they only really performed in two significant operations in Europe, and that was [the] Normandy invasion and the invasion of southern France. After the Americans got on the continent of Europe, the emphasis went immediately to the Pacific."

CHAPTER 2

Background details of UDT operations in the Pacific described in this chapter: "History of Commander Underwater Demolition Teams and Underwater Demolition Flotilla, Amphibious Forces, Pacific Fleet" (undated), Naval Special Warfare Command historical file; Mack M. Boynton, "An Informal Look at Operation Crossroads/Kili Operation" (undated), Naval Special Warfare Command historical file; Robert R. Baird, "The Journeys of Underwater Demolition Team 6," compilation of narrative, documents and maps (undated), courtesy Robert Baird; Phil H. Bucklew Oral History by John T. Mason Jr., 1980, Naval Institute, Naval Historical Center; microfilm collection of the UDTs, 1945, History of the Commander, Underwater Demolition teams and Underwater Demolition Flotilla, Amphibious Forces, Pacific, microfilm roll NRS II-490-511, Operational Archives, Naval Historical Center, Washington Navy Yard; and *The History and Organization of UDT, 1943–1960*, and the unit histories of UDTs 4, 5, 16, 18, and 21, all from the Naval Special Warfare Command Historical Files.

"They looked fantastic": Fane, *Naked Warriors,* p. 95.

"Our mission was to capture several military installations": John B. Dwyer, *Scouts and Raiders: The Navy's First Special Warfare Commandos* (Praeger, 1993), p. 33.

"Hell Week isn't designed to kill you": Rorke Denver and Ellis Henican, *Damn Few: Making the Modern SEAL Warrior* (Hyperion, 2013), p. 53.

Kauffman details and quotes in this chapter on UDT operations: Elizabeth K. Bush, *America's First Frogman: The Draper Kauffman Story* (Naval Institute Press, 2004), pp. 130–190.

"We don't want another blunder": Wyatt Blessingame, *Underwater Warriors* (Random House, 1964), p. 4.

"Not one plane appeared," "Get that damned thing out of here!," "Every single man": Fane, *Naked Warriors,* pp. 95–98.

OSS Maritime Unit operations: Tom Hawkins, with the assistance of Rima Magee, "Special Boat Legacy: History of the OSS Maritime Unit in the Arakan," undated, unpublished paper prepared for archive of *The Blast,* an edited version of a report by Lieutenant John E. Babb, USNR, at the time Chief Maritime Unit, India-Burma Theater, addressed to Lt. Commander A.G. Atwater, USNR, Chief MU, Washington, D.C., dated July 21, 1945, courtesy of Tom Hawkins.

Walter Mess biography and quotes: Stefanie Dazio, "Walter L. Mess, World War II spy, dies at 98," *Washington Post,* June 12, 2013.

UDT-10 frogman Robert Kenworthy comments: Patrick K. O'Donnell, *Operatives, Spies, and Saboteurs: The Unknown Story of World War II's OSS* (Citadel Press, 2006), pp. 136–138.

"The results achieved by these UDTs": Bush, *America's First Frogman,* p. 156.

Edward Higgins quotes on Okinawa operation: Edward T. Higgins, *Webfooted Warriors: The Story of a "Frogman" in the Navy During World War II* (Exposition Press, 1955), pp. 58–89.

August 28, 1945, Japanese surrender to Lieutenant Commander Clayton, of UDT-21: interview with Tom Hawkins; Naval Historical Center Photo NH 71599, http://www.history.navy.mil/photos/images/h71000/h71599c.htm.

"The UDTs were always the despair": Fane, *Naked Warriors*, p. 131.

CHAPTER 3

Dick Lyon's biography, quotes, and details of antimine operation in this chapter: interview with Dick Lyon and Carol Fleisher interview with Dick Lyon. The operation is also described in slightly different detail in Francis Fane's *The Naked Warriors*, p. 267.

"We were ready to do what nobody else could do": Michael E. Haas, *In the Devil's Shadow: UN Special Operations During the Korean War* (Naval Institute Press, 2000), p. 142.

Details and quotes of UDT operations in Korea described in this chapter are from interviews with Dick Lyon; Haas, *In the Devil's Shadow*, pp. 140–168; Orr Kelly, *Brave Men, Dark Waters* (Presidio, 1992), pp. 66–73; Francis D. Fane and Don Moore, *The Naked Warriors: The Elite Fighting Force That Became The Navy Seals* (Appleton-Century-Crofts, 1956), pp. 236–269.

"I was again assigned to a CIA clandestine program": http://www.navyfrogmen.com/Atcheson.html.

"It opened with a North Korean drive": David Winkler, "The Hungman Redeployment," *Sea Power*, December 2000.

CHAPTER 4

Bill Bruhmuller details, biography, quotes, account of Isle of Pines attack in this chapter: interview with Bill Bruhmuller and Carol Fleisher interview with Bill Bruhmuller. Also, interviews with three former SEALs then stationed in Florida with direct knowledge of the events and one former Cuban exile frogman with direct knowledge of the events.

There may have been parallel exile attacks or attempted attacks on the Isle of Pines facilities in this time period by different Cuban exile teams, including a CIA-created team called Commandos Mambises. Further identification of specific dates and individuals who took part is difficult, as the available declassified documentary record is limited, many of the individuals involved used code names with each other, many of the Cubans and Americans involved are deceased, and little information on these operations was shared laterally across different teams.

For accounts of the CIA's *Rex* spy ship, CIA and exile attacks on Cuba in 1962–1963, the Isle of Pines attack, and activities of CIA-trained Cuban exile frogman teams, including the team known as Commandos Mambises, see: Ted Shackley, *Spymaster: My Life in the CIA* (Potomac Books, 2006), pp. 66–67, 75; Brian Latell, *Castro's Secrets: Cuban Intelligence, the CIA, and the Assassination of John F. Kennedy* (Macmillan, 2013), pp. 86, 178; Warren Hinckle, William W. Turner, *The Fish Is Red: The Story of the Secret War Against Castro* (Harper & Row, 1981), pp. 138, 144, 145; Maurice Halperin, *The Rise and Decline of Fidel Castro: An Essay in Contemporary History* (University of California Press, 1972), pp. 285–286; John Prados, *Safe for Democracy: The Secret Wars of the CIA* (Ivan R. Dee, 2006), pp. 318–320; and Don Bohning, *The Castro Obsession: U.S. Covert Operations Against Cuba, 1959–1965* (Potomac Books, 2005), pp. 162, 165, 241.

Contemporaneous accounts of the *Rex* include Associated Press and UPI dispatches of October 31 and November 1, 1963. Fidel Castro publicly railed against the

CIA, *Rex* and Cuban exile missions against Cuba in this period. A contemporaneous account of the *Rex* and the Isle of Pines limpet mine attack appeared in Jeanne S. Perry, "Red Base on Isle of Pines," *Palm Beach Post,* June 6, 1964. In the 1st Quarter 2002 issue of *The Blast,* former Cuban exile frogman Jose Enrique Dausa wrote of an apparently separate, near-simultaneous attack on targets at the Isle of Pines using limpet mines.

Background on the formation of the SEALs was provided by a number of former SEALs who served in the early, formative first years of the SEALs, including David Del Giudice, Rudy Boesch, Gordon Ablitt, Leonard Waugh, Dennis McCormack, Rick Woolard, Bill Bruhmuller, Tom Hawkins, Maynard Weyers, and Dante Stephensen. Del Giudice detailed the formation of the SEALs in a February 2011 article in *Naval Institute: Proceedings* titled "Setting the Record Straight: The Origin of the U.S. Navy SEALs." In an e-mail to the authors, Del Giudice offered these additional notes on the origins of Naval Special Warfare: "If we are talking about genealogy, ADM [Draper] Kauffman begot NCDUs, ADM R.K. [Richmond Kelly] Turner begot UDTs and ADM Arleigh Burke begot SEALs." He added, "In November 1943 (prior to Tarawa) ADM Nimitz tasked the Seabees based in Hawaii to set up training facilities for programs in underwater demolition and experimentation to defeat coral reefs and man-made obstacles that impede amphibious landings. ADM Nimitz followed up with a letter to ADM Turner, Commander 5th Amphibious Group, to use the lessons learned from Tarawa to get men trained on the real thing. This letter also created the 'Reef Obstacle and Mine Committee' to develop tactics and doctrine for combating underwater obstructions and anti-boat mines. Turner meeting his committee in December 1943 determined that a unit was needed to conduct such operations and that unit was to be designated UDT to distinguish it from the NCDU. During the same month ADM Turner recommended to the office of the CNO [Chief of Naval Operations] that UDTs be formed as a permanent part of the Navy. In the meantime UDT-1 (Provisional) under the command of CDR Edward Brewster and UDT-2 (Provisional) under Lt. Tom Crist as CO were formed apparently assuming CNO's approval in advance. UDT-1 participated as an element of ADM Turner's Task Force for the Kwajalein operation (Jan–Feb 1944). Turner was somewhat critical of the UDT's performance in that operation as noted in his after action report. ADM Turner decreed at that time that henceforth, UDTs would be made up of Navy men only. Army and Marine personnel from UDT-1 and UDT-2 were returned to their original units. In March 1944 ADM Turner established a Naval Combat Demolition Training and Experimental (NCDT&E) base on Maui. Some reports indicate LCDR Kauffman may have been training officer of the NCDT&E for a short period of time prior to taking command of UDT-5 and participating in the Saipan operation in June 1944 along with UDT-5 and UDT-7." Del Giudice added that the "SEALs were always direct action oriented," and cited a June 5, 1961, letter by the Chief of Naval Operations that spelled out the missions: "a. To develop a specialized capability for sabotage, demolitions, and other clandestine activities conducted in and from restricted waters rivers and canals. b. Conduct training for selected U.S. and indigenous personnel in a variety of skills for use in clandestine operations. c. Develop doctrine and tactics for such operations. d. Develop support equipment, including special craft for use in the immediate objective area." In a June 6, 1962, speech at West Point, President Kennedy elaborated on his vision of non-conventional war: "This is another type of war, new in intensity, ancient in origins—wars by guerrillas, subversion, insurgents, assassins; wars by ambush instead of by conventional combat. . . . It requires a whole new kind of strategy, a wholly different kind of force, and therefore a new and wholly different kind of military training."

"My idea is to stir things up on the island": "Documents: JFK Snubbed Cuba Offer From Revolutionary Leader, *Associated Press,* April 29, 1996.

Background on CIA's Operation Mongoose, University of Miami, Zenith Technical Enterprises, CIA/exile attacks on Cuban targets: Evan Thomas, *The Very Best Men: The Daring Early Years of the CIA* (Simon & Schuster, 1995), pp. 270–309. Also see, for example, "Memorandum for the Special Group (Augmented), July 25, 1962, Department of Defense document: http://www2.gwu.edu/~nsarchiv /nsa/cuba_mis_cri/620725%20Review%20of%20Op.%20Mongoose.pdf.

"another attempt will be made against the major target": "Minutes of Meeting of the Special Group (Augmented)," October 4, 1962, White House document: http://www2.gwu.edu/~nsarchiv/nsa/cuba_mis_cri/621004%20Minutes%20 of%20Meeting%20of%20Special.pdf.

"the whole Mongoose thing was insane": *The Nation,* March 26, 2001.

"[Arleigh Burke] was a very forward-looking person": Carol Fleisher interview with David Del Giudice.

In an interview with Carol Fleisher, Tom Hawkins said this about SEAL secrecy: "The SEALs have never been 'secret.' The fact that SEAL Teams were formed and operating in Vietnam was kept classified at the secret level, but the SEALs were never secret within the Navy or within the military. The low visibility was intended to keep it out of the media, but they found us. What we do, even today, is secret but we are not secret, obviously, with all these damn movies and books."

"We were only ten officers": Carol Fleisher interview with David Del Giudice.

"The Company—the CIA—had been using men from the UDTs": Kevin Dockery and Bill Fawcett, *The Teams: An Oral History of the U.S. Navy SEALs* (William Morrow, 1998), pp. 12–16.

Conclusion and aftermath of the Isle of Pines limpet-mine attack: interview with Bill Bruhmuller.

Isle of Pines limpet-mine attack authorized as Operation 3117 by White House in declassified White House document: "Proposed infiltration/exfiltration operations into Cuba during November 1963," Cuban affairs coordinator to the "Special Group," November 8, 1963; Assassination Records Review Board, National Archives.

Account of former Cuban frogman: interview with veteran of Cuban exile frogman force based in Florida in 1961–1964.

CHAPTER 5

"exposure to almost impenetrable mangrove swamps": Kevin Dockery, *Navy SEALs: A History Part II: the Vietnam Years* (Berkley Books, 2002), p. 35.

"I don't know a single SEAL who operated in Vietnam": Robert A. Gormly, *Combat Swimmer: Memoirs of a Navy SEAL* (Dutton, 1998), p. 130.

"The SEALs and the Seawolves became a natural component": Carol Fleisher interview with Tom Hawkins.

SEAL POW rescues in Vietnam: George J. Veith, *Code-Name Bright Light: The Untold Story of U.S. POW Rescue Efforts During the Vietnam War* (Free Press, 1998), pp. 261–265. Details on prisoners freed by Couch's SEALs: p. 263.

Hawkins on SEAL formation: Carol Fleisher interview with Tom Hawkins.

"For two hours, the SEALs": T. L. Bosiljevac, *SEALs" UDT/SEAL Operations in Vietnam* (Random House, 1991), p. 145.

"You SEALs are assassins": Orr Kelly, *Brave Men, Dark Waters* (Simon & Schuster, 1993), p. 145.

"We had no status, no standing," "They were in small detachments": ibid., p. 146.

"harassment of the enemy, hit-and-run raids": Kevin Dockery, from interviews by Bud Brutsman, *Navy SEALs: A Complete History* (Berkley Books, 2004), p. 282.

"The first SEALs in combat": Carol Fleisher interview with Tom Hawkins.

"three SEAL [Team Two] Platoons handled themselves": Kevin Dockery, *Navy SEALs: A History Part II: the Vietnam Years*, p. 180.

Chau Doc operation details and quotes: Drew Dix and Maggie O'Brien, in Oral History for *Medal of Honor: Portraits of Valor Beyond the Call of Duty:* https://www.youtube.com/watch?v=-_nA8e0YDfI; Dockery, *Navy SEALs: A Complete History,* pp. 404–421.

Kuykendall operation: Carol Fleisher interview with Hal Kuykendall.

"We like to grab people", "Both SEALs and PRUs killed many VCI": Dale Andradé, *Ashes to Ashes: The Phoenix Program and the Vietnam War* (Lexington Books, 1990), p. 193.

"where principle is involved, be deaf": Karel Montor, *Naval Leadership: Voices of Experience* (Naval Institute Press, 1998), p. 523.

Kerrey operation: Kerrey Oral History for *Medal of Honor: Portraits of Valor Beyond the Call of Duty,* https://www.youtube.com/watch?v=hHAFZUOo8pY.

In April 2001, the *New York Times* and *60 Minutes* ran stories about a raid Kerrey and his SEALs conducted on February 25, 1969, to capture a Viet Cong leader, an operation that occurred three weeks before his Nha Trang operation, during which up to twenty civilians were reportedly killed. Eventually, the story receded into the historical mist of countless other tragedies of the Vietnam War.

Norris and Thornton operations details and quotes: Carol Fleisher interviews with Tom Norris and Michael Thornton. Thornton also recalled later being the inspiration for an iconic SEAL expression when he was a SEAL training instructor in 1983: "I was leading PT [physical training] and somebody yelled, 'Instructor Thornton, when are we gonna have an easy day?' And I said, 'The only easy day would be yesterday.'" In Thornton's honor, the class inscribed a PT platform with the words, "The only easy day was yesterday," which became a widely used SEAL axiom. "Yeah, there's no easy days," Thornton noted to Fleisher. "No use looking in the rear view mirror because that's gone. You better be looking forward."

Spence Dry and Operation Thunderhead: Carol Fleisher interview with Moki Martin; Michael G. Slattery and Gordon I. Peterson, "Spence Dry: A SEAL's Story," *The Naval Institute: Proceedings,* July 2005; Kevin Dockery, *Operation Thunderhead: The True Story of Vietnam's Final POW Rescue Mission—and the Last Navy Seal Killed in Country* (Penguin, 2008), *passim.*

SEALs freed some 152 Vietnamese captives, counting for 48 percent of POWs freed during the war: ibid., p. 226.

"By the end of 1970 SEALs," "I would like to have a thousand more like them": Dale Andradé, *Ashes to Ashes,* p. 199.

"Some people have said that if there were more SEALs": Carol Fleisher interview with Tom Hawkins.

"tactic in search of a strategy": Gormly, *Combat Swimmer,* p. 153.

"Although they were highly successful in their own districts": Bosiljevac, *SEALs: UDT/SEAL Operations in Vietnam,* p. 179.

"For the most part, we were relegated to the Navy river patrol": Gormly, *Combat Swimmer,* p. 153.

At least one SEAL proposed coordinated program of POW hunts: Veith, *Code-Name Bright Light,* p. 264.

Note on SEAL training from SEAL historian Tom Hawkins: "It was not known as BUD/S training until 1972, when all training was moved to Coronado. Little Creek training was called UDTR or UDT Replacement training. Coronado training was called UDTB or UDT Basic training. SEAL qualification training was accomplished at the unit level until 1972. When combined at the school in Coronado 1972 the name BUD/S was adopted. SEAL qualification continued at the unit level for several years after the school was established. Today, SEAL Qualification Training (SQT) is accomplished after BUD/S and only then can you go to a SEAL or SDV Team. SDV personnel receive yet another course of instruction before going to the team."

CHAPTER 6

Events, details, and quotes of operation at Grenada radio tower and escape to the ocean in this chapter: interview with SEAL veteran of Grenada, and "Naval Special Warfare Lessons Learned Case Study: Operation Urgent Fury (Grenada)" [unclassified, undated, c. 1995], Naval Special Warfare Command Historical File. Jason Kendall is a pseudonym.

William McRaven comments: commencement address at the University of Texas, May 17, 2014.

"It seemed like half the tough guys": Rorke Denver and Ellis Henican, *Damn Few: Making the Modern SEAL Warrior* (Hyperion, 2013), p. 106.

"one screw-up after another": interview with SEAL veteran of Grenada.

"Our Intel had been atrocious": Dockery, *Navy SEALs: A Complete History*, p. 603.

"We were like slow-moving turtles": Gary Ward, "Fury on Grenada," *VFW Magazine,* November 2013.

"A lot of our tactics, techniques, and procedures": interview with SEAL veteran of Grenada.

Gormly details and quotes on Grenada operation: Robert A. Gormly, *Combat Swimmer: Memoirs of a Navy SEAL* (Dutton, 1998), pp. 180–199; Dockery, *Navy SEALs: A Complete History*, pp. 590–596.

Details and quotes of Sir Paul Scoon's experiences at Governor-General's mansion during Grenada invasion: Paul Scoon, *Survival for Service: My Experiences as Governor General of Grenada* (Macmillan Caribbean, 2003), pp. 139–153.

"We achieved our mission, but took heavy casualties": John T. Carney Jr., Benjamin F. Schemmer, *No Room for Error: The Covert Operations of America's Special Tactics Units from Iran to Afghanistan* (Random House, 2007), pp. 110–111.

"I think we learned a lot about ourselves": interview with SEAL veteran of Grenada.

Achille Lauro operation: Gormly, *Combat Swimmer*, pp. 208–218.

Quotes and details of SEAL operations in Panama: interviews with Adam Curtis and four SEAL veterans of the operation; Orr Kelly, *Brave Men, Dark Waters* (Presidio, 1992), pp. 1–4 and 216–234; Kevin Dockery, *Navy SEALs: A Complete History* (Berkley Books, 2004), 644–667; Malcolm McConnell, *Just Cause: The Real Story of America's High-Tech Invasion of Panama* (St. Martin's Press, 1991), *passim.*

"If the mission was to take and hold the airfield": David Evans, "A Miscalculation Of Mission For The Seals In Panama?" *Chicago Tribune,* February 9, 1990.

"In Panama we violated our own doctrine," "They over-planned this operation": interviews with two SEALs who were on active duty in 1989.

Stubblefield letter: Orr Kelly, *Brave Men, Dark Waters*, pp. 231, 232. Kelly wrote of what he saw as a historical inability of the SEALs to learn from failure. "In the past," he argued, "the SEALs have not been very good at learning from their experiences, especially when things went wrong, and applying those lessons to plans for the future. The failure of UDT Sixteen during World War II at Okinawa is never spoken of. Neither is the SDV operation in 1972 in which Spence Dry lost his life. The SEALs took part in Urgent Fury in Grenada in 1983, but it was not until 1989, six years later, that three officers who served in that operation met with SEALs, other than their colleagues in Team Six, and shared their experiences. A meeting devoted to the SEAL participation in Just Cause, the invasion of Panama, was held shortly after the operation. But most of the SEALs present found the briefing unsatisfactory, and a few were so disturbed that they walked out." (*Brave Men, Dark Waters*, p. 245.)

"ass-end destroyed": Mir Bahmanyar, *SEALs: The U.S. Navy's Elite Fighting Force* (Osprey, 2011), p. 80.

Mina Saud operation details and quotes: interview with Tom Dietz. During the first Gulf War, the SEALs also seized an Iraqi oil platform and took twenty-three prisoners; captured Qarah Island, the first Kuwaiti territory to be liberated by the allied forces; and rescued a USAF F-16 pilot who was shot down and bailed out into the Gulf.

Mogadishu details: Carol Fleisher interview with Rick Kaiser.

"never used even once to track down terrorists": *Newsweek,* May 5, 2014.

SEAL Gulf operations during oil embargo: interviews and reporting by Dick Couch for *Down Range.* Sean Yarrow and Don Latham pseudonyms. On February 2, 2000, a highly dramatic SEAL operation occurred near the Persian Gulf when the Russian tanker *Volgoneft-147,* suspected of smuggling Iraqi oil in violation of United Nations (UN) Security Council Resolutions, was intercepted by a U.S. Navy cruiser. The Russian ship refused to obey orders to stop, so a heavily armed team of ten Navy SEALs fast-roped to the deck from helicopters and seized the vessel at gunpoint.

CHAPTER 7

Details and quotes of SEAL operations in Afghanistan and Iraq in this chapter, unless otherwise sourced: interviews and reporting by Dick Couch for his books *Downrange* and *The Sheriff of Ramadi.* In 2005–2007 Couch embedded with the SEAL platoon stationed in Ramadi, Iraq. In this chapter, the names Randy Lowery, John Seville, Jack Williams, Sean Smith, Lars Beamon, Chuck Forbes, Lou Taladega and Jim Collins are pseudonyms.

Development Group missions publicly described by U.S. Navy: "NSW Command Brochure," dated May 9, 2014: http://www.public.navy.mil/nsw/news/Docu ments/ETHOS/Brochure.pdf.

"In the SEAL teams, you train and train": Carol Fleisher interview with SEAL.

Phillips rescue detail is from contemporaneous press accounts.

"We think we found Osama bin Laden": Mike Allen, "Osama bin Laden Raid Yields Trove of Computer Data," *Politico,* May 2, 2011.

"What SEALs are good at": CBS *60 Minutes,* September 24, 2012.

Details of bin Laden raid are from contemporaneous press accounts and two books on the operation: Peter L. Bergen, *Manhunt: The Ten-Year Search for Bin Laden from 9/11 to Abbottabad* (Random House, 2012); and Mark Bowden, *The Finish: The Killing of Osama Bin Laden* (Atlantic Press, 2012).

Jessica Buchanan quotes and rescue details: Jessica Buchanan, Erik Landemalm, and Anthony Flacco, *Impossible Odds: The Kidnapping of Jessica Buchanan and Her Dramatic Rescue by SEAL Team Six* (Simon & Schuster, 2013), pp. 242–267; *Charlie Rose,* May 15, 2013; CBS *60 Minutes,* May 12, 2013.

EPILOGUE

Detail on knife ceremony, "On clear days, visitors to Rosecrans can often see": *Ethos,* Issue 22, 2013.

McRaven's apology is from contemporaneous press accounts, the accuracy of which McRaven confirmed to us by e-mail.

"There are a lot of mission areas out there": "Calland: SEALs Focus Is On Terrorism, Core Missions, Interoperability," *Defense Daily,* July 10, 2003.

Daniel Murphy comments: *NBC Nightly News,* May 3, 2011; CBS News, *The Early Show,* October 22, 2007.

APPENDIX A

http://www.public.navy.mil/nsw/Documents/USSOCOM_OrgChart.pdf.

APPENDIX B

http://www.public.navy.mil/nsw/news/Documents/ETHOS/Brochure.pdf.

APPENDIX C

Hawkins's sources include:

Sue Ann Dunford and James Douglas O'Dell, *More Than Scuttlebutt—The U.S. Navy Demolition Men in WWII* (2009) (http://ncdu-udt-ww2.com/).

"Hidden Heroes: Amphibious Scouts of Special Services Unit #1," June 2007, by Teresa "Pat" Staudt and Hank Staudt. A self-published research project provided to the Navy Historical Society.

Commander in Chief, United States Fleet, to Vice Chief of Naval Operations: Subject: Naval Demolition Units Project, May 6, 1943, Serial 01398 (National Archives, Textual Reference Division, Military Reference Branch, Suitland, Md.).

Vice Chief of Naval Operations to Chief of the Bureau of Yards and Docks: Subject: Personnel for Naval Demolition Units, May 15, 1943, Serial 01911223 (National Archives, Textual Reference Division, Military Reference Branch, Suitland, Md.).

Officer in Charge of Naval Demolition Unit to COMAMPHIBFORLANT: Subject: Recommendations for Naval Demolition Units, organization, training, and equipping of permanent units, May 27, 1943 (National Archives, Textual Reference Division, Military Reference Branch, Suitland, Md.).

Commander in Chief, U.S. Pacific Fleet, History of the Amphibious Forces, U.S. Pacific Fleet, "History of Naval Combat Demolition Training and Experimental Base, Kihei, Maui, T.H.," Section 150C, 166 (The Naval History and Historical Command, Washington, D.C.).

APPENDIX D

http://www.public.navy.mil/nsw/pages/ethoscreed.aspx

INDEX